Stopping the Trains to Auschwitz Budapest, 1944

Frank Baron

"In the tragedy of Hungarian Jewry . . . a dramatic turn came about with the disclosure of the Auschwitz Report."

Ernő Munkácsi, *How It Happened: Documenting the Tragedy of the Hungarian Jewry*

"By means of the propaganda of hate, it is possible to excite the masses to an uninhibited use of force and organized violence."

Sándor Török, "Szenes-Interviews"

First Printing by the University of Kansas Jayhawk Ink.

Copyright, 2020 by Frank Baron

Second, revised edition, 2020

Contents

	Preface	vii
I.	The July Crisis: Hungarian and Swiss Rescue Networks	1
II.	Soos and Wallenberg: Intrigues and Risks of Rescue	45
III.	Chronology and Documentation	61
IV.	Appendix A: The OSS Interrogations of Géza Soos	113
V.	Appendix B: The Auschwitz Report (OSS Translation, based on the Soos manuscript)	123
VI.	Appendix C: Sándor Szenes, *The Auschwitz Interviews*	175
	1. József Éliás	180
	2. Mária Székely	190
	3. András Zakar	196
	4. Sándor Török	202
VII.	Bibliography	213
VIII.	Index of Names	223

Preface

To write about the Horthy era in Hungary means to contend with limited options. At the heart of a continuing debate are the deportations of the Hungarian Jewish population to the Auschwitz death camp and the Hungarian head of state, Admiral Miklós Horthy. With his quarter of a century in power, he left a problematic legacy, restricting options that hardly allows for a middle ground: on the one hand, rationalizing Horthy's decisions during a tragic period of Hungary's history, or, on the other hand, focusing on the tragic consequences of his policies. Between those two positions a middle ground is difficult to imagine, much less to navigate. Rigid political positions appear to prop up both sides of this debate.

Randolph Braham has seen this problem in the following way:

> ... there are those who try to ease their conscience by emphasizing the number of Jews saved in Hungary. In their drive to rehabilitate Miklós Horthy—and by implication the entire Horthy era—these cleansers of history attribute the survival of the Jews of Budapest exclusively to the regent's decision of July 7, 1944, to halt the deportations. Eager to assure Hungary's historical continuity as a "chivalrous" nation, these nationalists fail to acknowledge the important role that others played.[1]

---

[1] Randolph L. Braham with Scott Miller (eds.), *The Nazis' Last Victims: The Holocaust in Hungary* (Detroit: Wayne State University Press, 1998), p. 43.

To appear to be a "cleanser" of history would totally invalidate the present effort. But later Braham amended his position to allow for a fresh look at this controversial topic. He wrote:

> The survival of most of the Jews of Budapest is attributed to Horthy's halting of the deportations on July 7, 1944. While this may largely be true, history cleansers fail to identify the political and military factors that induced the Regent to act at a time when all of Hungary, with the notable exception of the capital, had already been made *judenrein* [i.e., free of Jews]."[2]

This need to identify political and military factors must be, in any case, the priority. Braham's conditions for an acceptable interpretation of events are clear and point to the most reasonable approach. To understand how and why the deportations stopped, this investigation shifts the focus away from the formidable issues of Horthy's legacy, examining the critical events, without exclusive attention to Horthy's motivations or actions. Such a strategy will bring to the foreground events and initiatives that did not involve Horthy directly, but which led to the crisis during which he decided to act. How and why did events converge to provide an opportunity to end the deportations?

This approach permits the consideration of a particular time range, which appears to reach a critical climax in the end of June and in the first days of July. A strict chronological presentation of facts up to this point can bypass partisan politics. The question of whether an end to the deportations could have occurred earlier must

---

[2] Randolph L. Braham, "Assault on Historical Memory: Hungarian Nationalists and the Holocaust," in: Paul A. Shapiro and Robert M. Ehrenreich (eds.) *Hungary and the Holocaust Confrontation with the Past. Symposium Proceedings* (Washington D.C.: Holocaust Memorial Museum, 2001), pp. 45–75.
https://www.ushmm.org/m/pdfs/Publication_OP_2001-01.pdf
Accessed on August 5, 2020.

be put aside. Why Horthy acted becomes less important than what provided the necessary preconditions for a successful intervention. If this investigation of events can be persuasive, the question is no longer about Horthy's freedom or responsibility to act. As our investigation will show, developments in late June and early July reached a critical point at which freedom of action was no longer available. Horthy had no choice; he was forced to act.

In this critical historical situation, multiple forces merged. The deportations of the Jewish population were occurring in secrecy and with extraordinary speed. This efficiency had been the key to their stunning success. On the other hand, there were rescue efforts inside and outside Hungary. But the challenges to the extermination program had to contend with the policy of the Allies, who were intent exclusively on the military defeat of Germany. Rescue efforts appeared to political and military leaders as dangerous distractions. Only after the strict censorship barriers in Switzerland had been pierced, and facts about the extermination program had become known, was there a realistic chance of change. Decision makers at the highest levels, whether in Hungary, or in the United States, or Great Britain, were not inclined to act. Initiatives that finally impelled events in an unexpectedly new direction did not take place at those high levels. Who was left to undertake rescue efforts? The question how the decisive initiatives finally developed and achieved a surprising degree of success is the main concerns in the present study.

There has been a tendency in past research on this topic to see it from a Hungarian perspective, relying primarily on Hungarian sources and scholarship. Because important factors influencing events originated outside of the country, it is essential to expand the consideration of the most relevant facts and documents.

My research about the Auschwitz Report began in 1985 when I learned about the Szenes interviews from Mária Székely, who had translated the Auschwitz Report after it arrived in Budapest in late April 1944. Through her I became acquainted with

Sándor Szenes, whose investigative work about the Auschwitz Report's impact opened a revealing window to a tragic period of European history. Our conversations evolved into a collaboration and, finally, a book, which appeared in 1994 in Germany with the title *Von Ungarn nach Auschwitz: Die verschwiegene Warnung*. My contribution was to supply a broader context for the impact of that report, that is, in the countries outside Hungary, above all in Switzerland.[3] How the facts about Auschwitz finally awakened the conscience of the world outside Hungary are little understood, even today. Could Hungary without outside help impede the powerful momentum of the deportations? It had already consumed the Jewish population of Hungary outside of Budapest. The rescue of the Budapest population is an important issue that still deserves close attention. The Szenes interviews provide valuable material in this effort, but they require a historical context, which only a strict adherence to a precise chronological treatment can provide. This has been lacking up to now.

The work on this manuscript occurred during the crisis of Covid 19, a period in which the access to books and documents was severely limited. During this time I had help and advice from a number of generous persons, who gave me valuable access and advice. They are Duncan Bare, John Brewer, Fred Bleakley, Vernon A. Chamberlin, Lori N. Curtis, Marguerite DeHuszar Allen, Michael Fleming, Andrew Foat, Esther Gilbert, Jane Frydman, Russ Hutchins, Stephen Jaeger, Andrea Kirchner, Graham Kreicker, László Küllöi, Péter Küllöi, Pam Lerow, Paul Lim, Ferenc Laczó, László Magyar, Zsolt Mohi, Jonathan Paretsky, Hartmut Rudolph, Elizabeth Schultz, Michael and Anne Shaw, Ray Souza, Nóra Szekér, György Szőnyi, and, above all, my wife, Betty Baron.

---

[3] Sándor Szenes and Frank Baron. *Die verschwiegene Warnung* (Münster: Westfälisches Dampfboot, 1994).

I. The July Crisis: Hungarian and Swiss Rescue Networks

Recent scholars have argued that information about the death camps had become known to many at an early stage, even as early as 1942, when the Nazi drive was only beginning. Gerhart Riegner of the World Jewish Congress in Geneva relayed reliable information to the Allies that the Nazis intended to employ poison gas to exterminate Jews in the lands they occupied.[4] Less well known is the fact that Elizabeth (also Elisabeth) Wiskemann (1901–1971), press attaché at the Bern British legation and later a distinguished historian of interwar Europe, reported about an S.S. official who stated "in casual conversation that during the second half of 1942 about 30,000 Polish Jews had been killed by gas."[5] In the following years such reports came forward in a steady stream to Jewish leaders and the governments of the United States and Great Britain. Men such as Jan Karski had firsthand encounters with these Nazi actions and communicated information to the highest political leaders of the Allies. The steady stream of information, supplied, for example, by the Polish underground, encountered not only widespread disbelief but also resistance from political and military leaders, who believed that it was politically dangerous to make it appear that the war was being fought for the sake of the Jews. Decision makers at every level were not inclined to undercut well-established war aims.

Information about the death camps became available only gradually, at first only in bits and pieces and only to a limited number of people, out of the view of the

---

[4] Gerhart M. Riegner, *Never Despair: Sixteen Years in the Service of the Jewish People and the Cause of Human Rights* (Chicago: United States Holocaust Memorial Museum, 2006), pp. 39–43. Cf. Frank Baron, "The 'Myth' and Reality of Rescue from the Holocaust: The Karski–Koestler and Vrba-Wetzler Reports." *The Yearbook of the Research Centre for German and Austrian Exile Studies* 2 (2000): 171–208.

[5] Michael Fleming, *Auschwitz, the Allies and Censorship of the Holocaust* (New York: Cambridge University Press, 2014), pp. 352–353.

general public. Few people realized that rescue efforts were necessary, even if extremely difficult. A crucial point after which disbelief and political indifference were no longer an option came within and outside Hungary with public awareness of the Auschwitz Report by Rudolf Vrba and Alfred Wetzler, two prisoners of Auschwitz who had escaped from the camp on April 7, 1944. In late April Vrba and Wetzler were able to meet Slovak Jewish leaders and provide the fullest possible description of what had transpired in Auschwitz over a period of about two years: minute details about the size and national origins of the transports from different parts of Europe and about the methodical cruelties of the death camp.

The final form of the report was crafted by the escapees with the significant participation of Jewish leaders, who took care to verify all details and thus make the rejection of the report impossible. The facts presented had to withstand the most aggressive scrutiny from any direction. The report was completed by April 28. Because this effort occurred at a time when Slovakia was occupied by Germany, getting the report to Hungary and Switzerland quickly was dangerous and unpredictable. Nevertheless, the report did finally reach key people in Hungary and Switzerland. Although Vrba and Wetzler were not the first to escape from Auschwitz, in contrast to information that had trickled out of the camps before, their report possessed explosive force to make a difference.

Frustrating circumstances prevented the report from reaching key people quickly. There were unavoidable delays because of issues involving translation and transmission. In Hungary there was the threatening presence of the Gestapo. Neutral Switzerland contended with restrictions of strict censorship. In Hungary as well as in Switzerland the report reached officials representing the Allies relatively late, only in about the middle of June. Because of the delays, rescue efforts were not attempted. In Hungary the deportations were in progress, and by this time the number of deportees to Auschwitz reached about 300,000. A detailed list, prepared by Zoltán Tibori Szabó, showes 61 individuals who became aware of details in the Auschwitz Report, and when precisely they learned about it.[6] These individuals became the first to be confronted by the possibility or necessity of rescue. The following selection from Szabó's extensive list shows *only* the names that might be most relevant for the events to be treated here:

1. Rezső Kasztner (Rudolf Kastner), Vaada deputy head, on April 28th 1944[7]
2. Géza Soos (Soós), counselor of the Hungarian Ministry of Foreign Affairs, one of the leaders of the Hungarian Independence Movement, at the end of April or the beginning of May 1944.[8]
3. Reverend József Éliás, leader of the Good Shepherd Committee of the Hungarian Protestant churches, at the end of April or the beginning of May 1944.[9]
4. Miklós (Moshe) Krausz, head of the Palestinian Office in Budapest, at the beginning of May 1944.
5. Mária Székely, later Mrs. László Küllői-Rhorer, the Hungarian translator of the Vrba-Wetzler report, at the very beginning of May 1944.
6. Nathan Schwalb, head of the Hechalutz movement office in Geneva, on May 17th 1944.
7. Cardinal Jusztinián Serédi, Archbishop of Hungary, on May 10th 1944.

---

[6] Zoltán Tibori Szabó, "The Auschwitz Reports: Who Got Them, and When? The Auschwitz Reports and the Holocaust in Hungary," in: Randolph L. Braham and William J. vanden Heuvel (eds.), *The Auschwitz Reports and the Holocaust in Hungary* (New York: Columbia University Press, 2011), pp. 85–120. In his article Dr. Szabó provides details concerning the persons listed above.
[7] Kastner circulated the report among members of the Jewish Council.
[8] Géza Soos (1912–1953), (also Soós) lawyer and Calvinist theologian. Soos joined the youth movement *Soli Deo Gloria* in 1928 and eventually served as its president from 1940 to 1945. He received his doctorate in law in 1935. Together with Domokos Szent-Iványi, he was one of the founders of the Hungarian Independence Movement (MFM). He escaped from the Gestapo to Italy on December 9th 1944. He received a doctorate in theology in Switzerland and then emigrated to the United States, where he engaged in teaching and pastoral duties. He was killed in a car accident in 1953.
[9] On Éliás (1914–1995) see the Szenes interviews below.

8   Bishop László Ravasz, president of the Reformed Church General Synod, on May 12th–14th 1944.
9   Writer Sándor Török, acting member of the Committee of Christian-Jewish Alliance in Hungary, after the middle of May 1944.[10]
10 Giuseppe Burzio, representative of the Vatican in Slovakia, sending Cardinal Maglione the Auschwitz Report on May 24th.[11]
11 Countess Ilona Edelsheim Gyulai [Widow of István Horthy and daughter-in-law of the regent], at the end of May or beginning of June 1944.[12]
12 Miklós Horthy Jr., son of Regent Horthy, in June 1944.
13 Regent Miklós Horthy. Copy sent through Sándor Török, at the end of May or the beginning of June; the one sent by Ernő Pető through the Regent's son in June 1944; the regent also received copies from Cardinal Serédi and Bishop Ravasz, most probably about the middle of May.
14 Elizabeth Wiskemann, British representative in Bern, on June 13th 1944.[13]
15 Leland Harrison, American Minister in Bern, on June 13th 1944.[14]
16 Richard Lichtheim, head of the Jewish Agency [for Palestine] in Geneva, [and Gerhart Riegner of the Jewish World Congress], in the middle of June 1944.
17 Monsignor Mario Martilotti, Vatican legate in Switzerland, middle of June 1944.

---

[10] Cf. Török interview below. Bishop Ravasz heard about the report for the first time from Török, who escaped internment on May 16th. Miklós Mester, *Arcképek két tragikus kor árnyékában* [Portraits in the Shadows of Two Tragic Periods] (Budapest: Tarsoly Kiadó, 2012), p. 159.

[11] *Actes et Documents de Saint Sièges relatives à la Seconde Guerre Mondiale*, vol. 19 (Vatican: 1981), vol. 19, No. 204, p. 281). Quoted by György Haraszti, *Auschwitzi jegyzőkönyv* [The Auschwitz Protocols] (Budapest: Múlt és Jövö Kiadó, 2016), pp. 66, and 82. When the message arrived in the Vatican is still being debated. The Vatican claim is that it arrived only in October.

[12] Ilona Edelsheim Gyulai (1918–2013) played a key role in passing the Auschwitz Report through her mother-in-law to the regent. See the Szenes interview with Sándor Török below.

[13] Elizabeth [also Elisabeth] Wiskemann sent, according to Fleming, the telegram on the following day, June 14, 1944, to London. Fleming, *Auschwitz, the Allies and Censorship of the Holocaust*, p. 232.

[14] At the Bern legation Roswell McClelland, the represenatative of the War Refugee Board, was also informed.

18 Jaromir Kopecky, Swiss representative of the Czechoslovakian Government in Exile, on June [13th] 1944.[15]

19 Georg(es) Mantello (György Mandel), businessman from Beszterce (Bistrija), Northern-Transylvania, first secretary of the Consulate of El Salvador in Geneva, on June 21st 1944.

It should not be overlooked that George Klein was among the early readers of the Auschwitz Report, soon after it arrived in Budapest. At the age of eighteen, Klein served as an assistant to Dr. Zoltán Kohn, a member of the Jewish Council in Budapest, and had a chance to read the Vrba-Wetzler report. Klein, who became a prominent scholar in the field of cell biology in Sweden, later recalled the experience of reading the report. The truth of the report in his hands was impossible for him to doubt. These were simply facts. When he told his friends, they immediately understood the reality and gravity of the report. But it was totally different with the adults at a time when the deportation had not begun. Klein wrote: "My supervisor gave me permission to tell my relatives and close friends about the report so that they could go underground in time. Of the dozen or so people I warned, *not one believed me*." In a film interview Dr. Klein also related what he experienced when he tried to explain what he had learned to his uncle, a well-educated man, a dermatologist. The uncle became very angry. He almost hit Klein. He shouted: "Idiot. How can you believe such a thing?! That can't be real. Such things just cannot be done!"[16]

---

[15] Kopecky (with the reception date June 13th) must precede Wiskemann because Wiskemann acted on the basis of information from Kopecky. Cf. Szabó's source on this question: György Haraszti, *Auschwitzi jegyzőkönyv* [The Auschwitz Protocols], p. 18.

[16] George Klein, "Confronting the Holocaust: An Eyewitness Account," in: Randolph L. Braham and William vanden Heuevel (eds.), *The Auschwitz Reports and the Holocaust in Hungary*, pp. 255–284. George Klein, *Pietà* (Cambridge: MIT Press, 1989), p. 128. The German-language interview was produced by Michael Muschner and is available today with a brief summary. https://www.fbw-filmbewertung.com/film/leben_in_budapest_1944_1_der_auschwitz_report Accessed on 7/21/2020.

About the end of May, Horthy was still unwilling to accept that the destination was a death camp. This attitude had remained rigid ever since his disastrous meeting with Hitler at Kleßheim on March 18, 1944. Although no record of the fateful bargaining between Hitler and Horthy survived, it is evident, as British historian C. A. Macartney explained, that Horthy was willing "to make thousands of Jewish workers available for work in the German munitions factories. . . . Then he acted like Pontius Pilate: he washed his hands."[17]

Information about Auschwitz came to Horthy from many persons at different times. He tended to ignore that news until it became clear that too many people knew about the fate of the deported Hungarian Jews. One important source for that news came to him from his daughter-in-law. In her memoirs Ilona Edelsheim Gyulai wrote that she is convinced that the correct date was July 3rd, which is the date she had marked as a visit by Török. As it becomes evident in the Török interview below, she was mistaken. By that time the Auschwitz Report was no longer news at the palace. Török had the assignment to take the report to her, and that was clearly a priority for him. It is hard to imagine that he would not have accomplished this task by the end of May or in early June.[18]

Dr. Ernő Pető, member of the Jewish Council, met Miklós Horthy Jr., Horthy's son, at the end of May and gave him information about the ultimate fate of most deported Jews in the gas chambers of Auschwitz.[19] Moreover, there is reason to believe that Soos, who had close ties to the "kiugrási iroda," [office conspiring to leave the Axis], would have informed Horthy Jr. about the Auschwitz Report even before the middle of May. That would explain why he did not ask Éliás to undertake

---

[17] C. A. Macartney, *October 15th: A History of Modern Hungary. 1929–1945*, II, pp. 236–237.
[18] Gróf (countess) Ilona Edelsheim Gyulai, *Becsület és Kötelesség* [Integrity and Responsibility] (Budapest: Európa, 2001), p. 263.
[19] Ernő Munkácsi, *How it Happened: Documenting the Tragedy of the Hungarian Jewry* (Montreal: McGill-Queen's University Press, 2018), p. 203.

this task. Domokos Szent-Iványi, the leader of the Hungarian Independence Movement (MFM) explained the crucial role that Soos played through his many contacts in government and church circles. He was responsible for building a huge MFM network. ("egy hatalmas komplexum építés[e]"), and after the death of István Horthy, Soos was able to create a positive relationship with Horthy's other son, Miklós Jr., with whom he and his closest associates often met ("akivel viszonylag gyakran találkoztak").[20]

Regent Horthy also dated his acquaintance with the Auschwitz Report later than he should have. He provided numerous dates. Not even what he remembered after the war at the Nuremberg trials can be considered reliable. There he stated that he only learned of the extermination camp in about the end of June 1944.[21] Lieutenant-General Gábor Faragho (Faraghó), administrative leader of the provincial police (the *csendör* units), remembers talking to Horthy about his experience reading the report in the middle of June. Horthy had probably known about it much earlier (perhaps suspecting the truth from the beginning), but by this time he must have realized that there was no way to deny it.[22]

---

[20] Domokos Szent-Iványi, *Visszatekintés 1941–1972.* [Taking a Look Back] Edited by Nóra Szekér and Gyula Kodolányi (Budapest: Magyar Szemle Könyvek, 2016), p. 89. Cf. *The Hungarian Independence Movement 1939–1946.* Edited by Gyula Kodolányi and Nóra Szekér (Budapest: Hungarian Review Books, 2013). Géza Kádár in: *Evangéliomot Magyarországnak,* p. 281. Bálint Török, "A Magyar Függetlenségi Mozgalom zsidómentő tevékenysége," in: "Az Auschwitzi jegyzőkönyv 1," [The Auschwitz Protocol, part 1]. In: *Magyar Szemle,* New Series 12 (2003).
[21] Mario D. Fenyo, *Hitler, Horthy, and Hungary: German-Hungarian Relations, 1941–1944* (New Haven: Yale University Press, 1972), p. 194.
[22] László Karsai and Judit Molnár (eds.), *Az Endre-Baky-Jaross Per* (Budapest 1994), pp. 371–372. A meeting between Faragho and Horthy took place on June 22nd, at which Horthy indicated that he wished to end the deportations. Sebők, *A titkos alku. Zsidókat a függetlenségért. Horthy-mítosz és a holocaust* [The Secret Bargain: The Jews for Independence; the Horthy-Myth and the Holocaust] Budapest 2004, p. 177. Miklós Horthy, *Memoirs,* (London: Hutchison, 1956), p. 219. On May 27, 1947, during an interrogation in connection with the Nurnberg trials, he stated that he learned of the extermination of the Jews and Auschwitz about the end of June ("gegen Ende Juni 1944, als ich ausführliche Berichte von Vernichtungslager Auschwitz bekam.") Quoted by Fenyo

When Calvinist Bishop László Ravasz, who had been supporting efforts to restrict the rights of Jews, saw the report, he rushed to make arrangements to meet Horthy. As Ravasz recalled, Horthy insisted that Hitler had asked for many thousands of workers. He had been promised that they would be treated humanely. He held fast to this fiction until the middle of June, when he was being confronted by the Auschwitz Report, passed to him from different directions, partly through his daughter-in-law, Ilona Edelsheim Gyulai, and through his son, Miklós Horthy, Jr. He had to realize at last that his previous efforts to explain the deportations were untenable. Now the question became: What could be done about it? Under pressure from Hitler, Horthy had put the apparatus of the Hungarian government at the disposal of Nazi collaborators, the Hungarian provincial police (the *csendör* units), and Adolf Eichmann's efficient program. The deportations acquired a powerful momentum. The provincial police served to collect and concentrate the Jewish population of the countryside and force them into waiting trains. In the meetings of his council of ministers Horthy was confronting men he had appointed, now committed to the continuation of the deportations. Lone voices, such as those representing the ministry of foreign affairs, reminded those ministers that the news about Auschwitz had reached the outside world.

The mass deportations in Hungary had begun at the middle of May 1944. There were serious efforts to get the Auschwitz Report out of Slovakia to Switzerland and the Allies. Rabbi Michael Dov Weissmandl's and Gisi Fleischmann's desperate coded messages from Bratislava had arrived in Switzerland about the middle of May. A telegram of May 16th pleaded for the bombing of the railway lines to Auschwitz at Kassa (Kaschau) in Hungary and Presov in Slovakia.

---

from NA Record Group 238, World War II War Crimes Records. National Archives. Mario D. Fenyo, *Hitler. Horthy and Hungary. German-Hungarian Relations 1941-1944* (New Haven: Yale University Press, 1972), pp. 194–195.

A similar telegram arrived in Lugano on May 24th. On May 25th Roswell McClelland, representative of the War Refugee Board at the Bern legation, felt that the proposal to bomb was a matter more of "a military nature" and contacted the military attaché for the War Department, Colonel Alfred R. W. de Jong.[23] This action may speak for others in a critical period. The result was further delay.

The most significant communication to arrive at this time in Switzerland was addressed to Nathan Schwalb, director of the Zionist international Hechalutz (Hehalutz) office in Geneva, who, in turn, was also in touch with Roswell McClelland. Thus, a German copy of the Auschwitz Report, dated May 17th, eventually found its way into the archives of the War Refugee Board, but it is not clear why it was not translated into English, or when it was actually seen in the U.S. by the World Refugee Board or the Department of State. The Vrba-Wetzler Report, dated May 17th designated as *Tatsachenbericht ueber Auschwitz und Birkenau* [Factual Report about Auschwitz and Birkenau], in its original German language form, was evidently copied in the office of Nathan Schwalb, Weltzentrale des Hechaluz, Geneva. But the drawing of the Auschwitz camp was retained in its original form, prepared by Rabbi Dov Weissmandl in Bratislava.[24]

Such efforts to transmit information during the war met with delays and, in certain cases, a lack of urgency that the messages demanded. Despite Schwalb's

---

[23] All these documents are found in David S. Wyman (ed.), *America and the Holocaust* (Amherst: University Press, 1989*)*, XII, pp. 82–87.
[24] Preserved at the Roosevelt Library, War Refugee Board, Miscellaneous Documents & Reports Concerning Extermination Camps in Poland, Box 64. This copy has a drawing of the camps that is precisely the same as that of Rabbi Dov Weissmandl. See illustration in Abraham Fuchs, *The Unheeded Cry: The Gripping Story of Rabbi Weissmandl, the Valiant Holocaust Leader, Who Battled Both Allied Indifference and Nazi Hatred* (Brooklyn, NY: Mesorah Publications, 1986, 2nd ed.), p. 137. Weissmandl translated the report into Yiddish, which explains why the illustration shows that language. Cf. David Kranzler, *The Man Who Stopped the Trains to Auschwsitz: George Mantello, El Salvador, and Switzerland's Finest Hour* (Syracuse: University Press, 2000), pp. 68–71. See p. 173 below.

consistent flow of messages and documents to McClelland's office (generally in the German language), and also to Jewish leaders in the United States and Israel, no clear impact can be detected as a result of these efforts. There is no evidence that McClelland's office forwarded the information from Schwalb in any form except summaries until about October, despite the fact that McClelland valued Schwalb's active work and input. McClelland wrote to J. Klahr Huddle, counselor of the legation, in Bern on May 12th, 1944: "The following is a wire sent to me by a very reliable Jew, Nathan Schwalb, head of the Zionist 'Hechalutz' office in Geneva, for transmission . . . Schwalb's organization is doing very creditable work in rescuing people, and I should accordingly recommend that we send this wire for him." [25] Censorship in neutral Switzerland slowed down such communication efforts. But there appeared to be an unwritten policy in place that communication on the Jewish crisis was not a priority for the Allies. C. A. Macartney, in charge of the Hungarian section of the Foreign Office Research Department, articulated this approach for the British side. He advocated the "marginalization and exclusion of information concerning Jews from broadcasts to Hungary." The need to win the war was the priority.[26]

A period of about a month, from about May 17th to about June 14th, elapsed from the time the revelations of the Vrba-Wetzler report arrived in Switzerland until they actually reached the public's attention. What can explain and justify this lengthy delay? In retrospect, it would appear that if a breakthrough had occurred earlier, the

---

[25] Franklin D. Roosevelt Presidential Library, Administrative Matters–Personnel, Box 61. On Schwalb's communications with Slovak Jewish leaders Gisi Fleischmann and Rabbi Michael Dov Weissmandl see Hanna Zweig-Strauss, *Saly Mayer (1882–1850). Ein Retter jüdischen Lebens während des Holocaust* (Köln: Böhlau, 2007).

[26] Michael Fleming, "British Narratives of the Holocaust in Hungary," *Twentieth Century British History* 27/4 (2016): 555–577. https://academic.oup.com/tcbh/article/27/4/555/2525311 Accessed on 8/21/2020 and Gabriel Milland, "The BBC Hungarian Service and the Final Solution in Hungary." In: *Historical Journal of Film, Radio and Television* 18 (1998): 362.

pressure to stop the deportations could have had greater success. After all, the deportations in Hungary had only begun at the middle of May. Certainly the censorship in neutral Switzerland is one explanation. On the other hand, the general policy of marginalizing of rescue efforts by the Allies posed a daunting barrier. The most responsible officers at the legations of the Allies in Switzerland were not inclined to act. The secret services were silent. Only when individuals outside the normal chain of command took initiatives did a new direction emerge.

Dr. Jaromir Kopecky, the Geneva representative of Czechoslovak government-in-exile in Geneva, made the adherence to the policy of marginalization difficult. He had obtained the reports not only of Vrba and Wetzler, but also of two other men, Czeslaw Mordovicz and Arnošt Rosin, who had escaped from Auschwitz on May 27th and reported on the arrival of deportations trains from Hungary. These reports finally reached Geneva on June 13th.[27]

Reading this report, Gerhart Riegner, representative of the World Jewish Congress, suddenly realized what was about to happen in Auschwitz. The six-month "quarantine" program that the Nazis had organized, according to the Vrba-Wetzler report, was about to be carried out again. According to the Vrba-Wetzler Auschwitz Report, an entire family transport from Terezin (Theresienstadt) had been allowed to continue an exceptionally favorable existence. This section of the camp was designated for what the German officials called *Sonderbehandlung* [special treatment]. In a death camp it was certainly special not to require the usual prisoner clothing and to permit families to stay together, without demands for work day and night. This special camp segment served as a showcase model camp to the outside world. But the Vrba-Wetzler report revealed what special treatment really meant: a

---

[27] Martin Gilbert, *Auschwitz and the Allies* (New York: Henry Holt, 1981). p. 232.

six-month pause before death in the gas chambers. So ended this first so-called *Sonderbehandlung* experiment on March 6th, 1944.[28]

But now Riegner held in his hands the new follow-up report on Auschwitz, provided by Mordovicz and Rosin, who had escaped just when the first Hungarian transports were arriving. They provided information about what had transpired in the camp after the escape of Vrba and Wetzler, including, on June 13th the arrival of a second group from Terezin (Theresienstadt), again receiving the special assignment of *Sonderbehandlung*. Immediately, Riegner grasped what this could mean: after six months this family camp would experience the tragic fate of its predecessor. Martin Gilbert, who interviewed Riegner, recalled his words, which he directed to Kopecky, at the moment of this realization: "Have you seen this paragraph? These people are going to be killed in seven days. We must act. We must telegraph to London at once. The BBC can alert the world."[29]

On the same day they contacted Elizabeth Wiskemann at the British legation in Bern. Wiskemann, educated at Newnham College, Cambridge, served in Bern as assistant press attaché, working on intelligence, with a focus on Czechoslovakia. According to Michael Fleming, Wiskemann had been sending regular intelligence

---

[28] Independent reports confirm that postcards, written by inmates from the quarantine camp, gave an idyllic return address: *Waldsee* (forest by the lake). Rudolf Kastner, *Kastner-Bericht über Eichmanns Menschenhandel in Ungarn* (Munich: Kindler, 1961), p. 83.

[29] Martin Gilbert's interview with Riegner took place in Geneva on October 1st, 1980. Cf. Martin Gilbert, *Auschwitz and the Allies*, p. 232. A later interview of April 1995 at the Jewish World Congress in Geneva gives essentially the same information about Riegner's experience and actions, indicating that Gilbert obtained his information directly from the Riegner interview. About Mordowicz and Rosin see Eduard Nižňanský, "The History of the Escape of Arnošt Rosin and Czeslaw Mordowicz from the Auschwitz–Birkenau Concentration Camp to Slovakia in 1944." In: *Resistance of Jews and Efforts to Inform the World on Genocide Conference Proceedings in Žilina, Slovakia, 25–26 August 2015 International Christian Embassy Jerusalem Historical Institute of Slovak Academy of Sciences.*
http://vrbawetzler.eu/img/static/Prilohy/Proceedings_from_Conference_Zilina_2015.pdf
Accessed on July 15, 2020. Cf. Riegner, *Never Despair*, pp. 85–86.

reports from Bern to the Foreign Office in London.[30] She immediately prepared a summary of the facts and sent the requested telegram.

The telegram of June 14th was a plea to prevent the planned massacre, while reporting on the gas chambers. As a result, the outside world learned previously unknown details about Auschwitz. BBC radio broadcast the news and a warning on the following day, and this was reported by German radio monitors:

> Important news! London has been informed: The German authorities in Czechoslovakia have ordered that 3,000 Czechoslovakian Jews are to be murdered in the gas chambers of Birkenau on June 20. These 3,000 Czechoslovakian Jews were sent to Birkenau last December from the Theresienstadt [Terezin] concentration camp [sic] on the Elbe. 4,000 Czechoslovakian Jews who in December 1943 were taken from Theresienstadt to Birkenau were murdered in the gas chambers on March 7. The German authorities in Czechoslovakia and their subordinate offices are notified that in London there is a most detailed record of the mass murder. All those responsible for the mass murder, from the superior authorities through the intermediaries to the organs carrying out the orders, shall be brought to account.[31]

Thus, the Geneva-Bern network achieved a significant breakthrough. News about Auschwitz was reaching the wider public. When he met with Erich Kulka after the war, Riegner learned that even in Auschwitz prisoners heard the news that the BBC

---

[30] After 1958 she held the post of professor for international relations at Edinburgh University. Subsequently, 1958-1971, she served as tutor in modern European history at the University of Sussex. She died in 1971. Cf. Fleming, *Auschwitz, the Allies and Censorship of the Holocaust*, pp. 232 and 369.

[31] Henryk Świebocki, *London Has Been Informed... Reports by Auschwitz Escapees* (Auschwitz: The Auschwitz-Birkenau State Museum, 2008), p. 56. Cf. Gilbert, *Auschwitz and the Allies*, p. 233.

had transmitted. Kulka said: "I was in Auschwitz and can confirm that we had radio transmitters in Auschwitz, and we heard those warnings by the BBC."[32]

Wiskemann passed on the information about Terezin and Auschwitz to Allen Dulles, who, in turn, forwarded it to Roswell McClelland on about June 20th. Wiskemann made a notation that reflected the importance and urgency of the information: "I have just wired this—could you also?" Allen Dulles, the responsible OSS administrator in Bern, sent the information not to Washington, but just to McClelland with the note: "Seems more in your line."[33] For Dulles this was a way to do something in response to Wiskemann, but it was also a way to let the message die a slow death.

New reports arrived. A so-called Polish major (a cover for the actual person of a young medical student named Jerzy Tabeau) confirmed independently that an estimated one and a half million persons had been killed in the death camp. Tabeau escaped from Auschwitz in November 1943. He had prepared a report even before Vrba and Wetzler escaped. He arrived in Budapest in March 1944, just as the Nazis invaded Hungary. Tabeau asserted in an interview that he had no chance to communicate with Hungarians about his report. Because of the German invasion of March 19th he was forced to return to Poland. Tabeau was in Budapest six weeks before the Vrba-Wetzler report arrived. If it had reached the MFM (Magyar Függetlenségi Mozgalom, i.e., the Hungarian Independence Movement), for example, Tabeau's report could have had significant impact in Hungary.

---

[32] The previously mentioned interview of April 1995 at the Jewish World Congress in Geneva mistakenly transmitted the name of the Auschwitz prisoner as Kulpa. He was, in fact, Erich Kulka. See his article "Five Escapes from Auschwitz," in: Yuri Suhl, *They Fought Back: The Story of the Jewish Resistance in Nazi Europe* (New York: Crown Publishers, 1967), pp. 196–218. Kulka refers to the BBC report on p. 215, though not to Riegner's recollection of the incident in Auschwitz.
[33] Gilbert, *Auschwitz and the Allies*, p. 233. The War Refugee Board records show no evidence that the information was sent to or received in Washington.

Nevertheless, when it finally came to light in Switzerland, in combination with the Vrba-Wetzler, it contributed to a significant turning point.[34]

Despite the lack of active US participation, the pressure generated by the new revelations in Switzerland meant that censorship regulators could no longer hold back the avalanche of these revelations. Significant news arrived a few days later also from Moshe (Miklós) Kraus, head of the Palestine Certificate Office in Budapest. He had taken refuge in the compound of the Swiss legation, and from there transmitted reports to George Mantello (György Mandel), first secretary of the El Salvador consulate in Geneva. His was a five-page abridgement of the Vrba-Wetzler report, along with the abridged testimony of Mordovicz and Rosin and, finally, a six-page description of the ghettoization and deportation of Hungarian Jews from the provinces, beginning on May 15th.

Allen Dulles also passed the new Krausz reports to McClelland, after a delay of several days, on June 28th, 1944: "My British friends gave me the attached, which may have reached you through other channels." The fact that Dulles mentioned "British friends" reflects that his contact in this instance, as in the previous one, was probably Elizabeth Wiskemann. In fact, the relationship between Dulles and Wiskemann was close. Douglas Waller remembers: "Elizabeth Wiskemann, a temperamental English journalist and historian working as a press and propaganda attaché for the British legation, who had a trove of old sources in Germany. Dulles charmed her reports out of her with flowers, flirty notes, and fancy meals his cook prepared."[35]

---

[34] Reference to an interview with Jerzy Tabeau in: "The 'Myth' and Reality of Rescue from the Holocaust: The Karski-Koestler and Vrba-Wetzler Reports." *The Yearbook of the Research Centre for German and Austrian Exile Studies* 2 (2000): note 54. Cf. Świebocki, *London Has Been Informed*, p. 23.

[35] Douglas Waller, *Disciples: The War II Missions of the CIA Directors Who Fought for Wild Bill Donovan* (New York: Simon and Schuster, 2015), p. 136.

The close relationship between Dulles and Wiskemann is also illustrated by an incident of July 20, 1944: Wiskemann and Dulles were chatting in the office at the American Bern legation when the news of the assassination attempt on Hitler occurred. "After we had talked a few things over," she recalled, "his telephone rang. He answered it very briefly, as if accepting a piece of news he had rather expected. He put back the receiver and said to me, 'There has been an attack on Hitler's life at his headquarter.' I was not surprised either, but rather excited: we neither of us knew whether it had succeeded. Not until midnight, when he heard Hitler's voice on the radio, did Dulles learn that the plot had failed."[36]

In a pencil note McClelland confirmed that he had also received the information from Krausz in Budapest from another source.[37] Again, it appears that Dulles was not taking the information as seriously as Wiskemann had. Neal H. Petersen asked: "Why did Dulles choose not to emphasize the Holocaust in his reports to Washington?" Peterson proceeded to suggest an answer about Dulles's motivation:

> Given the range of his contacts, associates, and friends, one must assume that he was neither ignorant of nor insensitive to the fate of the Jews. Perhaps he believed that in view of German and European anti-Semitism, highest priority denunciation of the Holocaust would be counterproductive for the purpose of Western psychological warfare.

Peterson also speculated that Dulles might have feared that there would be a flight of refugees and that such would interfere with his espionage activities. For Peterson this subject is among the most controversial and most perplexing about Dulles in

---

[36] Richard Harris Smith, *The Secret History of America's First Central Intelligence Agency* (Guilford CT: The Lyons Press, 2005), p. 221.
[37] Franklin D. Roosevelt Presidential Library, World Refugee Board archives. "Jews in Hungary," Box 66.

Bern. Perhaps the positions taken by Dulles would be more easily understood in the context of the Roosevelt administration's policy, which was to regard the issue of rescue as one that must be put aside in light of the primary goal, the defeat of Germany.[38]

The dramatic new information, which had been held back for about a month and which the American officials of the legation did not take very seriously, suddenly burst forth in the open with an explosive force. These reports became the basis for press releases distributed by Mantello and David Garrett of the *Exchange Telegraph*. The following excerpt found its way into all corners of the country, and beyond:

> FOLLOWING DRAMATIC ACCOUNT ONE DARKEST CHAPTERS MODERN HISTORY REVEALING HOW ONE MILLION 715 THOUSAND JEWS PUT DEATH ANNIHILIATION CAMP AUSCHWITZ BIRKENAU . . . REPORT COME **EX** TWO JEWS WHO ESCAPED BIRKENAU CORRECTNESS WHEREOF CONFIRMED RESPONSIBILITY THEREFORE ACCEPTED **EX** ONE NEUTRAL DIPLOMAT TWO HIGH FUNCTIONARIES **STOP** FROM THE BEGINNING JUNE 1943 NINETY PERCENT INCOMING JEWS GASSED DEATH **STOP** . . . THREE GAS-CHAMBERS FOUR CREMATORIUMS BIRKENAU-AUSCHWITZ STOP EACH CREMATIORIUM . . . TWO THOUSAND CORPS DAILY. GARRET ADDS ABSOLUTE EXACTNESS ABOVE REPORT UNQUESTIONABLE AND DIPLOMAT CATHOLIC FUNCTIONARIES WELL KNOWN VATICAN DESIRE WIDEST DIFFUSION WORLD-WIDE END EXCHANGE.

---

[38] Neal H. Peteresen, *From Hitler's Doorstep: The Wartime Intelligence Reports of Allen Dulles, 1942–1945* (University Park: Pennsylvania State Press, 1996), p. 570. Cf. Rafael Medoff, *The Jews Should Keep Quiet: Franklin D. Roosevelt, Rabbi Stephen S. Wise, and the Holocaust* (Lincoln, NE: University of Nebraska Press, 2019), p. xvi.

In one efficient strike, this initiative ended censorship in Switzerland. The information distributed by Mantello and Garret succeeded in reaching 384 Swiss papers, leading to headlines throughout the country. The world was forced to take notice.[39]

This crucial turning point in the crisis put pressure on Leland Harrison, U.S. Minister in the Bern office, who sent a telegram to Cordell Hull, Secretary of State in Washington. His June 24th telegram reported on the large scale deportations, beginning about May 15th:

> The movement involved 12,000 persons per day. . . . People were deported 60 to 70 per sealed freight wagon for a trip of two to three days without adequate water or food probably resulting in many deaths en route. . . . It is urged by all sources of this information in Slovakia and Hungary that vital sections of these lines especially bridges along one be bombed as the only possible means of slowing down or stopping future deportations.

But then Harrison quickly added his reservations. "This is submitted by me as a proposal of these agencies and I can venture 'no opinion on [the] utility' of this bombing mission, despite the fact that Hungarian Jews are being sent to Auschwitz where at least 1,500,000 Jews have been killed."[40]

There appears to have been a general lack of urgency in getting information to Washington from McClelland's office, which was, after all, the most vital center for knowledge about the Holocaust. It is difficult to explain why essential information, which was acquired in the crucial moments of the middle and late June, was telegraphed only on October 12th, on the same day in which McClelland sent

---

[39] John S. Conway, in the afterword for Rudolf Vrba, *I Cannot Forgive* (Vancouver: Regent College Publishing, 1964), p. 428. Cf. Kranzler, pp. 86–91.
[40] Michael J. Neufeld and Michael Berenbaum, *The Bombing of Auschwitz: Should the Allies Have Attempted It?* (Lawrence: University of Kansas Press, 2003), pp. 256–257.

the message with the Auschwitz Reports. He wrote to John W. Pehle, the director of the War Refugee Board in Washington: "I had occasion to speak here in Bern [June interview!] with a member of the Bratislava Papal Nunciature who had personally interviewed these two young men [on June 20th!] and declared the impression they created in telling their Auschwitz story to be thoroughly convincing. I further understand the responsible members of the Bratislava Jewish community closely crossexamined the authors of this report so that the material finally incorporated into it includes only that about which there was no uncertainty or equivocation in their minds of their examiners."[41]

John Pehle of the War Refugee Board in Washington was far away from the excitement that the stream of news about Auschwitz created in Switzerland. He took up the proposal to bomb the railway lines to Auschwitz and sent it to John McCloy, the Undersecretary for the Army. He wrote: "I made it very clear to Mr. McCloy that I was not, at this point at least, requesting the War Department to take any action of this proposal other than to appropriately explore it. McCloy understood my position and said that he would check into the matter."[42] As could be expected, nothing was done about this half-hearted proposal. Consequently, valuable time was lost.

On June 24th McClelland sent a telegram to the Refugee Board, in which he detailed deportations from the Hungarian provinces. He concluded that he did not doubt that the deportations were directed to Auschwitz and indicated, as had Harrison, the American Minister in Bern, that since 1942 1,500,000 Jews had been killed.[43] When McClelland finally sent the full texts of the Auschwitz Reports of Vrba and Wetzler and the Polish major on October 12, 1944 to Washington, he

---

[41] David S. Wyman (ed.), *America and the Holocaust,* XII, pp.75–76.
[42] Ibid., p. 104.
[43] Ibid., pp. 147–149.

wrote: "While it is of course impossible to directly vouch for the complete authenticity of these reports," he had every reason to believe that they were, "unfortunately, a true picture of the frightful happenings in these camps." But then McClelland concluded his text with reservations about the usefulness of what he was sending:

> Although, in the main, I personally feel that the handling of such material as the enclosed reports cannot be considered as a positive contribution to real relief or rescue activities, it does constitute a tragic side of the whole problem, an awareness of which plays a necessary role in developing and implementing programs destined to bring whatever aid possible to these people.[44]

The comment that these reports "cannot be considered as a positive contribution to real relief or rescue activities" reflects a general tendency that McClelland shared with Harrison and Dulles, namely to restrict information. But in an extraordinary situation, in which secrecy allowed the extermination program to function, it now appears that much could have been achieved by granting wider publicity to those reports. Such publicity materialized eventually, but not because of actions by McClelland, Harrison, or Dulles. The U.S. Bern legation generated relatively weak information, without effective proposals for rescue.

As a result of the uproar that began with the Swiss press, political pressure on the Allied governments intensified. The pressure came in the form of warnings. They

---

[44] Franklin Delano Roosevelt Presidential Library, Records of the Department of State relating to the problems of relief and refugees, (War Refugee Board), Miscellaneous Documents and Reports re Extermination Camps for Jews in Poland (1), Box 69.

hailed down on the Hungarian government from different directions: from President Roosevelt, the Pope, and the king of Sweden.[45]

At a ministers' meeting of June 26th Horthy declared that the deportations must stop. It turned out, however, that words were not enough to produce results; the momentum of the deportations, which Horthy himself had allowed to proceed, was not easily halted. Even if he had wanted to act, Horthy had lost the political and military basis for making sure that he was taken seriously.

Nevertheless, the pressure to halt the deportations continued to mount on Horthy. In this respect an initiative in Switzerland requires special attention. After the publication of his *Auschwitz and the Allies*, Martin Gilbert published an article in *The London Times*, which he based primarily on an interview with Gerhart Riegner. In that interview Riegner was able to supply new information that had not been seen in its proper context. Gilbert's delayed article deserves to be quoted extensively; it supplies a neglected link in the chronology of the decisive sequence of events in Budapest:

"Should the Allies Have Bombed Auschwitz?"
The London Times, January 27th, 2005:

---

[45] Roosevelt's warning of June 26th, relayed by Secretary of State Hull, presented the text which the president had formulated on March 24th. Tsvi (Zwi) Erez asserted that this warning also came down on Budapest in the form of flyers. But he presented no evidence of such a flyer being dropped or found at this particular time. His source only refers to Roosevelt's earlier warning. Tsvi Erez, "Hungary–Six Days in July 1944" in: Randolph Braham (ed.), *Holocaust and Genocide Studies* 3 (1988): 38. Oláh shows, on the other hand, that the particular leaflet that Erez referred to was dropped, but considerably later! András Pál Oláh, "A magyarországi és a légiháború magyar zsidók deportálásának kapcsolatai a II. Világháború idején," [The connection between the deportation of Hungarian Jews and the air war over Hungary during World War II] In: *Belvedere Meridionale* 30 (2018): 69–87.

Gilbert argues here that the bombing was unnecessary because, as a result of initiatives of Richard Lichtheim and Elizabeth Wiskemann, the deportations had ended and bombing no longer made sense. Apparently frustrated by the fact that governments had not acted decisively in the crisis of the deportations, Lichtheim and Wiskemann composed and sent a provocative telegram to the Foreign Office in London. They made specific requests. The most noteworthy for subsequent events are the following:

> [. . .] for the precision bombing of the death camp installations.
>
> The final request was for the target bombing of all collaborating Hungarian and German agencies in Budapest.
>
> The telegram gave the names and addresses of 70 Hungarian and German individuals who were stated to be most directly involved in sending Jews from Hungary to Auschwitz.

Then came a daring calculation, to all appearances a simple twist: "On Wiskemann's inspiration, this telegram was sent uncyphered, to enable Hungarian Intelligence to read it." That agency did read it, as predicted, "and took it at once to the Hungarian Regent, Admiral Horthy, and his Prime Minister, Döme Sztójay . . . "[46]

---

[46] Gilbert continues to discuss the revelations and their consequences. But because there are mistakes in Gilbert's text regarding actions of Horthy and Veesenmayer, corrections are necessary. As we will see further below, Horthy met with Edmund Veesenmayer on July 4th, but Horthy did not demand, as Gilbert contends, the stopping of the deportations at that particular time. Only on the 6th did Veesenmayer learn from Sztójay that Horthy had decided to order definitely to prevent the deportations in Budapest. Veesenmayer did not halt the deportations, as Gilbert writes. Horthy and the tanks from Esztergom did. In Gilbert's presentation it would appear that there was a single telegram. But, as will become evident further below, when Prime Minister Szójay described the decoded telegrams in his conversation of July 6th with the German ambassador, he reported that

Gilbert believed that on the basis of the serious warnings contained in the decoded telegram Horthy was impelled to stop the deportations. That may be true. But the events of early July demonstrate that its impact was actually most dramatic on Horthy's prime minister, Döme Sztójay, and the German Ambassador Edmund Veesenmayer, and thus they played an equally important role in shaping the same outcome.

Without a detailed consideration of all relevant events in Budapest, Gilbert's brief presentation appears to be an oversimplification. The political situation in the summer of 1944 was far too complex to allow for a single explanation for the halting of the deportations in Budapest. There were simply too many powerful forces and events converging with the winding up of the deportations in the provinces. Gilbert seems to be exaggerating the significance of the initiatives taken by Wiskemann and Lichtheim. It is hard to believe that their telegram could really become the decisive factor, as Gilbert believes.

Was Gilbert off the mark by celebrating Wiskemann's role? Her name, at any rate, has not received serious attention from Hungarian historians. What might justify at least certain aspects of Gilbert's assertions? To better understand the initiatives taken by Lichtheim and Wiskemann, it is necessary to consider what had happened a few days earlier.

An increasing stream of alarming news reached Geneva and Bern. Gerhart Riegner, more than anyone else, was taken seriously about the Nazi plans to use gas to destroy the Jewish population of Europe. That was in 1942, but his revelations did not lead to any response in political or military terms. But disturbing news continued to intensify. By June 1944 Riegner could share his frustrations with many

---

the seventy names and addresses were part of a different telegram (one of the three that the Hungarian intelligence agency decoded).

others. Joined by Jaromir Kopecky, Richard Lichtheim, George Mantello, and Elizabeth Wiskemann, he was now part of a concerned network, pleading for the attention of US and British authorities to take the shocking information seriously.

Certainly Willem A. Visser 't Hooft was close to this network. He represented the World Council of Churches, whom Soos had contacted in early 1943. In March of that year Lichtheim and Visser 't Hooft submitted a joint proposal to the governments of Great Britain and the United States suggestions for saving European Jews. Although Nathan Schwalb had valuable contacts in Slovakia and Hungary and had received crucial information directly from Bratislava as early as May, he was secretive and tended to share information only with Roswell McClelland, not with others in Switzerland.[47]

A similar low-level network existed in Hungary, where the disaster for the Jews in the provinces and its impending extension to Budapest were felt most acutely. But here it seemed that here the German army and the Gestapo controlled everything, and actions against them could entail life-threatening risks. Nevertheless, an effective secret Hungarian independence movement (MFM) existed underground. The founder and leader of the MFM, Domokos Szent-Iványi, placed the tasks of Jewish affairs primarily in the hands of two men, Géza Soos and József Éliás, who recognized the impending crisis and the urgency for action. A degree of cohesiveness existed in the MFM in Hungary through numerous affiliations with Calvinists, such as Horthy. Soos, a Calvinist youth leader (president of the organization SDG [Soli Deo Gloria]), was the first in the country to acquire and actively distribute the Auschwitz Report, which he shared immediately with Éliás.[48] Both Soos and Éliás realized that the report represented a matter of great

---

[47] Riegner, *Never Despair*, p. 123.
[48] Éliás, as head of a service organization associated with the Calvinist Church and the Red Cross, was partly Jewish and had contacts to the Jewish population of Budapest.

urgency and had to be passed secretly to all Hungarian religious and political leaders. At a critical point in the subsequent developments, another Hungarian patriot, also a Calvinist, Lt. Col. Ferenc Koszorús, leader of a Hungarian tank division north of Budapest, was won over to prevent deportations from the capital.

Éliás is reported to have taken the regent's daughter-in-law, the Countess Ilona Edelsheim Gyulai, to the Budapest ghettos to show her the deplorable conditions there. Upon her return, she is reported to have said to Horthy "that the deportations from the provinces were continuing and that preparation were being made to remove the Jews of Budapest.[49] At the time when the Budapest deportations were imminent, Soos and Éliás worked out a plan to have young Jews come out of the ghettos and demonstrate against any removal from the buildings.[50]

Considering the initiatives in Hungary and Switzerland, it is possible to recognize that two networks, independently, intensified the series of warnings directed at the collaborating Hungarians and Germans. Soos and Éliás achieved this by revealing the "crime of the century" with the distribution of the Auschwitz Report to key religious and political leaders. A closely related effort was the content of telegrams that Martin Gilbert described in the Lichtheim-Wiskemann telegram, which became evident during the crisis of July 6th. At a critical moment it became a force causing fear, fear in collaborators such as Prime Minister Sztójay about the risk in taking aggressive initiatives and in Horthy about the personal consequences

---

[49] This information, which Soos presented during his OSS interrogation, may not be accurate. Perhaps Soos confused what he had heard about the Valéria Kovács report on the preaprations for deportations in Budapest. Cf. *Rádai Gyüjtemény,* p. 254. See about her report further below.

[50] Bálint Török, "A Magyar Függetlenségi Mozgalom zsidómentő tevékenysége. Az Auschwitzi Jegyzőkönyv 2. Rész." [The Actions of the Hungarian Independence Movement to Save Lives of Jews. The Auschwitz Protocol. Part 2.] *Magyar Szemle,* New Series, 2003. Török explains that Éliás, József Cavallier, and András Sebestyén made this plan, but a number of others are named as participants in the planning, including Soos.
http://www.magyarszemle.hu/cikk/a_magyar_fuggetlensegi_mozgalom_zsidomento_tev%C3%A9kenysege_2_resz Accessed on July 27th, 2020.

of inaction. The telegram evidently unsettled the German Ambassador Edmund Veesenmayer. By causing general disorientation, the telegram established the favorable conditions for Horthy's decision to order a halt to the deportations. The potential significance of the telegram, as suggested by Gilbert, deserves consideration, but not as the single explanation for what occurred, but rather in the broader context of the crisis facing the Hungarian government and Horthy.

As early as June 26th, Horthy had announced at a Crown Council meeting with considerable fanfare that "the deportation of the Jews of Budapest must cease! The government must take the necessary steps!"[51] But the regent's weakened authority became evident when needed actions failed to follow Horthy's words. As decisive as his voice might have sounded, the following days actually reflect developments in the opposite direction, toward the actual implementation of the deportations in Budapest.

The provincial police, the *csendőr* units, rooster-feathered gendarmes with bayonetted rifles, arrived in late June in Budapest.[52] These units had served well for the concentration and entrainment of Jews in the provinces, but now the deportation in the capital provided their most challenging prospect. It is clear that Adolf Eichmann needed them, and now he met with Hungarian Nazi leaders, including László Baky, to discuss how to organize with these units the final, but also most challenging stage of the Nazi vision, to rid Hungary of Jews completely.[53]

---

[51] Braham, *The Politics of Genocide* (New York: Columbia University Press, 1994), II, p. 873.
[52] Ibid., p. 880.
[53] Ibid., pp. 879 and 932. Faragho is said to have participated in the meeting with Eichmann to plan the Budapest deportations. Faragho denied taking part. Cf. C. A. Macartney, *October 15th: A History of Modern Hungary. 1929–1945* (Edinburgh: University Press, 1957), p. 304. On the controversy about Faragho's mysterious behavior see Duncan Bare, "Hungarian affairs of the US-Office of Strategic Services in the Mediterranean Theater of Operations from June 1944 until September 1945," Master Thesis presented at the University of Graz, 2015, p. 89. Cf. Zwi Erez, "Horthy and the Jews of Budapest," in: Michael R. Marrus (ed.), *The "Final Solution" Outside Germany*, II, in: *The Nazi Holocaust* (London: Meckler, 1989), IV, pp. 616–642, here 625.

At about the same time, an assassination attempt took place on the life of István Bárczy, the secretary of the Council of Ministers and Horthy's close friend. He held a key to the secret passage leading from the Sándor palace, the prime minister's residence near the castle, to the residence of the regent. It never became clear whether the intent behind this failed attack was a serious challenge to Horthy. The leader of the MFM, Domokos Szent-Iványi, believed that it was just a bungled burglary attempt, not an act with a political design, organized by a far-right-wing group of Baky's people with German support.[54] At any rate, the attempt, happening at the arrival of the provincial police, served to increase the sense of danger for Horthy.

This danger became abundantly clear when Colonel [Lajos] Kudar, a member of the MFM, was able to win the confidence of a leading provincial policeman, probably Colonel István Láday, chief officer of the Galánta battalion. When he became drunk, Kudar heard him declare "that it was ridiculous for an 86-year-old lunatic king (king of Sweden) to give advice to a 75-year-old nut (Horthy), that they were only fooling themselves if they believed they had stopped the deportations, and that, if necessary, his two battalions would take away the Jews together with their regent." Without hesitation, Kudar informed Horthy's chief bodyguard, Lieutenant-General Lázár, about the danger threatening Horthy. At the same time, he also briefed the leadership of the MFM.

---

[54] Domokos Szent-Iványi, *The Hungarian Independence Movement 1939–1946* (Budapest: Hungarian Review Books, 2013), pp. 492–494. Domokos Szent-Iványi, *Visszatekintés 1941–1972.* [Taking a Look Back] Edited by Nóra Szekér and Gyula Kodolányi (Budapest: Magyar Szemle Könyvek, 2016), pp. 151–155. Szent-Iványi, Domokos. "A Bárczy elleni merénylet [The Assassination Attempt against Bárczy], 1944. június 28–29." In: *Magyar Szemle,* New series, 25, 3–4 (2014).

When precisely the incident with Kudar and the Galánta officer took place is not immediately evident. Swedish King Gustaf V sent his telegram on June 30th.[55] How could the Galánta officer learn about it? It is difficult to imagine that the provincial police officer would have had quick access to the arrival of such a message on a diplomatic level. On the other hand, as a high-ranking intelligence officer Kudar certainly would have learned about the telegram upon its arrival. In other words, the anecdote that spread quickly to a number of persons was probably the result of a conversation in which Kudar revealed that the Swedish king had given advice to the regent. That means that the incident could have taken place as early as July 1, which, in turn, would have provided the members of the MFM urgent need to alert Koszorús about the crisis. Urgency was of the essence.

Valéria Kovács, Horthy's personal friend, whom Horthy had sent to Szeged to report on the conditions under which deportations were taking place, returned on July 2nd. On the following day she told the regent that the provincial police were intending to carry out the deportations without regard to the wishes of the Regent. This news tended to confirm what Kudar had learned from the Galánta officer. It became evident that the successful deportation substantially undermined Horthy's authority.[56]

---

[55] Zoltán Vági et al., *The Holocaust in Hungary* (Lanham, MD: Alta Mira Press, 2013), p. 135. Péter Bajtay, *Emberírtás; Embermentés* [Extermination; rescue] (Budapest: Katalizátor Iroda, 1994), p. 87. If the Galánta officer was István Láday, he was a major figure in the persecution of the Jews. He participated in the deportations and became a leading figure in the Arrow Cross government. He was executed after the war. Elek Karsai and Ilona Benoschofsky (eds.), *Vádirat a nácismus ellen. Dokumentumok a magyarországi zsidóüldözés történetéhez* [Indictment of Nacism in the context of the history of Jewish Persecution in Budapest] (Budapest: Balássi Kiadó, 2017, new edition), IV, p. 1105. See also Láday's recollections below about his confrontation with Horthy and the forced departure of his units.

[56] László Karsai and Judit Molnár (eds.) *Az Endre-Baky-Jaross Per*, (Budapest, 1994), pp. 309–318. See also [Valéria] Istvánné Kováts [Kovács], *Visszapilantó Tükör* (Budapest: GO-Press, 1983), pp. 148–159. Ernő Munkácsi, *How it Happened*, 2018, pp. 199–201. The Washington Holocaust Museum has recorded an interview in Hungarian with Valéria Kovács in which she also

As the result of the new revelations about the intentions of the provincial police, the MFM took decisive steps. The leaders of the MFM delegated two young army officers to Esztergom and advised Ferenc Koszorús about the crisis and the need to respond to the crisis promptly. For a soldier like Koszorús the immediate need to support Horthy in his crisis provided a sufficient cause. As a result, Koszorús lost no time and located Lázár. After hearing about the frustrations of the regent, Koszorús offered the use of his tank division, which the German authorities did not know was in readiness. Koszorús remembered that he met Lázár *by chance* at the banks of the Danube. This statement could be misunderstood to mean that he had no previous interchanges with the MFM about the urgent need to contact Lázár.[57]

The meeting of Koszorús and Lázár took place on July 2nd, the same day a massive bombing attack on the industrial complex south of Budapest occurred. A number of bombs also fell on the city. Although the bombing missions were not part of the Allied effort to influence political events in Hungary, it turned out that they were, in fact, seen that way by many in Budapest. The bombing definitely reinforced the earlier warnings by President Roosevelt.[58]

Koszorús's offer to put his tank division at Horthy's disposal substantially improved the regent's ability to be taken seriously. He wasted no time and assigned special powers to Lázár and Gábor Faragho to take control of the city. He ordered Koszorús to work out the plans to prepare his tank division for the removal of the provincial police. These preparations put Horthy in charge and in a strong position

---

describes the above events. https://collections.ushmm.org/search/catalog/irn509840 Accessed on July 5th, 2020.

[57] Ferenc Koszorús, *Emlékiratai és Tanulmányainak Gyüjteménye* [Collection of Memoirs and Essays], published by the Universe Publishing Company, Englewood, N.J., 1987. (Written in Washington on November 17, 1961.), pp. 55–58.

[58] Richard Davis, "The Bombing of Auschwitz: Comments on a Historical Speculation," in: Michael J. Neufeld and Michael Berenbaum (eds.), *The Bombing of Auschwitz: Should the Allies Have Attempted It?* pp. 214–226.

to end the deportations. On the following day, July 3rd, Koszorús received Horthy's order to outline a plan for the occupation of Budapest.[59]

On July 4th, Horthy asked for a meeting with Veesenmayer. At this meeting the regent did not mention the information from the decoded telegrams. He did not reveal that he had decided to stop the deportations with the aid of tanks. Instead, he provided Veesenmayer with the kind of anti-Semitic sentiments that he expected the ambassador to appreciate. He insisted that he was no friend of the Jews.[60] Instead of announcing his intentions, he expressed concern about the weakening situation on the Russian front and a desire to visit his soldiers to help the cause. The most revealing fact about this exchange is what Horthy did not say. He did not reveal that he had important cards in his pocket: that he had been informed about the decoded telegrams sent from Bern to London on June 26th with serious warnings; nor did he reveal to the German ambassador that he had already given orders to the tank division to expel the provincial police. Horthy's silence on these relevant issues

---

[59] Prominent questions in debates about events in Budapest have been: When did the provincial police units leave Budapest and why. The sequence of events suggests that the threat of force by the tanks was the direct cause for their departure. Faragho's strange, self-serving assertions at the trials after the war that the provincial police came to Budapest to save the Jews, are impossible to believe. László Karsai and Judit Molnár (eds.), *Az Endre-Baky-Jaross Per* (Budapest 1994), pp. 370–372. Cf. Braham, *The Politics of Genocide,* II, p. 879–880. See note 40 on p. 932. Cf. C. A. Macartney, *October 15th: A History of Modern Hungary. 1929–1945*, II, pp. 304–305. Tsvi (Zwi) Erez, "Hungary–Six Days in July 1944" in: Randolph Braham (ed.), *Holocaust and Genocide Studies* 3 (1988): p. 43.

[60] Veesenmeyer reported on this meeting with Horthy two days after it took place. Braham, *The Destruction of the Jewry*, p. 420. Horthy's anti-Semitism was actually also on display in his conversation with the Swedish ambassador on the same day, July 5th. Horthy asserted that the Jews in the eastern provinces were Communists, and he would understand the need to take them away. Per Anger's report to Foreign Minister Christian Günther. Péter Bajtay (ed. and transl.), *Emberirtás; Embermentés. Svéd követjelentések 1944-ből. Az Auschwitzi Jegyzőnyv* [Extermination (and) Rescue: Swedish Diplomatic Reports of 1944. The Auschwitz Protocol] (Budapest: Katalizátor Iroda, 1994), p. 89.

reflected a delay tactic, to withhold from the Germans any information that would alert them about what was about to happen.[61]

The Council of Ministers met on the 5th of July and actively debated the reports about Auschwitz and the planned deportations from Budapest. It is clear from the discussions that took place that by this time the government had knowledge of decoded telegrams. Sztójay referred to the reports as ones originating with the British and American officials in Switzerland.[62]

In the evening of the same day, July 5th, Koszorús received the order from Horthy to occupy the city. Writing in his diary on this day, General János Vörös, chief of the Hungarian general staff, confirmed that the units from Esztergom had occupied the northern sector of Budapest. That same night, Ernő Munkácsi, a member of the Jewish Council, recalled the following events. Two leaders of the provincial police, Colonels Tölgyessy and Paksy-Kiss, experienced leaders of the deportations, could be expected to guide the actions planned for the deportations in Budapest. They were staying at the Pannonia Hotel on Rákoczi Avenue, just a few steps away from the center of Jewish life in Budapest and the headquarters of the Jewish Council on Síp Street.

> Around two o'clock in the morning, a car from the office of the regent pulled up in front of the hotel. A high-ranking officer got out and brought Tölgyessy to the royal castle, where he had to report to Lieutenant-General Lázár, commander-in-chief of the royal guards. Lázár handed him orders made out specifically in his name, to the effect that the command of the consolidated law enforcement troops in Budapest had been transferred to Lázár by the regent. Around four in the morning, the car from the regent's office returned to the hotel and

---

[61] Braham, *Destruction of Hungarian Jewry. A Documentary Account*, pp. 419–424. The text in Hungarian translation is also in: Zsuzsa Hantó and Nóra Szekér (eds.). *Páncélosokkal az életért*, pp. 279–281.
[62] For a general description of the Crown Council meeting on July 5th Cf. Braham, *The Politics of Genocide*, II, p. 881.

took Paksy-Kiss to the castle. In both cases, the vehicle was escorted by sidecar motorcycles armed with submachine guns. Paksy-Kiss was also given his personalized orders by Lázár.[63]

There is, in addition, a testimony of one of Horthy's personal guard, Ernő Bangha, major of the royal guard, written by hand and without date. János Sebők assumes the date might be July 1st. In light of the above description of the dramatic circumstances it would be logical to assume that the confrontation with Baky also occurred during the night of July 5th–6th. Lieutenant-General Lázár explained to Major Bangha and his officers what was going on: László Baky was planning a coup d'état and the deportation of the Jews.

> To prevent this the royal guard invaded the buildings of the castle and with loaded weapons they awaited the expected visitors. . . . Cars appeared at the entrance of the palace door. Officers of the provincial police with the typical rooster-feather hats got out. They crowded around a single person in civilian attire: this was Baky, the secretary of state for internal affairs. . . . The visitors found themselves at a secret double-wing door, Lázár confronted them. . . . In response to a tapping signal the guards stepped forward on both sides of the steps, while closing their ranks in the rear. Hardly disguising alarm, the men followed Lázár up the stairs between the extended bayonets. . . . During the subsequent audience the regent ordered that those provincial police units that had come to Budapest must return to their home bases without delay. If this does not occur, the regent will draw on the army to make sure that his order is obeyed. Without any sign of protest, Baky took note of the order and promised to have it carried out completely.[64]

---

[63] Munkácsi, *How It Happened*, p. 210.
[64] *Magyar Hírlap*, July 5, 1993, quoted by Sebők, *A titkos alku. Zsidókat a függetlenségért. Horthy-mítosz és a holocaust* [The Secret Bargain: The Jews for Independence; Horthy-myth and the Holocaust] (Budapest 2004), pp. 191–192. Jenő Lévai dates this event on July 7th. Cf. *Fekete Könyv a Magyar zsidóság szenvedéseiről* (Budapest: Officina, 1946), p. 177.

Colonel István Láday recalled that later in the morning, at 11:00 a.m., July 6th, he also was called to the palace and reprimanded by the regent. Horthy accused the provincial police of betrayal and insisted that Láday's battalion leave by 4:00 p.m. Láday and his battalion were forced to face the embarrassment when they departed from the city. The men removed their decorative rooster feathers as they marched under the threatening eyes of the Esztergom armored division.[65]

The events of the critical days in early July have been fiercely debated, and there is fundamental disagreement about what Horthy and Koszorús accomplished, precisely when they did and why. Motivations are questioned. It would be helpful, however, to set aside the contention that all these men acted with the primary aim of saving the lives of Jews. Such an interprepation could be the result of an assumption from a later point in time, when the whole world knew about Auschwitz. At this time Horthy was seriously threatened by the prospect of the deportations; the rescue of his own life and political future was evidently a primary motivation for his decisive actions. For a nationalistic career soldier such as Koszorús the primary goal was probably to defend the nation's leader in a serious crisis, at a time when the independence and future of the country had suffered under German occupation.[66]

---

[65] Attila Bonhardt, "The Role of Colonel Ferenc Koszorús in the Prevention of the Deportation of the Jews of Budapest," in: Géza Jeszenszky (ed.), *July 1944: Deportation of the Jews of Budapest Foiled* (Reno, Nevada: Helena History Press, 2017), pp. 203–218, here pp. 215–216. Cf. Hantó and Szekér (eds.), *Páncélosokkal az életért*, p. 39. Láday was a fanatical Hungarian Nazi. See note 54 above.

[66] Ferenc Koszorús, *Emlékiratai és Tanulmányainak Gyüjteménye* [Collection of Memoirs and Essays], published by the Universe Publishing Company, Englewood, N.J., 1987. Written in Washington about November 17, 1961, pp. 55–58. Just as it is with Horthy, views about Koszorús are sharply divided. Peter Pastor questions the motivations that Attila Bonhardt in his essay attributed to Koszorús's actions. Pastor writes that "Bonhardt twisted Koszorús's story in order to show that saving Jews was Horthy's and Koszorus's primary preoccupation." Although that does not appear to be Bonhardt's intention, it would be wrong, at any rate, to claim that Koszorús had been acting mainly to save the lives of Jews. László Karsai has joined Pastor in questioning the historical significance of the Koszorús mission. Pastor quotes Karsai's impressive rhetorical flourish that Koszorús had been, in effect, wasting his time: "By the time Koszorús and his steel chariots rumbled into Budapest, there were no gendarmes there." László Karsai, "Koszorús és a

The same motivation can be assumed for the Hungarian officers, along with other members of the MFM, who had persuaded Koszurús to intervene. Even if Soos, in contrast to the others, had been consistently motivated by the wish to rescue the Jews of Budapest, for him saving the Jews was equivalent to saving Horthy and the nation.

These events set the stage for a climax in the crisis: the lengthy and crucial telephone conversation between Prime Minister Sztójay and the leading figure of the German occupation, Edmund Veesenmayer. On July 6th Sztójay presented dramatic facts to Veesenmayer. He reported Horthy's firm decision to halt the deportations and provided a detailed explanation for this decision. Horthy reportedly argued that in other countries such as Romania and Slovakia, Jews were allowed to remain in their respective countries, that the emigration of rich Jews to Portugal raised serious questions about the justice of the actions against Jews in general, and, that a barrage of telegrams, appeals, and threats had been directed at the regent and the Hungarian government because of the Jewish question.

Finally, stressing the need for the strictest confidence, Sztójay revealed to Veesenmayer the contents of three telegrams that the British and American diplomats in Bern sent to their governments, all of which had been decoded by the Hungarian intelligence agency. Veesenmayer recorded all relevant details for Foreign Minister Ribbentrop in Berlin meticulously:

---

pesti zsidók," ["Koszorús and the Jews of Budapest'] *Népszabadság,* June 8, 2014."Steel chariots" would imply that the tanks were antiquated and worthless. This argument ignores the fact that the provincial (csendör) units probably decided to leave precisely because of the potential use of tanks against them. Cf. Bálint Török, "Legenda vagy Tény?" In: *Új Szemle,* New series, no. IX, pp. 5–6. For Pastor's article see Peter Pastor, "A New Historical Myth from Hungary: The Legend of Colonel Ferenc Koszorús as the Wartime Savior of the Jews of Budapest" in: *Hungarian Cultural Studies.* e-Journal of the American Hungarian Educators Association, Volume 12 (2019): 133–149. Pastor's review focuses on the book edited by Géza Jeszenszky: *July 1944: Deportation of the Jews of Budapest Foiled.* Reno, Nevada: Helena History Press, 2018. See also in that book Attila Bonhardt's article on pp. 214–217.

The telegrams Sztójay had [received] described in detail what was happening to the Jews who were deported from Hungary. The telegrams reported that 1.5 million Jews had already been exterminated, and the same fate awaited the majority of Jews being deported now. The following proposals were made in these telegrams: the bombing and destruction of the destination of the Jewish transports, and, in addition, destruction of the rail lines connecting Hungary with this location. The targets of the bombing, in addition, would be every participating Hungarian and German official buildings—their exact street addresses in Budapest being made available—and a massive propaganda campaign should let the whole world know exactly what was happening. A further telegram named 70 prominent Hungarians and Germans who bore the primary responsibility.

Besides reporting the contents of the telegram, Veesenmayer also reported precisely how the prime minister had reacted to the new information:

> Sztójay told me that he is personally unmoved by these threats because, in the event of our victory, he would view the whole business as uninteresting, and in the alternative scenario, his life would be definitely over. Nevertheless, it was clear that these telegrams had made a strong impression on him. I have heard in the meantime that the council of ministers had also been informed about these telegrams and that there the telegrams had a similar impact.[67]

The prime minister and his colleagues were taking the threats very seriously, not the least because of the bombing threats because, as Veesenmayer noted, the July 2nd bombing "damaged residential areas as well—have been rather unpleasant, and there is widespread worry that after the removal of the Jews, Budapest will perish."

---

[67] IMT, NG–5523 in: Braham, *Destruction of Hungarian Jewry. A Documentary Account*), pp. 425–428. Lévai has published the same report but refers to it as telegram no. 301, NG 5684. Jenő Lévai, *Abscheu und Grauen vor dem Genocid in aller Welt* (New York: Diplomatic Press, 1968), p. 204.

Veesenmayer, together with Eichmann, a chief administrator of the deportations, now realized that there could be a serious argument against them.

What unsettled Sztojay and Veesenmayer, the prospect of Budapest's destruction, added pressure on Horthy. Having had earlier access to these telegrams, they could have influenced him in his decision to stop the deportations. His fate was directly linked to the fate of the city. In this sense the telegrams contributed an additional warning that intensified the previous ones: He must act before it was too late.

When Elizabeth Wiskemann and Richard Lichtheim, frustrated with the lack of Allied action, composed the essential components of these telegrams, they could not have imagined a more effective result of their efforts. The messages fell into the hands of the two perpetrators at a decisive moment. Sztójay and Veesenmayer had to pay attention to what was happening around them. They had important decisions to make. But suddenly they faced directly what they were accustomed to suppress: the consequences of Germany's defeat. The bombing of Budapest on July 2nd (though not actually planned as a warning, being directed to the industrial complex south of Budapest) could have provoked such thoughts, but the present confrontation with a future precision bombing of Budapest, targeting Sztójay and Veesenmayer, together with their associates, must have been devastating. They had to imagine Budapest's destruction. They realized that the deportations could be the direct cause of such an outcome. For the prime minister there was the additional suggestion: if the Germans lost the war, then the consequence for himself would be his execution (which, in fact, was the actual outcome). The two men, while they had been confidently directing the execution of others, were now unprepared to face their own demise.

The segment of the telegrams that revealed seventy names and addresses of collaborators to be targeted was missing from the otherwise identical telegram of

June 26th that Lichtheim sent to the secretary of the Jewish Agency for Palestine in London. It is not clear whether the names of seventy collaborators were actually listed in one of the other telegrams. How such a list was inserted, together with the warning about precise bombing of governmental buildings, remains a mystery. [68]

There are indications that a number of persons worked together to accomplish this result. A person involved in intelligence work at the British or Hungarian legations might have been able to provide such a list. At any rate, the mere reference to such list and the precision bombing could function to increase fear. To solve this mystery historian Jenő Lévai provided a tempting clue:

> Colonel F. M. West, the British military attaché in Bern, and the air attaché Colonel Gripp, with the concurrence of the British Minister Norton, agreed to a request from George Mantello, a diplomat from San Salvador, of Hungarian-Jewish extraction, and conveyed through intermediaries some passages from radio signals, to the Hungarian military attaché, Colonel Dr. László Rakolczay. He passed them on, saying they had been decoded by Hungarian radio monitors. [69]

---

[68] As Veesenmayer indicated, there were three telegrams. One, initiated by Lichtheim, was sent by John Clifford Norton, British minister in Bern, on June 26th to the Foreign Office in London. Norton telegram, No. 2949. Martin Gilbert, *Auschwitz and the Allies*, p. 251–252. This particular telegram is also to be found in: Francis R. Nicosia, *Archives of the Holocaust*. Volume 4, Central Zionist Archives Jerusalem (New York: Garland, 1990), pp. 297–298. The same telegram was decoded by the Germans. It was sent to Kaltenbrunner by Horst Wagner. At the Foreign Office Wagner dealt with Jewish affairs in *Abteilung Inland II*, which worked with Adolf Eichmann on the deportation. The document with the telegram to Ernst Kaltenbrunner has been published in "Akten zur deutschen Auswärtigen Politik 1918–1945", Series E, vol. VIII, p. 165–166. These two telegrams are identical; they both lack, however, the final points that Veesenmayer is referred to in the report he received from Sztójay. What was precisely in the second or third telegrams is a mystery. At the very least one of these would have had information about seventy collaborators.
[69] Lévai, *Abscheu und Grauen vor dem Genocid in aller Welt*, p. 204. Tsvi Erez translated the original German text. Tsvi Erez, "Hungary–Six Days in July 1944," in: Randolph Braham (ed.), *Holocaust and Genocide Studies* 3 (1988): 47–48 and 52.

What were the "passages" from radio monitors and to whom did they have to be transmitted? This transmission of messages suggests that George Mantello, who had been working with Lichtheim and Wiskemann earlier, was again involved in an effort to make sure that the truth about Auschwitz became known. Moreover, it appears that Colonel Dr. László Rakolczay became a willing participant in the conspiracy to get information to key persons in Hungary. The number of conspirators hoping to trick the Germans was increasing. Unfortunately, we have no information about the content of the messages that Rakolczay sent. They could explain how the reference to the seventy names of collaborators became a factor in the July crisis.

The appearance of the name of the Hungarian military attaché in Bern, Dr. László Rakolczay, in this context adds still another mysterious element. It confirms that he was keenly aware of the need to enlighten the Hungarian authorities about German intentions. In early July, he appears, once again, as an informant in support of Regent Horthy. He had been invited, together with the chief secretary of the Hungarian legation, Imre Tahy, to a small gathering to view a film produced by the German Propaganda Ministry.

The "documentary" had two parts. The first part showed the Hungarian provincial police in Nagyvárad (today Oradea, in Romania), beating women with rifle butts, chasing children with whips, and tearing wedding rings off the helpless victims. The Hungarian officers with their rooster-feather hats pressed the Jews into the freight cars. No Germans were present in this segment of the film. But in the second part they appeared to show how they took over the transports in Slovakia from the cruel Hungarians. At this point there was the shock of the German Red Cross nurses as they opened the sealed cars. Horrified, they removed corpses, and distribute fresh water and food to emaciated victims still alive. While the first part of the film probably reflected reality, the second part was clearly staged.

At the conclusion of the film there was applause. The diplomats were convinced. Only a few in the audience knew that the first part of the film was genuine and reflected a sad reality, but the other part was a staged film prepared by Eberhard Taubert, the film producer for Propaganda Minister Goebbels. The purpose of this trick was to undermine the vehement press campaign in Switzerland.[70]

The Hungarian government reacted immediately. Baron Károly Bothmer, the Hungarian Chargé d'Affaires in Bern, at the request of Mihály Arnóthy-Jungerth, the Deputy Foreign Minister in Hungary, lodged a protest against the film. Mantello also indicated the need to withdraw the film. The German authorities soon realized that the film was not achieving the desired effect and put it aside. No copy is known to have survived. Historian Randolph Braham believes that Horthy, after learning of the news about this film, became more determined to stop the deportations.[71]

The intended disorientation and distractions intruded into the political crisis at a critical moment. Such incidents cannot be considered as major factors in the

---

[70] Lévai, *Abscheu und Grauen vor dem Genocid in aller Welt,* pp. 223–224. The second part of the film was staged in Theresienstadt. Sebők believes that the news of the film arrived about June 22nd. János Sebők. *A titkos alku. Zsidókat a függetlenségért. Horthy-mítosz és a holocaust* [The Secret Bargain: The Jews for Independence; Horthy-myth and the Holocaust] (Budapest 2004), pp. 177–178.

[71] Braham, *The Politics of Genocide,* I, pp. 679-680. Braham's source is Révai in the previous note. Braham does not provide dates or further documentation. In the meeting of minister's council of July 5 there appears to be reference to this affair when, according to a report by the Bern minister, the Hungarians were committing brutal acts against the Jews. The fact that the active foreign minister, Arnóthy-Jungert, informed Horthy about the film supports the thesis that the news had a significant impact. Mester suggests that Faragho at this time switched sides against Baky and became more supportive of Horthy. Miklós Mester, *Arcképek két tragikus kor árnyékában* [Portraits in the Shadows of Two Tragic Periods], pp. 76–77. Cf. Sebők, pp. 177–178 and Gellért, pp. 103–104. To be sure, a fictional dramatization by Leo Kanawada, *Holocaust Diaries, V* (Bloomington, IN: Author House, 2010), p. 571, asserts that the news of the film came to Horthy on July 4th.

course of events, but they add crucial elements to those decisive factors. The news about the telegrams and the propaganda film became known when the responsible German official needed to pay attention to what was actually happening. At this time the maneuver to drive out the provincial police was already in progress. Baky, the Hungarian Nazi leader directly involved in the deportations, hoped that S.S. units would be called in. No such action had been planned or approved by the Germans; Veesenmayer insisted that the deportation had to be a Hungarian mission. It was his job to make sure that Hungary could be held peacefully, without the use of military resources needed at the Russian front. In fact, he had promised Hitler that there would be no more demands on military force in Hungary. Adolf Eichmann, the model organizer of the next and final steps in his ambitious deportation project, the momentary paralysis and the inability to respond, created a new political situation. The machinery of the deportations could not proceed as previously planned.

As Veesenmayer reported to Berlin in his telegram on the following day, the Budapest deportations were not about to take place. On July 8th he complemented the information: "In the course of the last forty-eight hours I received reliable information that State Secretary Baky and the provincial police had intended to carry out a coup d'état. The regent reacted by alarming the Budapest garrison and forcing the provincial police to return to their home bases." As an afterthought, Veesenmayer complained to the regent that he was sorry that the latter had neglected to tell him in advance what measures he was about to have carried out.[72] For Horthy,

---

[72] Braham, *Destruction of Hungarian Jewry. A Documentary Account* (New York: Pro Arte, 1963), pp. 436–438. In a telegram of July 9th Veesenmayer asserted to the minister of interior affairs, Andor Jaross that the Budapest deportations had to be carried out by the Hungarians and not by the units of the S.S. Ibid., p. 441. In other words, there was an attempt by Jaross to get help from the Germans in an effort to carry out the deportations. This would support the claim that Koszorús makes about the desperate telephoning of the Baky people. Veesenmayer had assured Hitler that the calling of S.S. troops would not be necessary. Mario D. Fenyo, *Hitler, Horthy, und Hungary: German-Hungarian Relations, 1941–1944* (New Haven: Yale University Press, 1972), p. 205. Cf. Lévai, *Black Book*, p. 325.

the element of surprise, achieved with the aid of the tanks from Esztergom and the distraction of the Wiskemann-Lichtheim telegrams, helped to stop the deportations.

Eichmann still succeeded in secretly slipping transports from the camps at Kistarcsa and Sárvár toward Auschwitz. But a relative peace and security for the Jewish population prevailed until October 15th, 1944, when Horthy was arrested and forced to abdicate. Despite this setback, which brought on the renewed, devastating persecution of Jews by the Nazi Arrow Cross Party, the deportations could not be renewed. It is undeniable that the actions of early July that halted the Budapest deportation can be considered a singular rescue effort of the war.

Although Regent Horthy's decisive actions were partly responsible for this outcome, it would be a mistake to ignore the role of the resistance and rescue networks within Hungary, led in Budapest by Géza Soos, József Éliás, Ferenc Koszorús, and networks operating in Switzerland with Gerhard Riegner, Richard Lichtheim, Jaromir Kopecky, George Mantello, and Elizabeth Wiskemann, among others. They made it possible for Regent Horthy to recover from his initial, disastrous adherence to the deportations.

Several Hungarian historians have attacked what they consider a widespread myth, namely that Horthy and Koszorús acted in July 1944 to save the Jews of Budapest. Randolph Braham also referred to the promotion of Horthy and Koszorús in a heroic context as a cleansing of history. He viewed this false historical writing as an effort to rehabilitate Miklós Horthy and the entire Horthy era. Available evidence fails to prove that the primary motivation behind the actions of Horthy and Koszorús was to save Jews. Because there is no convincing evidence to prove such an intention, the exclusive focus to explain the course of events in early July 1944 has been misleading. After all, during the July crisis, interests in self-preservation, represented by Horthy, and attaining independence from Hitler's Germany, represented by Koszorús and Soos, converged to prevent further deportations.

The chronology lays out a complex situation in which the revelations of the Auschwitz Report became the decisive catalyst for public awareness and rescue efforts. In Hungary, Géza Soos and the MFM recognized that the facts about Auschwitz necessitated even military action. But such bold initiatives in Hungary required outside support. Corresponding initiatives by networks in Switzerland to make the Auschwitz Report public succeeded, despite the efforts of authorities to marginalize the report. Because of the publicity, urgent telegrams from different directions, from President Roosevelt, the Pope, and the King of Sweden, warned Hungary to stop the deportations. Because of these powerful pressures, Horthy resolved to act. But to provide credibility to his orders, Horthy relied on the tanks under Koszorús's command. As a result of this show of force, all preparations to carry out deportations in Budapest ceased.

For Horthy the window of opportunity to abandon his tragic pact with Hitler opened only briefly. When Soos, Koszorús, Wiskemann, and others in Switzerland finally created conditions to stop the deportations, Horthy recognized that delaying was not an option. Views diverge about his personal or political calculations. He might have feared a coup d'état in Hungary or punishment by the victorious Allies. Nevertheless, Horthy's resolute action was instrumental in saving many thousands of Jews in Budapest.

II. Soos and Wallenberg: Intrigues and Risks of Rescue

Following closely upon the tumultuous events of early July, when Raoul Wallenberg arrived in Budapest, one of his first consultations with Géza Soos took place. This was predictable. Both men were intensively concerned with rescue missions in response to the unrelenting Nazi war against the Jews. In response to the initiatives of the War Refugee Board (WRB) in Washington, Herschel Johnson, head of the American legation in Stockholm, wrote that Wallenberg had made a "very favorable impression." He would be able to "act intelligently and with discretion" to accomplish whatever the WRB delegated to him.[73] Sven Grafstöm, the head of the Swedish foreign ministry's political department, understood that the very delicate arrangement would also involve Per Anger in the Budapest Swedish legation. He confided in his diary that Wallenberg had been sent to Budapest "with American money, to help the persecuted Jews."[74]

After his arrival, on July 11th, Wallenberg met with Soos at the home of Per Anger, who served as second secretary at the Swedish legation in Budapest. A few days later, Wallenberg, also met with József Éliás, fellow member of the MFM.[75]

---

[73] June 28th, 1944. Franklin Delano Roosevelt Presidential Library, Records of the Department of State relating to the problems of relief and refugees, (War Refugee Board), cable no. 2360. Cf. Rebecca Erbelding, *Rescue Board: The Untold Story of America's Efforts to Save the Jews of Europe* (New York: Doubleday, 2018), pp. 171–172. Rebecca Erbelding, "The United States War Refugee Board, the Neutral Nations and the Holocaust in Hungary," in: *Bystanders, Rescuers, or Perpetrators? The Neutral Countries and the Shoah* (Berlin: Metropol Verlag, 2016), pp. 183–197.
[74] Johan Matz, "Sweden, the United States, and Raoul Wallenberg's Mission to Hungary in 1944," in: *Journal of Cold War Studies* 14 (Summer 2012): 97–148, here 124–125.
[75] Mária Ember, *Wallenberg Budapesten* (Budapest: Városháza, 2000), pp. 32–33.

Having been assigned by the MFM to deal with the Jewish crisis, it was only natural that Soos would be put in touch with Wallenberg as soon as he arrived in Budapest. Soos recalled: "I was one of the first persons he looked up. Then I spent a long evening of discussion with him and his friend Anger."[76] These meetings did not occur by chance. In preparation for Wallenberg's arrival, there were efforts in Stockholm to supply him with useful contact information for his initial orientation. Andor Gellért, a person well known to both Soos and Wallenberg had played a role in the preparation of these meetings

Wallenberg recorded in his diary, shortly before he left for Budapest, on July 1st: "Gellért visiting me."[77] As a journalist, Gellért was in an ideal position to advise Wallenberg for his Budapest assignment. Gellért remembered that he had given Wallenberg letters of introduction to forty Budapest residents. Of these he considered Soos most important.[78]

Another person in an ideal position to provide help for Wallenberg with orientation in Budapest was Vilmos Böhm, an exiled Hungarian politician. A former war commissioner and lieutenant-general of the Hungarian Red Army, he had command of information about Hungary. Böhm worked closely with Gellért. As a result, there was a potential hazard for Wallenberg. There are reasons to believe that

---

[76] In: Ilona Tüdős [Mrs. Géza Soos] (ed.), *Evangéliumot Magyarországnak. Soos Géza Emlékkönyv* [The New Testament for Hungary. The Legacy of Géza Soos] (Budapest: Bulla, 1999), pp. 254–255.

[77] Ember, *Wallenberg,* pp. 32–35 and 63–64.

[78] Soos was "...not only personally always at the disposal [of Wallenberg], but provided him with many valuable staff." Duncan Bare, "Hungarian affairs of the US-Office of Strategic Services in the Mediterranean Theater of Operations from June 1944 until September 1945," Master Thesis presented at the University of Graz, 2015, pp. 84–85, note no. 422. I am grateful to the author for making his original research results available. See also a relevant study by the same author: "Angleton's Hungarians. A Case Study of Central European Counterintelligence in Rome 1945/46," in: *Journal for Intelligence, Propaganda and Security Studies* 9/1 (2015): 8–24.

Böhm, a fervent socialist, passed on information to the Russians.[79] In view of the political situation that developed with the defeat of the Germans and Russians taking full control of Hungary, the association with Gellért and his circle could come back to haunt Soos and well as Wallenberg.

The mysterious figures of Gellért and Böhm lead us into a realm of intelligence intrigues, the implications of which perhaps neither Soos nor Wallenberg was fully aware. For them rescue work was the matter of utmost concern; they were not inclined to be critical of any help offered. Wallenberg's associations were primarily with the newly established War Refugee Board, the board that reached out to neutral governments to find a way to help threatened people in Hungary. At the U.S. Stockholm legation, Iver Olsen and Herschel Johnson acted quickly to identify Wallenberg as the ideal person for this task. Olsen was primarily responsible for financial affairs at the legation, but his simultaneous duties also linked him to the OSS, one of the CIA's forerunners. As a result, from the beginning the appointment of Wallenberg acquired an invisible, but still indisputable, link to the American intelligence service.

Who was Andor Gellért? How did he play a pivotal role in the subsequent days for both Soos and Wallenberg? Gellért (1907–1990), combined his career as a journalist with work for the Hungarian foreign service, but from the beginning his work was never what it appeared.[80] In 1938 he arrived in Berlin under cover of a reporter, representing a Budapest newspaper, *Pesti Hírlap*. His real task was intelligence work. In Germany's capital he may have demonstrated his efficiency by acquiring contacts with members of the American embassy. His work in Berlin

---

[79] Ember, pp. 34–36. Wilhelm Agrell, *The Shadows around Wallenberg: Missions to Hungary, 1943–1945* (Lund: Historiska Media, 2019), pp. 175 and 189–190. Originally in Swedish: Wilhelm Agrell, *Skuggor runt Wallenberg: Uppdrag i Ungern 1943–1945* (Lund: Historiska Media, 2006).
[80] In the years 1954–1957, in the period when the Hungarian revolution occurred, Gellért was director of Radio Free Europe in Munich.

earned him new tasks when disillusionment set in about Hungary's role in the war on the side of Germany. The new Hungarian government, under Prime Minister Miklós Kállay, organized secret diplomatic contacts for peace with the Allies. After moving to Stockholm in the summer of 1942, Gellért was encouraged to contact responsible British subjects, communicating efforts of Prime Minister Kállay to prepare a possible abandonment of the alliance with Germany. These efforts, which were also conducted by a variety of messengers in other countries, in Turkey, the Vatican, and Switzerland, had failed. The failure was due to the fact that Hungary had to offer unconditional surrender, which, given the entanglement with Nazi Germany and its geographical position, it was unable to do.[81]

There existed a mistaken assumption that such discussions, conducted in several locations, could be kept secret from the Germans. Hitler soon learned of them, and he knew how to put a quick end to them: by means of the March 19th, 1944 invasion that ended all behind-his-back discussions of peace. But he also accomplished potentially something else that concerned him very much: the solution in Hungary of the Jewish question, which, in his view, Hungary had not dealt with properly.[82]

---

[81] C. A. Macartney, *October 15th: A History of Modern Hungary. 1929–1945*, II, pp. 121–143; Code name for Gellért was Willard, but Agrell knew of the designation Mountaineer. Agrell, *The Shadows around Wallenberg*, p. 189. According to Duncan Bare, records reveal efforts by Gellért and Antal Ullein-Reviczky to make contact with the Allies, meeting from December 1943 until at least February 1944 with OSS and State Department representatives on behalf of the Kállay Government. Duncan Bare, "Hungarian affairs of the US-Office of Strategic Services in the Mediterranean Theater of Operations from June 1944 until September 1945," pp. 83–85. Cf. Gellért Kovács, *Alkonyat Budapest felett. Az embermentés és ellenállás 1944–45-ben* [Dusk over Budapest: The History of Rescue and Resistance in 1944–45] (Budapest: Libri, 2013), pp. 127–130. László Veress, a Hungarian Foreign Ministry official, was dispatched in February 1943 by Kállay to contact the British in Istanbul. Agrell, *The Shadows around Wallenberg*, p. 142. Veress was seriously involved in preparing for Hungary a surrender agreement with the British on September 18th, 1943, but it was not finalized. Macartney, II, pp. 184–187.

[82] Allen Dulles explained the causes of the German invasion of Hungary: "(1) They knew that the Hungarians were carrying on discussions with the Anglo-Saxons; (2) they did not want a *Badoglio* [i.e., the overthrow of Mussolini] in Hungary; (3) there were approximately 1,000,000 Jews behind

After the German army invaded Hungary in March of 1944 and after the new government dictated by the Nazis had been established, both Andor Gellért and the head of the Hungarian legation in Stockholm, Minister Antal Ullein-Reviczky, were dismissed. Gellért turned first to the British authorities to seek employment. They refused to help him. Creating a complication that was to have significance for both Soos and Wallenberg, he then began working for the American secret services, the Office of Strategic Services (OSS). The generous helping hand he offered to Wallenberg at their meeting of July 1 had to be seen at the time as welcome aid for orientation in a hostile Budapest.[83] But later events throw a different light on the consequences of Wallenberg's association not only with Gellért, who was soon to become an OSS man, but even with the War Refugee Board, which was his employer and had its goals set on rescue. Gellért's activities, however, may have been viewed differently by agents at the Soviet legation in Stockholm, who were certainly aware of his projects and contacts.[84]

---

the German armies, and this the Germans could not stand." RG 226, Entry 97.box 35, cable no. 2548–2549. Schlomo Aronson, "OSS X-2 and Rescue Efforts During the Holocaust," in: David Bankier, *Secret Intelligence and the Holocaust* ((New York: Enigma Books, 2006), p. 91, also in: Schlomo Aronson, *Hitler, the Allies, and the Jews* (New York: Cambridge University Press, 2004), p. 221.

[83] Ingrid Carlberg, *Raoul Wallenberg: The Biography* (London: MacLehose Press, 2016), p. 222. Ilona Tüdős [Mrs. Géza Soos] (ed.), *Evangéliumot Magyarországnak, Soos Géza Emlékkönyv* (Budapest: Bulla, 1999), p. 142. Johan Matz, "Sweden, the United States, and Raoul Wallenberg's Mission to Hungary," *Journal of Cold War Studies* 14 (2012): 97–148. Kovács, *Alkonyat Budapest felett*, pp. 127 and 130.

[84] British services expressed reservations about Gellért. Agrell, *The Shadows around Wallenberg*, pp. 179, 187–190, and 209. Such reservation could have been based on Gellért's associations with Vilmos Böhm, who had connections to the secret services of the Soviet Union. Böhm actually tried to recruit Gellért for the Russians, but was unsuccessful. It was about this time that Gellért was recruited by the Americans. "In July Taylor Cole, head of SI in Stockholm, wants to recruit G[ellért] for contacts in Hungary." On December 23rd, 1944 Roosevelt actually ordered some records to be turned over to the Russians. Agrell, *The Shadows around Wallenberg*, pp. 38–39 and 206. Antal Ullein-Reviczky, *German War; Russian Peace: The Hungarian Tragedy* (Paris: Éditions de la Baconnière, 1947), p. xxiii.

On August 15th, 1944, by the time the United States army was securely established in southern Italy, Gellért's American secret service superiors made arrangements for Gellért to travel to Bari, the base for Secret Intelligence Central Europe (SICE), with which Gellert was in constant contact. His instructions constituted a response to discussions about sending agents to become active within Hungary.[85] There were plans to deliver two radio transmitters (WTs) to specific persons in Budapest, whom Gellért was asked to identify. Thorston Akrell (Acrel), as a Swedish diplomat accepted the task as courier.[86] He arrived in Budapest on September 4th. A cryptic communication of November 7th between OSS members in Italy appears to indicate that Soos did, in fact, receive access to one of the transmitters: "[Géza Soos] may be contacted only through Per Anger, Swedish legation in Budapest. Raoul Wallenberg of the same legation will know if he is not in Budapest. Soos has a Swedish signal plan, the whole affair was administrated by Swedes. . . . "[87] Although Soos later denied that he actually received a radio transmitter intended for him by Gellért, he had, nevertheless, access to the communication facilities of the Swedish legation. Here we have, coincidentally, confirmation of the close collaboration between Soos and Wallenberg.

It is important to consider this murky background and evolution of the American intelligence agency's activities. Much that took place at this time has come to light primarily in the records of the American secret services. They help to explain the tragic consequences for Wallenberg when he was arrested, soon after the Soviet army encircled Budapest and laid siege to the castle with its German retreating defenders. Confident of imminent victory, Russian leaders were by this

---

[85] OSS in Bari wanted Gellért in Italy to plan for "a penetration into his homeland." Agrell, *The Shadows around Wallenberg*, pp. 201 and 207.
[86] Ibid., p. 210.
[87] Ibid., pp. 214–215. "Willard [code name for Gellért] sent an American radio set to Soós through the Swiss pouch. This Soós never received." 423–424.

time consolidating their political hold on this country against potential enemies. On January 16th 1945, they located Wallenberg and considered what to do with him. A few weeks later the embassy of the Soviet Union informed Wallenberg's mother that Wallenberg was under the protection of the Red Army in Budapest.[88] But months earlier, starting in the middle of October, just when the Arrow Cross Party came to power, the consequences resulting from the Russian capture of Budapest could not be imagined yet; in that earlier time there were still the threatening wild raids and killings by the German and Hungarian Nazis to contend with. The Gestapo was searching for Soos. There were several instances when only a few minutes separated his escape from the serious consequences of arrest.[89]

In October 1944, having realized that that there was no hope of winning Allied support, Horthy turned, in desperation, to Russia to make peace. He sent MFM members Szent-Iványi and Faragho to negotiate with the Soviet Union. While Szent-Iványi was in the Soviet Union to negotiate with the Russians, Soos was left as the leader of the MFM. On October 16th, the day after Horthy's announcement of this desperate decision for an armistice, he was arrested and overthrown. The Germans took Horthy and his family to Bavaria as prisoners.[90]

The far-right Nazi Arrow Cross Party took control of the government and restarted the violent persecution of the Jews. While Szent-Iványi was in Moscow, Soos remained in Budapest as the leader of the MFM. Although the MFM had an estimated membership of about 2,700, it was helpless to prevent the rampages of the

---

[88] Ember, p. 129
[89] Soos writing to his wife on December 10th 1944. Ilona Tüdős (ed.), *Evangéliumot Magyarországnak,* p. 159.
[90] Macartney has provided a detailed description of these dramatic events. Macartney, II, pp. 391–443. Thomas Sakmyster, *Hungary's Admiral on Horseback: Miklós Horthy 1918–1944* (Budapest: Columbia University Press, 1994), pp. 366–380.

Arrow Cross people.[91] Soos hoped to make contact with the advancing Russians to create conditions that would avert the destruction of Budapest. Not being able to establish safe communications with the advancing Russian army, Soos turned to the Americans. His decision was influenced by Andor Gellért, who advised Soos to find a way to get to Italy and to meet there.

The OSS at Bari in Italy had indicated that it wanted Gellért for assistance on projects involving "penetration of his homeland."[92] Gellért welcomed this news in Stockholm. He prepared to leave for Italy and hoped Soos could escape to meet him there. Gellért transferred to Bari in September 1944, to be part of the upcoming Budapest City Unit.[93] He hoped that Soos would be a partner in the adventure.

The decision to join Gellért and the Americans meant that Soos would be making contact with the OSS. It was not the first time that Soos had contact with the world of the American intelligence services. The OSS documents reveal that in early 1943 Soos, an official of the Hungarian Foreign Ministry, was entrusted to travel to Switzerland, ostensibly to participate in a conference of the World Council of Churches (WCC). Soos and Elek Boér (1899–1954), a judge and member of the Hungarian parliament, were assigned to deliver a message from Bishop László Ravasz.[94] The bishop's presentation to the conference revealed extremely

---

[91] Elek Karsai, "Soos Géza és Hadnagy Domokos tájékoztatása a magyarországi helyzetről és a Magyar Függetlenségi Mozgalomról 1944 decemberében" [Report of Géza Soos and Domokos Hadnagy about the Hungarian Situation and the Hungarian Independence Movement in December 1944], in: *Raday Gyüjtemény Évkönyve*, [The Annual of the Raday Collection], IV–V (Budapest, 1986), pp. 238–287, here p. 243. Cf. Duncan Bare, "Hungarian Affairs of the U.S.-Office of Strategic Services in the Mediterranean Theater of Operations from June 1944 until September 1945," p. 84.
[92] Agrell, *The Shadows around Wallenberg*, p. 207.
[93] Duncan Bare, "Hungarian affairs of the U.S.-Office of Strategic Services in the Mediterranean Theater of Operations from June 1944 until September 1945," p. 84.
[94] A letter from the ministry of foreign affairs to the ambassador of Hungary in Switzerland, Baron György Bakách-Bessenyey, indicates that Soos was being assigned to go to Switzerland for two to three weeks as a courier in cultural matters ("kulturális futárként"). Dated January 13th, 1943. The Hungarian National Library (i.e., Magyar Nemzeti Levéltár (MNL) K 448 15 cs.

conservative views of the dangers of Communist Russia. Visser 't Hooft met the delegation but refused to receive the document from Ravasz formally because he considered it to be too mild in its formulations on National Socialism and thought it exaggerated the wickedness of the Communist ideology and practice."[95]

Soos and Boér had at least two different, unrelated assignments in Switzerland in 1943. In fact, their participation in the international church conference was a cover for a secret diplomatic mission, not unlike Gellért's, initiated once again by Prime Minister Kállay.

This dual function becomes evident in OSS records. In the period May–June, Soos was in Bern to conduct secret talks with two men, [Zsolt] Aradi and [Tamás] Perczel. They represented Baron Gábor Apor, the Hungarian ambassador in the Vatican. The latter was considered a reliable anti-Nazi among the Hungarian ambassadors. All indicators point to real focus of discussions: once again Prime Minister Kállay's desperate need to force the United States to listen, to facilitate Hungary's escape from Germany's stranglehold. It was Visser 't Hooft who helped Soos to make contact with Allen Dulles, who represented the OSS in Bern.[96]

---

[95] László Gonda, "The Service of Evangelism, the Evangelism of Service: The Influence of John R. Mott, Hendrik Kraemer, Willem A. Visser 't Hooft and Johannes C. Hoekendijk on the Development of the Understanding of Mission in the Reformed Church in Hungary (1910–1968)" Ph.D. diss. 2008, p. 127.
http://www.bratislavachurch.net/file/BRATI/s_board/20131008143309350/Gonda%20Laszlo%20-The%20Service%20of%20Evangelism%20The%20Evangelism%20of%20Service.pdf
Accessed on 27/8/2020.

[96] On the Aradi-Perczel-Apor contacts in 1943 see the OSS report on pp. 122–123 below. Visser 't Hooft was a Calvinist. Other contacts mentioned: "Lipot Baranyai, Visser 't Hooft, Allen Dulles (th[r]ough Visser 't Hooft), and Elizabeth Wis[ke]eman[n]." OSS record of Jan. 5th, 1945. Cf. Appendix at the end of this chapter. It is not likely that an approach to Dulles at this time would have favorable results. Allen W. Dulles (OSS Chief in Bern, Switzerland) expressed his attitude toward Hungarians when he stated "there is, on the part of these people [the Hungarians] a tantalizing tendency to consider that they deserve special treatment because their table manners happen to be better than their neighbors, to say nothing of their irritating insistence on some deserved heritage from their history of one thousand years." Cable 4158, Section Two, 14 July

MFM member Kálmán Saláta remembered the Soos trip to Switzerland in 1943. His brief comment implies that the Soos mission had two different aims: one religious and the other national: "to enlighten people about the true situation of Hungary."[97]

The trip to Switzerland in 1943 was significant for Soos in other ways. He was able to renew his contacts at the British legation. His earlier communications had followed the German invasion of Poland, which caused many Poles to escape to Hungary. There were rescue efforts in Hungary to aid these refugees, and Soos played a role by administering money that came from the British legation for that purpose. The significant contact that might have been established at that early point was Elizabeth Wiskemann, who may have become the intended addressee for the Auschwitz Report. Soos probably hoped to reach Visser 't Hooft or Dulles with that report. On the other hand, Wiskemann had the most impressive record as someone who could act to rescue the imperiled Jewish people.[98]

Although after the halting of the deportations in early July a period of relative peace set in for the Jewish population, German authorities, the Gestapo, and the Hungarian collaborators, having recovered from the brief challenge in early July, asserted themselves as the real powers in the country. It was no secret that the Soviet

---

1943, in: Petersen, *From Hitler's Doorstep: The Wartime Intelligence Reports of Allen W. Dulles, 1942–1945*, p. 82.

[97] Saláta's recollection, which clearly refers to the effort to make peace with the Allies, is in: Ilona Tüdős (ed.), *Evangéliumot Magyarországnak*, p. 255.

[98] Communication on Nazi persecution within the circle of Visser 't Hooft, Wiskemann, and Dulles was taking place as early as March of 1943. Dulles reported "public protests by the affected spouses of some of the [detained] Jews." A month later Wiskemann told Dulles that one of her sources had confirmed Visser t' Hooft's account of the arrest of "half-Jews"; she also reported that many religious people in Berlin were hiding Jews. Some of Dulles's information about Nazi measures against Jews in Berlin went from the OSS to the White House." Wiskemann's letter [15th Apr. 1943–B arrived from Berlin on 13th Apr.] to Dulles, see NA, RG 226, entry 210, box 376, folder 5. Richard Breitman, Norman J. W. Goda, Timothy Naftali, Robert Wolfe (eds.), *U.S. Intelligence and the Nazis* (New York: Cambridge University Press, 2005), pp. 29–30.

army was approaching the borders of Hungary. Horthy sent Domokos Szent-Iványi to Moscow to negotiate a peace settlement. Soos remained as the leader of the MFM in Budapest. He attempted get help from a contact in Sweden with good connections to the Allies. It was an act of desperation to seek assistance from the past head of the Hungarian legation in Stockholm, Minister Ullein-Reviczky. He had been Soos's colleague during the early 1940s. In September Soos described the situation in Budapest. Soos believed that resorting to armed resistance had become necessary. He described such efforts. Although Ullein-Reviczky informed the British about this, nothing appears to have resulted from this desperate initiative.[99]

After the German invasion of Hungary and the Arrow Cross control of the government, borders became dangerous to cross. The invitation that Soos had received to meet Gellért in Italy was difficult to accomplish. Soos and his fellow MFM partner, the Hungarian Air Force Pilot Major Domokos Hadnagy, worked out an intricate and dangerous plan to make that escape to Italy.

The confusion and desperation existing as the Soviet army approached Budapest actually worked in their favor. Soos left Budapest with his small party in an army car, heading for an airfield at Pápa, southwest of Budapest. Hadnagy, on the other hand, went to the Budapest airport, and, using the excuse that he needed to test the airplane of a high Hungarian Nazi leader, he simply flew away with it.

The stolen plane had been intended to take General Vilmos Hellebronth, the Hungarian Nazi armaments minister, to Germany for a conference with Hitler. Thus, Hadnagy commandeered a plane with sufficient fuel, a German Heinkel–111 bomber, and, after evading the attention of the responsible guards, was able to meet Soos, who arrived at the Pápa airfield southwest of Budapest, by car.

---

[99] Agrell, *The Shadows around Wallenberg*, p. 216.

German Henkel-111 Bomber

Soos was not alone. His refugee group included Hadnagy's wife, daughter, the mechanic István Rákovits, Lt. Árpád Toperczer, and a Dutch Lt., Baron Johannes Bentinck. They had to be pressed into the small airplane's tight space behind the pilot. The plane took off without the aid of a radio, at 9 A.M. on the 9th of December 1944.[100] Hadnagy piloted the stolen airplane in the direction of Rome, but bad weather caused him to change directions; it forced a landing at San Severo, to the east of Rome, near the Adriatic.

> The arrival of Soos and the Hungarian air force major was considered an intelligence breakthrough for the OSS concerning Hungary because fresh and detailed information was now forthcoming about conditions right up until the final battle for Budapest and the westward evacuation of the Hungarian administration.[101]

Intensive interrogations of Soos and Hadnagy took place shortly after the arrival of the small party. They began on December 13th and continued until January

---

[100] Duncan Bare, "Hungarian affairs of the U.S.–Office of Strategic Services," pp. 86–87.
[101] Agrell, *The Shadows around Wallenberg,* p. 216.

26th. The interrogators included Major Abraham G. Flues, 1st Lt. Richard Burks, Andor Gellért, Eugene Fodor,[102] and Márton Himler[103].

Hadnagy's wife recalls a brief visit to OSS headquarters in Bari, where the debriefing was in progress. The interrogators were keenly studying the Auschwitz Report that Soos had brought along in microfilm form. This document was subsequently translated into English [presumably from the original German form], and classified as secret; it is preserved in the National Archives. Transmitted by the commanding officer, Major A. G. Flues, it shows the date of May 1st 1945.[104] The classification of such a document as secret may reflect, once again, the position of the Allies to put aside the persecution of Jews and rescue efforts a potential distraction from the need to defeat Nazi Germany.

Soos and Hadnagy were obliged to remain in Italy under OSS protection until April of the following year, when they finally had a glimpse of the transcript of their interrogation, a summary report with numerous shocking mistakes. Extremely upset, Soos and Hadnagy complained with a four-page rebuttal.[105] When it appeared that the OSS might show the report to members of the Soviet Union embassy, it became for Soos and Hadnagy crucial to have corrections made. Although Márton Himler promised to make the corrections, he did not keep the promise. The final form of the report states, for example, that Szent-Iványi hated the Russians, an outrageous

---

[102] Later famous for his travel guide books.

[103] In April of 1945 the Budapest Desk (later in the summer of 1945 renamed the Hungarian Section) departed for Austria, where the group, under the leadership of Márton Himler, was engaged in rounding up and arresting numerous Hungarian war criminals after escaping from the Russians in Hungary. Bare, "Hungarian Affairs of the US-Office of Strategic Services," p. 97.

[104] Duncan Bare, "Hungarian affairs of the US-Office of Strategic Services in the Mediterranean Theater of Operations from June 1944 until September 1945, pp. 85–88. Cf. p. 124 below.

[105] Ilona Tüdős (ed.), *Evangéliumot Magyarországnak,* pp. 154–157. The final report is found in Elek Karsai, "Soos Géza és Hadnagy Domokos tájékoztatása a magyarországi helyzetről és a Magyar Függetlenségi Mozgalomról 1944 decemberében," pp. 238–287. Duncan Bare, who is the most knowledgeable historian of the OSS involvement with Hungary for this period, observed that "both Soós and Hadnagy were extremely altruistic and not interested in personal glory or status." Bare, "Hungarian Affairs of the US-Office of Strategic Service," p. 86.

statement that a careful diplomat like Szent-Iványi, whom Horthy had sent to negotiate with the Russians, could not have made or permitted.[106] This was the moment when such false information in the wrong hands could spell disaster for persons in territories in control of the Soviet Union.

In the meantime, as the Russian army took military control of Hungary, the political life in Hungary began its radical transformation. Whatever had been planned before, such as the intention to send Gellért and Soos to Budapest, was no longer valid. For Soos thoughts of public service in Hungary were about to be permanently destroyed. After the siege of Budapest ended, the Russians quickly began to exert pressure to establish a government comparable to the Soviet dictatorship. When Soos finally returned to Hungary in 1946, he was offered a position in the Hungarian government, but there was a serious condition: membership in the Communist Party was an absolute requirement. Soos refused. He expressed his bitterness about the change that had taken place: "The Russians tolerate only three kind[s] of Hungarians in public life: corrupt politicians who accept bribes openly, former Nazis who serve the new sponsors for fear of prosecutions, and insignificant bureaucrats without political conviction."[107] At the same time, it became apparent that former members of the Independence Movement were now in great danger, being persecuted as potential enemies of the state. Previous coworkers such as Szent-Iványi were arrested, put on trial, and imprisoned. Soos escaped just in time.

---

[106] Elek Karsai, "Soos Géza és Hadnagy Domokos tájékoztatása a magyarországi helyzetről és a Magyar Függetlenségi Mozgalomról 1944 decemberében," pp. 243 and 278. Cf. note #428 in Duncan Bare "Hungarian Affairs of the U.S.–Office of Strategic Services in the Mediterranean Theater of Operations from June 1944 until September 1945," p. 86.

[107] Duncan Bare, "Hungarian affairs of the US-Office of Strategic Services in the Mediterranean Theater of Operations from June 1944 until September 1945," p. 16.

Rescue work in war-time, such as that of Soos and Wallenberg, could not be easily separated from its political implications. Rescue efforts required the risk of intrigues. Misunderstandings were unavoidable. It was unfortunate that in the case of both Soos and Wallenberg, the cause of rescue, in collaboration with Americans, implied being the enemy of the Soviet Union. That was undoubtedly the cause for Wallenberg's disappearance and death.

Soos escaped this fate. But his tragic death years later reflects an important aspect of his historic role in Budapest. After immigration to the United States, he renewed his friendship with Ferenc Koszorús, who also immigrated to the United States. Soos and Koszorús were devoted Calvinists. They shared this faith with Horthy. In 1953, both were on route from Washington to Pittsburgh for a church conference when, driving in a mountainous range of Pennsylvania, they encountered a violent storm, during which their car accidently hit the side of a bridge. Both men were seriously injured: Koszorús lost consciousness, but Soos, though also injured, set out on foot to find ambulance help. When it arrived, Soos also lost consciousness, and then, losing blood fast, died on the way to the hospital. Koszorús, though requiring lengthy hospital treatment, survived.[108]

In the last moments of his life Soos was once again engaged in an effort that had been the essence of his actions in Budapest, together with those of Koszorús: intent on rescue, even at the cost of his own life. In that sense he shared a significant legacy with Wallenberg.

---

[108] Ferenc Koszorús in: Ilona Tüdős (ed.), *Evangéliumot Magyarországnak,* pp. 238–242.

III. Chronology and Documentation

Admiral Miklós Horthy, the Regent of Hungary, who became leader of his nation after the end of World War I, had been an admiral of the dual monarchy with Austria, but when the country lost the war, it also lost its monarch. Horthy took the initiative in a chaotic period to become the head of state, governing a nation, ostensibly until a legitimate successor in the royal line could return. For almost a quarter of a century Horthy led his country as regent. He became entangled in World War II on the side of his powerful neighbor, Hitler, at a time when Germany appeared invincible. But soon the tables began to turn, and once again Hungary found itself on the losing side of a great war. In order to prevent Hungary from switching alliances, Hitler decided to invade Hungary.

The final solution of the Jewish question had been meticulously outlined during the Berlin Wannsee Conference of January 20, 1942. Implementation followed, according to plan, in most of the projected countries of Europe. A notable exception was Hungary. According to the estimates available to the members of the Wannsee meeting, Hungary possessed a Jewish population of 742,800. In March of 1944, Germany was losing the war, but Hitler, obsessed about the "final solution," ordered the German army to invade Hungary. Adolf Eichmann, S.S. officers, the Gestapo, and the collaborating Hungarian provincial police, received the assignment to carry out the deportations to Auschwitz. The German ambassador to Hungary, Edmund Veesenmayer, accepted the task of reporting the number of transports and the precise number of individuals that had been successfully sent on their way. The key to success was secrecy. But Regent Horthy's participation was necessary. Hitler demanded the participation at their meeting Austria.

DAILY EXPRESS

HOW HUNGARY FELL: First full story tells of stormy 'Schuschnigg interview' at which the Admiral refused ten demands

HITLER RAVED AT HORTHY, SENT IN PARATROOPS

Tommy-guns shot down guards in Budapest

And now BULGARIA

JAP DRIVE ON INDIA OPENS

'Put out your ear lights'— though the mountain was on fire

Vesuvius

Hitler raged at Horthy, and he ordered his army and paratroopers to invade Hungary. This country had been Germany's ostensible ally. Italy had also been an ally, but in 1943 that country attempted to extricate itself from Germany. Now Hungary was engaging in secret correspondence with the Allies to switch sides. Hitler accused the Hungarian leader of being a traitor, who, in addition, was not doing enough to solve the so-called Jewish problem. Horthy protested and considered resigning. But British historian C. A. Macartney explained what happened then behind closed doors: " . . . a private meeting between the two leaders took place.

There is no record of the fateful bargaining between Hitler and Horthy. But in the end, under considerable pressure, Horthy made concessions, first, to appoint a government favorable to the Germans and second, to make thousands of Jewish workers available for work in the German munitions factories. This turned out to be a disastrous concession. After returning to Hungary, Horthy transferred responsibilities for dealing with the Jews to a newly formed government. Then he acted like Pontius Pilate: he washed his hands."

C. A. Macartney, *October 15th: A History of Modern Hungary. 1929–1945,* II, pp. 236–237. See the correspondence of Heinrich Himmler about the use of 100,000 prisoners for underground factories. *Trial of the Major War Criminals before the International Military Tribunal. Nuremberg*, vol. 3 [in Nov. 14 – Oct. 1, 1946] (Nuremberg: US Printing Office, 1948), pp. 355–357. The figure being discussed is confirmed by Veesenmayer during his trial: "The 100,000 Hungarian workers required by the Todt Organization for labor allocation in the Reich would have to be requested from the S.S. Main Administrative and Economic Office." *Trial of the Major War Criminals before the International Military Tribunals under Control Council Law No. 10,* vol. 14 [in Oct. 1946–Apr. 1949] (Washington: US Printing Office, 1949–1953), p. 814.

April 28th, 1944

Calvinist Bishop László Ravasz recalls:

"The Regent listened to my proposals with a certain air of dissatisfaction, as if under the impression that I was overstepping my competence. Yet my boldness had ensued from the situation itself, and I had no choice but to undertake that risk. In reply, the regent told me that, as soon as he had heard about the atrocities, in Nyíregyháza, he called the minister of the interior, raised hell with him, and immediately dispatched the two state undersecretaries, who, as far as he knew, put an end to the outrageous treatment of the detainees. Then he talked about the Germans' demand for a large number of hands for labor service. . . . Consequently, a few hundred thousand Jews would be taken out of the country but they would no more have the hair on their heads hurt than the hundreds of thousands of Hungarians who had been working in Germany since the beginning of the war. From this I was dismayed to conclude that the regent had been misled. I had barely stepped out the door when a young gendarme lieutenant entered his room. I only found out later that it was Undersecretary László Baky."

Ernő Munkácsi, *How it Happened: Documenting the Tragedy of the Hungarian Jewry* (Montreal, 2018), p. 168.

Ca. April 30th / Beginning of May, 1944

József Éliás recalls how the Auschwitz Report came to his attention through Géza Soos:

"In 1944, on one of the last days of April or on one of the first days of May, Géza Soos invited me to meet with him. He indicated in advance that he wished to discuss an important matter at length. As I recall, we met in the café of the National Museum. Géza, who was a person of great energy but otherwise calm and collected, seemed on this occasion to vibrate with excitement. I sensed that he had something extraordinary to communicate. He said that a secret organization of prisoners in a concentration camp of the Germans in Poland was successful in bringing about the escape of two young Jews. The escape bordered on the miraculous.

These men had the task of informing the world about what was going on in Auschwitz. Having reached a place of safety, the escapees prepared a detailed report about Auschwitz, which they supplemented with drawings. They referred to it as a kind of official record in order to emphasize its factuality and reliability. A representative of our opposition movement on the border of Slovakia received one of the German copies of the report; the messenger had arrived with it in Budapest on the morning of our meeting. . . . During our conversation there was an empty chair between us, and we put our briefcases on it. I can still visualize how Géza slipped the report into mine. After he listed the addresses (among them those of the highest ranking church leaders), he added, 'The government officials must not learn that the report is in our hands. It is not necessary to enlighten them because,' he emphasized, 'the head of the government and most of the ministers under him know about Auschwitz and its function. The opposition movement wants to orient the church leaders, above all, so that the government will not mislead them and so that these influential individuals can exert pressure on the government to prevent the tragedy awaiting the Jews.'"

See the interviews below. Sándor Szenes, " . . . akkor már minden egyházfő asztalán ott volt az Auschwitzi Jegyzőkönyv . . ." [By then all church leaders had the Auschwitz Report on their desks] *Valóság* 10 (October 1983): 75–90.

Ernő Munkácsi, member of the Jewish Council, assesses the significance of the Auschwitz Report:

"History provides evidence of momentous events that lead in an unpredictable, new direction. This phenomenon is replicated in the structure of drama, the poetic form of history, in which developments necessitate a totally new path. In the tragedy of Hungarian Jewry, such a dramatic turn came about with the disclosure of the Auschwitz Report, which, on the one hand, dispelled the culpable optimism that had dulled the minds of the vast majority of Jews, and, on the other hand, stirred up the conscience of certain Christian leaders and revealed the final destination of their policies."

Ernő Munkácsi, *How it Happened: Documenting the Tragedy of the Hungarian Jewry*, p. 130.

Ca. April 30th / May 1st, 1944

Mária Székely recalls the experience of translating:

"I had to concentrate on the translation so that I could complete it as soon as possible. For six to eight days I worked day and night. The report revealed the total and terrible reality of the extermination of human beings, organized methodically and pedantically, planned as a crime of massive proportions. I have not been able to blot this out, nor the brutal fact that people who planned and carried this out could sink to such low depths.

My work on the translation was also the cause of dramatic moments, as a result of my own fault, to be sure. It was warm in my room, and I went outside with my papers and dictionary to the ground-level terrace, which was only three to four meters from a loose wire fence. A strong gust of wind came along and caught one page of my German text, including drawings, and it flew against the fence, where it got stuck. On the other side of the fence an armed German soldier was on guard, walking back and forth.

On Érmelléki Street the Germans occupied the houses all around. I became greatly frightened by the loss of my paper, but by the time I got to it, the guard had reached over the fence; he removed it and returned it politely. I was lucky that he showed no interest in the text or the drawing. . . Of course, I went back to my room in order to continue my work.

József Éliás gave me the assignment to take the translation to Soos in Úri Street in the castle. The foreign ministry has an office there. This trip was full of excitement. I started off for the castle from Széna Square. But just then the sirens sounded for an air raid. I had to stop and seek refuge in a basement. I started off, but then there was another siren, and I had to hide again, on this occasion for a short time. After finally reaching the castle I encountered the police checking for documents. It was a great relief when I finally reached Géza Soos and was able to give him the German and Hungarian Auschwitz Reports. He also sighed for relief. Then he gave me the new assignment to make a translation to English. I worked day and night. It turns out that there was an opportunity to get the document to Switzerland."

Cf. Szenes, *Befejezetlen múlt*, pp. 109–125. The location of the Foreign Ministry, where Soos had an office, was Úri utca 18. *Külügyi közlöny* (*A m. kir. Külügyminisztérium ügybeosztása*) [The Royal Hungarian Foreign Ministry Organisation], Budapest, 1943), p. 8.

The fate of the English translation, intended by Soos to be taken to contacts in Switzerland has not been clarified. This particular copy of the Auschwitz Report has never come to light. On the basis of previous contacts, that report should have been delivered to Visser t'Hooft, Allen Dulles, or Elizabeth Wiskemann about the second half of May. Censorship in Switzerland and the reluctance of Allied authorities to focus attention on the persecution of Jews may explain the silence about this report, which only became known through Jaromir Kopecky and George Mantello about the middle of June 1944.

According to American intelligence records, Soos had been in Switzerland in 1943. That visit led to acquaintance with the prominent Dutch ecumenical church leader Willem Adolf Visser 't Hooft and the press agent of the British legation in Bern, Elizabeth Wiskemann. We cannot be sure about what happened with the English Auschwitz Report that Soos sent to Switzerland. According to Soos, through Visser 't Hooft he was able to make contact with Allen Dulles. But it is known today that Dulles was inclined not to share news about Jews with Washington; in the best case, he passed such information to the representative of the War Refugee Board, Roswell McClelland.

Bálint Török suspects that the addressee of the English translation was the World Congress of Churches (i.e., Visser 't Hooft) or Bakách-Bessenyey György at the Hungarian ambassy in Bern. Bálint Török, "Az Auschwitzi jegyzőkönyv 1," [The Auschwitz Protocol, part 1]. In: *Magyar Szemle,* New Series, 12 (2003).

Ca. second half of May, 1944

After having received a report about Auschwitz, Calvinist Bishop László Ravasz, is reported to have spoken with Regent Horthy: Géza Soos, who was a friend of Bishop Ravasz, reported that the latter had asked Horthy whether he knew what crimes were being committed in his name. The Regent Horthy replied that

"the Germans asked for a half a million workers to be sent to German war plants . . . . Hitler had promised that these Jews would be treated exactly as Hungarian workers." Soos also reported that Ravasz was dismissed with the reproach that the regent was not accustomed to have his word questioned."

Géza Soos in the OSS report, in: *Raday Gyüjtemény Évkönyve,* IV–V (Budapest, 1986), p. 253. Although the reliability of the OSS report may be questioned, the accuracy of this report is confirmed by other sources. Cf. the Török interviews about the way Ravasz reacted to the Auschwitz Report. Ravasz himself reported about his meetings with Horthy at the trials after the war. László Karsai and Judit Molnár (eds.), *Az Endre-Baky-Jaross Per* [Budapest]: Cserépfalvi, 1994), p. 343. Munkácsi may also be referring to this same meeting when he reports Ravasz saying the following: "[I] fervently beseeched the regent to oppose these developments with all his might instead of letting the perpetrators hide behind his name. My experience told me that people would have no qualms about using the regent's authority as an excuse in their own defense. My visit was not a pleasant one, for the head of state or myself, and it was never my habit to make such appeals. This was the first and last time I ever did something like this. The regent told me that those unfit for military service were being taken to work, along with their families so they could all stay together." Munkácsi, p. 197. Bishop Ravasz appears not to have been precise in remembering when he discussed these matters with Horthy. It is also unclear whether Ravasz actually told Horthy the details that he had learned in May from reading the Auschwitz Report.

Second half of May or the beginning of June, 1944

Sándor Török recalls the experience of transmitting the Auschwitz Report to the royal palace into the hands of the Regent's daughter-in-law. The connections to the palace were prepared for him by the MFM:

"As a result of my charge I immediately went to the Red Cross, and I requested help. At the end of May or the beginning of June I was taken along to the royal palace and introduced to Mrs. Horthy, Countess Ilona Edelsheim Gyulai, the Regent's daughter-in-law. While in the outside world the events took their course, here in and about the royal residence a strange situation developed: On the one side there was the residence of Angelo Rotta, the ambassador, representing the Vatican, who helped us a great deal, and on the other side there was the German embassy surrounded by the different offices of its headquarters; here in the center of the royal residence, in the rooms of Mrs. Horthy [Countess Ilona] a "conspiratorial" group gathered. I was part of this group, and we discussed and tried to reach a consensus about the news that Mrs. Horthy brought from those close to the Regent as well as the news we had brought from the outside world. Of course, in order to understand what went on, one must imagine, at the same time, the strange situation that was characterized by danger, complexity, lies, attempts to help, attacks, and confusion that affected those who lived in the royal residence and from which they could not isolate themselves.

On the square directly opposite the Hungarian court guards, a German tank and a line of German guards stared right back. They observed what was going on at the Regent's residence, the royal palace on the Buda hill, and I believe that they knew a lot.

We had to go up into the residence from the side of the Elizabeth Memorial Museum through a small side entrance, and then we saw bodyguards in green uniforms with machine guns posted in what I believe to have been a naively vulnerable position. They protected the residence. I had the task of calling Ilona Horthy [Countess Edelsheim Gyulai] every day for several weeks on a special phone number, and after introducing myself as the bookbinder Bardócz, I asked if she had any work for me. If she said that there was a bookbinding job, I could go safely to get the news or to discuss what would have to be done in a certain matter. The people I met in the royal residence all knew that the war would end with a German defeat. They were afraid of the Germans and did not respect them, but at the same time they were somehow helpless, hesitating, and paralyzed in their presence.

Later I heard from the countess about Regent Horthy's reaction to the report about Auschwitz. He accepted all of it as the truth."

Connections to the royal court were made possible by the secret influence of the MFM leader Domokos Szent-Iványi. Cf. Sándor Szenes, *Befejezetlen múlt,* p. 194.

May 15th, 1944

German Ambassador Veesenmayer reports on April 23rd:
"Negotiations about transportation have begun, and, starting May 15th, we expect that every day the trains will take 3,000 Jews. . . ."

Randolph Braham, *Destruction of Hungarian Jewry. A Documentary Account* (New York: Pro Arte, 1963), I, p. 356.

> **Total persons deported by May 31st, 1944: 217, 236**

> **Ca. June 10th, 1944**

Ernő Munkácsi, member of the Jewish Council, describes new developments:

"After much bickering, around June 10 an opportunity presented itself for the two camps to face each other. The disgruntled Jews sent a message to the president of the Council saying they wanted to speak with him to voice their concerns. Around five in the afternoon, Samu Stern received a large delegation led by Dr. Imre Varga, a young physician from Pest. Among the members of the delegation were some Zionists of the younger generation and, making a first appearance at Síp Street, left-wing Jews hardened by forced-labor service and not shy about active resistance. Two members of the Pest prefecture and the chief secretary of the Support Office were also present. This was the first time that the detractors, who had been grumbling for months, were given a chance to speak their minds face to face with the Council, the repository of absolute discretion over the internal affairs of the organization. Dr. Varga spoke passionately: "Can't you see?" he said in great agitation: "Don't you understand that our fathers, mothers, brothers, and sisters are being shoved into freight cars by the Gendarmerie at the point of bayonets, seventy of them at a time, to be dragged away into the unknown, into annihilation, smothered in human excrement? How can we stand for this any longer? How can we content ourselves with mere petitions and servile supplications instead of revealing it all to

Christian society? We must resist instead of slavishly obeying their orders!" The executive meeting was full. Everyone was carried away by Varga's sincere indignation and incitement to take a brave stance. His speech was accompanied by utter silence, and although the solemn promises made previously led one to expect further commentary, no one else rose to speak. The president replied calmly in a dry tone of voice: "The Jewish Council is doing everything humanly possible. The news of the deportations has been relayed to every important official and clerical entity whose support we can count on. Unfortunately, the Germans are in command, and the Hungarian authorities cannot or dare not oppose them. Any resistance on the part of us Jews would only lead to futile bloodshed and could collapse almost instantly. Aggravating the situation of others unimaginably. The Council has fulfilled its duty and will continue to do so." His brief address finished, the president rushed out of the room. Those who remained entered into a heated discussion about Dr. Varga's plea and possible ways of administering affaris with better results than the Council was capable of. The following day we learned that Varga had committed suicide in his despair over the inadequate reception to and impact of his speech."

Ferenc Laczó writes: "The morally charged question why those (and again this probably includes several members of the Council) with access to the Auschwitz protocols [i.e., report] did not do more to publicize Vrba and Wetzler's eye-witness account of the atrocities. Of all the many excruciatingly difficult decisions made by the Hungarian Jewish Council, the decision to suppress or not broadcast the Auschwitz Protocols is widely considered the least comprehensible and least defensible. Arguably, however, this controversial decision fully conformed to a chief aim of the Council: to avoid mass panic." Laczó adds: "Varga's speech and subsequent suicide appear to have been a turning point for Ernő Munkácsi, Immediately afterward, Munkácsi's work as scribe for the Jewish Council ended, and he joined activists. . . . in writing and distributing an underground pamphlet informing Gentile Hungarians about the murder of Jewish Hungarians – and asking for their help." Cf. the introduction to Ernő Munkácsi's, *How it Happened: Documenting the Tragedy of the Hungarian Jewry*, pp. xxxix, lxvii, and pp. 139–140.

Total persons deported by June 19th, 1944: 340,142

When, finally, about 400,000 persons had been deported from the provinces and the Auschwitz Report had been circulated among church and government leaders, Regent Horthy was forced to take a stand against the deportations. He received urgent messages from the Vatican and the president of the United States to halt the deportations.

Ca. June 22nd, 1944

Gábor Faragho, Lieutenant-General, commander-in-chief of the Provincial Police remembers Horthy's reaction to the Auschwitz Report:

"I talked about these matters with [Horthy], and he used expressions that I cannot repeat here: 'These gangsters! They do even this kind of thing! It is impossible that children—I read it and saw it in black and white—that they put children into gas chambers!' This was the big turn. It must have been the middle of June."

László Karsai and Judit Molnár (eds.), *Az Endre-Baky-Jaross Per* (Budapest 1994), pp. 371–372. A meeting between Faragho and Horthy took place on June 22nd, at which Horthy indicated that he wished to end the deportations. Sebők, *A titkos alku. Zsidókat a függetlenségért. Horthy-mítosz és a holocaust* [The Secret Bargain: The Jews for Independence; Horthy-myth and the Holocaust] (Budapest 2004), p. 177. Faragho probably began a gradual shift away from his support of the deportations about this time. At the June 21, 1944 Council of Ministers session, Faragho was still defending them: "If we take into consideration that we had already deported 400,000 Jews to labour camps and resettlements, the fact that complaints were lodged against a few of the 20,000 gendarmes participating in the operation, we must consider the problem as equal to zero." Quoted by Braham, 1997, p. 887. http://degob.org/index.php?showarticle=2011 Accessed on 8/30/2020

On the 25th of June, a telegram from Pope Pius XII expresses to Regent Horthy the wish that the suffering of "unfortunate people, because of their nationality or race, may not be extended and aggravated."

See the the text of Pius XII's message in: *Actes et Documents,* vol. 10: *La Saint Siège et les Victims de la Guerre. Janvier 1944 – Juillet 1945* (Libreria Editrice Vaticana, 1981), p. 328. Although the pope's message did not mention the simple fact that the "unfortunate people" were actually Jews, the message, despite its vagueness, can be understood as a shift in the pope's position as a result of the Auschwitz Report. Martin Gilbert, *The Holocaust: A History of the Jews of Europe during the Second World War* (New York: Henry Holt and Company, 1985), p. 701. For Archbishop Serédi, the leader of the Hungarian Catholics, the pope's silence about the deportations was a reason for him not to speak out against them. Cf. Török interviews below. Cf. John Cornwell, *Hitler's Pope: The Secret History of Pius XII* (New York: Viking, 1999), p. 325.

June 26th, 1944

Cordell Hull sends a message from President Roosevelt to Horthy:

"Above all, the United States demands to know whether the Hungarian authorities intend to reduce food rations in a discriminatory fashion, whether to deport Jews to Poland or to any other place, or to employ any measures that would in the end result in their mass execution. Moreover, the United States wishes to remind the Hungarian authorities that all those responsible for carrying out those kind of injustices will be dealt with in the manner stated by the President of the United States in his public warning of March 24, 1944."

Jenő Lévai, *Fehér Könyv*, (Budapest: Officina, 1947), pp. 56-59.

Admiral Horthy at a Royal Council of Ministers speaks out against the deportations:

"I shall not tolerate this any further! I shall not permit the deportations to bring further shame on the Hungarians! Let the government take measures for the removal of Baky and Endre! The deportation of the Jews of Budapest must cease! The government must take the necessary steps!"

Randolph L. Braham, *The Politics of Genocide: The Holocaust in Hungary* (New York: Columbia University Press, 1994), II, p. 873.

June 26th, 1944

British Historian Martin Gilbert writes about initiatives in Switzerland:

". . . the reports from both sets of escapees [Vrba-Wetzler and Mordovicz-Rosin] reached the Jewish and Allied representatives in Switzerland. "Now we know exactly what happened, and where it has happened," wrote Richard Lichtheim, the senior representative of the Jewish Agency in Switzerland, to his superiors in Jerusalem. The reports made clear, Lichtheim noted, "that not only Polish Jews had been sent to Auschwitz but also Jews from Germany, France, Belgium, Greece etc," and that they had been murdered there. . . . On Elizabeth Wiskemann's inspiration, this telegram was sent without codes, to enable Hungarian Intelligence to read it."

The London Times, January 27, 2005. Cf. Veesenmayer's telegram of July 6 to Ribbentrop. (See also the discussion in Chapter I above.) "On reading the cable Churchill scribbled a note to Eden: 'What can be done? What can be said?' The British had lost control of the news agenda, according to Michael Fleming, "because of the wide publicity given to the news of Auschwitz published in neutral Switzerland." Fleming, *Auschwitz, the Allies and Censorship of the Holocaust,* pp. 235–

236. About the drantaic impact of this initiative on Hungary see the events described below for July 5th and 6th.

Historian Randolph Braham reconstructs the steps taken by Eichmann and the provincial police for the deportation of Jews from Budapest:

"Under the plan [to have been prepared by Eichmann and Hungarian collaborators], thousands of experienced gendarmes [i.e., provincial police units] were to be concentrated in Budapest and its environs without attracting suspicion, on the pretext of participating in a flag-award ceremony honoring the gendarmerie unit of Galánta. The ceremony was scheduled for July 2 at Heroes' Square [Hősök Tere] [plans later cancelled because of the bombing raid]. During the three days following the ceremony, the gendarmes were to spend their 'furlough' in Budapest getting acquainted with the size and location of the Yellow-Star houses and working out plans to prevent Jews from escaping. The preparations for the deportations were to be completed within a few days and the trains were expected to begin rolling on the 10th of July."

Braham, *The Politics of Genocide,* II, p. 879. The plans were cancelled because of the bombing raid.

June 28th, 1944

Domokos Szent-Iványi, leader of the Hungarian Independence Movement (MFM), describes the assassination attempt on the life of István Bárczy:

"On the afternoon of June 28th Bárczy and I drove to Szentendre, north of Budapest, and thus I became a witness to what happened after a failed assassination attempt. On that same evening we were sitting on the porch of [a friend] when we heard gun shots, coming from the house where Bárczy was residing for the evening. I went immediately over to the [house, where] we heard shots and learned from Bárczy what had happened. At 10:30 p.m. the bell rang, and because he was the only man in the house, he went to see who it was. The women in the house did not permit it, however. Instead, the cleaning girl went down, and, without opening the door, asked who it was. The response came that they wanted to speak with the honorable Bárczy and requested that the door be opened at once. Of course, the girl refused, but even before she could have done anything, shooting began in front of the house. Later it turned out that one of the men thought better of it, and did not want to have Bárczy killed, and, in the course of an argument, he killed the leader of the gang. After this the entire gang, including the individual who had been shot, disappeared.

People concluded later that this was simply a bungled burglary attempt. In fact, it was a political assassination attempt, which a far-right-wing group organized with Baky's people with German support."

Szent-Iványi was residing in the house of Count A. H. Khuen-Héderváry. Bárczy was residing in the Ábrányi–Goldberger house. Domokos Szent-Iványi, "A Bárczy elleni merénylet, 1944. június 28–29."
http://www.magyarszemle.hu/cikk/20160408_visszatekintes_1941_1972_reszletek. Accessed in January 2020. Cf. *Visszatekintés,* [Taking a Look Back] pp. 148–151.

June 28th. General János Vörös, chief of the Hungarian general staff, notes in his diary:

"His majesty had informed me that news had filtered out that one of the right-wing parties—probably Baky and his group—recently held meetings with the Gestapo.

The subject of the meeting was how to get rid of the government. The Regent instructed me to take the necessary measures."

Vörös diary for June 29, Mario D. Fenyo, "The War Diary of the Chief of the Hungarian General Staff in 1944," *East European Quarterly* 2 (1968): 315–333, here p. 323.

Total persons deported by June 29th, 1944: 381,661

June 29th, 1944: Bárczy remembers:

"I have never seen the Regent in such an agitated state and he had never treated me in such an intimate way. He treated me as if we were brothers. Curiously, his anger turned against Baky and the Hungarian Nazis."

Visszatekintés, [Taking a Look Back] p. 154. Cf. *The Hungarian Independence Movement 1939–1946*. Edited by Gyula Kodolányi and Nóra Szekér (Budapest: Hungarian Review Books, 2013).

June 30th, 1944: King Gustaf of Sweden sends a telegram to Horthy:

"I have decided to turn personally to your Serene Highness to ask, in the name of humanity, that you intervene on behalf of those among these unfortunate people who can still be saved."

Zoltán Vági et al., *The Holocaust in Hungary* (Lanham, MD: AltaMira Press, 2013), p. 135. Michael Fleming reports about the British Political Warfare Executive's caution: "Use any British press comment on the King Gustaf of Sweden's statement and on any subsequent statement from authoritative Allied sources. Keep any BBC comment to the bare minimum, suggesting only that the fact that Hungary has allowed many thousands of Jews to be deported to Poland, to almost certain death, in the public opinion of the United Nations, one of the greatest sins of Hungary's war record." Fleming, *Auschwitz, the Allies and Censorship of the Holocaust*, p. 237.

Last days of June, and July 1, 1944

Historian Randolph Braham:

"Thousands of cock-feathered gendarmes with bayonetted rifles in fact appeared on the streets of Budapest."

Braham, *The Politics of Genocide,* II, p. 880.

Kálmán Saláta describes the leading role that Soos played at this time:

"[Soos] had a key role in the small group organizing the steps in the political and military operations that halted the deportations."

Kálmán Saláta, "Soos Géza," In: Ilona Tüdős [Mrs. Géza Soos] (ed.), *Evangéliumot Magyarországnak. Soos Géza Emlékkönyv* (Budapest: Bulla, 1999), pp. 254-255.

Soos, in a report to the Office of Strategic Services (OSS,) in Caserta, Italy, remembers:

"A few days after the attempt on Bárczy, László Endre, secretary of state for the Jewish question in the ministry of interior, ordered two battalions of gendarmes, normally stationed at Nagyvárad and Galánta, to Budapest. Neither General Faragho, superintendant of the provincial police, nor the Regent had been consulted. The commander of the battalions, when drunk, declared that it was ridiculous for an 86-year-old lunatic king (King of Sweden) to give advice to a 75-year-old nut (Horthy), that they were only fooling themselves if they believed they had stopped the deportations, and that if necessary his two battalions would take away the Jews together with 'their Regent.

Soon after hearing about this, Lt. Col. Ferenc Koszorús of the general staff, a member of the MFM, ordered the Hungarian tank combat units at Esztergom to Budapest, and they arrived within a few hours."

According to Soos in the final OSS report, in: *Raday Gyüjtemény Évkönyve, IV–V (Budapest, 1985)*, text, p. 255. About the identification of the Galánta officer see note no. 54 above.

Last days of June, and July 1, 1944

Dr. Kálmán Saláta also reports information he received from Colonel Lajos Kudar, the chief intelligence officer of the provincial police, also one of the founders of the MFM:

"Colonel [Lajos] Kudar, acting with the aid of his two assistant officers, succeeded in getting one of the provincial police unit's top men totally drunk. In the drinking establishment called *Négy Szürke* the drunken officer related that seven battalions were on location in order to deport the Jews from Pest, and if the old man (meaning the Regent) did not like this, his people would take care of him, too. The two intelligence officers took him home, but then made a record of what they had learned. Kudar handed the report over to Horthy's bodyguard, Lieutenant-General Lázár, who was also a member of the MFM. Of course at the same time, the circle of Szent-Iványi was also informed."

István Csicsery-Rónay, *Első Életem* [My First Life] (Budapest, 2002), p. 244. The same story is recalled by Csicseri-Rónai in "A Magyar függetlenségi mozgalom története." [The History of Hungarian Indepencence Movement] *Magyar Szemle*, new series 28, nos. 9–10 (1999). Both Kudar and Soos were close associates of Domokos Szent-Iványi within the MFM. Cf. Domokos Szent-Iványi, *Visszatekintés*, [Taking a Look Back] p. 56. *The Hungarian Independence Movement 1939–1946*. Edited by Gyula Kodolányi and Nóra Szekér (Budapest: Hungarian Review Books, 2013).

István Csicsery-Rónay confirms the role played by the Esztergom tank division:

"At this time in the vicinity of Esztergom there was a tank division, the existence of which was kept secret from the Germans. This division needed to be ready and available as the regent's resource for breaking Hungary out of the grip of the Germans. I was present when we had to decide whether the division should continue to remain secret for that later use, or, on the other hand, whether it should be used immediately to stop the massive deportations. Of course, we decided for the latter alternative, and we sent two officers (as we learned later, both members of the secret organization of *Magyar Közösség*), to Colonel Koszorús, who represented the leadership for the officer on duty at the front."

István Csicsery-Rónay, *Első Életem* [My First Life] (Budapest, 2002), p. 244. On the history of the *Magyar Közösség* or Magyar Testvéri Közöség [i.e., the Hungarian Fraternal Community], including details about the role of Géza Soos, see Nóra Szekér, "A Magyar Közösség Története" dissertation of the Péter Pázmány University in Budapest, 2009.
http://mek.oszk.hu/08400/08480/08480.pdf Accessed on July 26, 2020.

Dr. Géza Soos remembers how the MFM contacted Koszorús:

"When the Galánta provincial police battalion officer, in a drunken party, spilled the story about the King of Sweden's advising Regent Horthy to prevent the deportation and to save Jews, Major Károly Chemez and Major László Beleznay, both of whom were in touch with the underground movement, approached Lieutenant-Colonel Koszorús about the need to act."

Excerpt from Géza Soos, "Ellenállás és zsídómentés," Ráday-Archíve, Géza Soos, C_230, Karton 16. The photograph of the following page identifies these two officers as close associates of Koszorús and members of the tank division that was about to enter Budapest.

Balról jobbra: Chemez Károly vk. őrnagy, Koszorús Ferenc vk. ezredes Beleznay István v. őrnagy.

Major Károly Chemez and Major László Beleznay with Lieutenant-Colonel Koszorús

Cf. "Photo gallery," in: Jeszenszky (ed.), *July 1944.*

Dr. Géza Soos describes the central role that Koszorús played:

"Colonel Ferenc Koszorús, the chief of the Esztergom armored corps, influenced by two young Hungarian officers in his circle of acquaintances, energized his armored units for the sake of the persecuted people. . . . I need to point out that the initiative of the Esztergom division occurred with knowledge that it undercut its primary goal, which was to support the possibility of an armistice. They had succeeded in "hiding" this division from the German army. Its function was to serve the Regent, if an opportune moment materialized, assuring him some freedom of action. Because the Esztergom division was activated for the purpose of saving the Budapest Jews, its existence came to the attention of the Germans, who immediately made it part of their strategic calculations. For this reason these resources were no longer available to Regent Horthy during the fateful hours October 15 [when Hungary attempted to abandon the alliance with Germany]."

Ráday-Archíve. Géza Soos papers, "Amióta emigrácioban élek," C_230 Box 18, pp. 2–3. Cf. Sebők, *A titkos alku* (Budapest 2004), pp. 192–193 and Vigh Károly in *Magyar Nemzet*, Jan. 29, 1993. In: Ilona Tüdős (ed.), *Evangéliumot Magyarországnak. Soos Géza*, p.135.

July 2nd 1944, Bombing of Budapest

The American carpet bombing on this day was estimated to have resulted in 136 killed, 111 wounded, and 370 destroyed buildings. Military Historian Richard Davis interprets the significance of the bombing that took place on July 2nd. Although the bombing mission was not planned to influence political events in Hungary, the result was to exert an impact influence because it appeared to be connected to the warnings by the Allies and other leaders about the deportations:

"On July 2nd 1944 the Fifteenth Air Force put 509 heavy bombers and 1,200 tons of bombs over targets in or near Budapest. The attack, [although flown primarily against the industrial plants south of Budapest], was the only bombing raid of the war with a direct and significant effect on the Holocaust."

Richard G. Davis, *Bombing the Europen Axis Powers: A Historical Digest of the Combined Bomber Offensive 1939–1945* (Maxwell Air Force Base: Air University Press, 2006), p. 398. Richard Davis, "The Bombing of Auschwitz: Comments on a Historical Speculation," in: Michael J. Neufeld and Michael Berenbaum (eds.), *The Bombing of Auschwitz: Should the Allies Have Attempted It?* (Lawrence: University of Kansas Press, 2003), pp. 214–226.

Last days of June, and July 1, 1944

Horthy asks a friend, Valéria Kovács (Mrs. István Kovács), to observe the deportation process in the city of Szeged:

Valéria Kovács remembers:

"I was told that as a woman I had a better chance of gaining access to certain places. So I traveled to Szeged and there I made up a story for the officer of the provincial police (*csendőr*) about needing to get inside the brickyard to deliver a package to a doctor to whom I was indebted. The lieutenant-colonel said this was out of the question; nobody was allowed to enter. Conversing with this officer for an hour and a half, I managed to gain his confidence, and he told me about certain things. Pretending, I told him that I found it impossible that the Jews of Budapest were to be passed over when all the Jews of the provinces were being taken out of the country. This would be unjust. The lieutenant-colonel believed that I was on his side. 'Come now, madam,' he said. 'We will begin removing the Jews from the brickyard this evening and will finish by Wednesday and then deal with the Budapest Jews.' 'Nonsense,' I answered. 'How can you possibly get them all out on such short notice?' The officer then told me that the trains were waiting in Óbuda at the edge of the city, six thousand gendarmes had been transferred to Budapest, and that Eichmann, the chief deporting expert, who possessed substantial experience in that field, had arrived in the capital as well. At that moment, an S.S. officer entered the room, and I had to come clean. He said he was going to have me arrested and thrown into the brickyard if I wanted to see the inside of it."

(Although Kovács was not given permission to enter the brickyard, she was able to observe the removal of the Jews as they were driven through the streets to the waiting trains.)

"The Jews were led away at half past one, amid much terrible abuse by the gendarmerie. The elderly were kicked around. The bystanders felt sorry for them. 'Sorry, eh?' the gendarmes replied to them. 'You want to go with them, is that it?' The rear was brought up by a big black automobile carrying the S.S. colonel, another man I did not know, and someone wearing dark glasses whom I recognized as László Endre. They all followed the whole scene until it was over. I was standing in the crowd. As the black car rolled by slowly along the narrow road, I crouched against the wall of a small peasant cottage some four or five meters away.

. . . One example was an elderly couple, the old man, who must have been around eighty, apparently having a problem with a stiff neck or something. The policeman (the gendarme) gave him a blow on the back with the butt of his rifle. The old man fell over, and the gendarme kicked him, probably in the face. I could see his face was all bloody.

. . . . I arrived in Budapest on Sunday. [July 2nd]. At three o'clock on Monday [July 3rd] I reported to the Regent about the atrocities in Szeged."

Istvánné Kováts [Kovács], *Visszapilantó Tükör* (Budapest: GO-Press, 1983), pp. 148–159. Ernő Munkácsi, *How it Happened*, 2018, pp. 199–201.

Domokos Szent-Iványi, the leader of the Hungarian Independence Movement (MFM) confirms that his secret organization was in touch with Colonel Koszorús:

"The office concerned with escaping from the alliance, under the leadership of Horthy's son, Nicholas Horthy, with Germany and the MFM were in regular contact with Colonel Koszorús through an intermediary."

Domokos Szent-Iványi, *Visszatekintés,* [Taking a Look Back] p. 153. Cf. *The Hungarian Independence Movement 1939–1946* Edited by Gyula Kodolányi and Nóra Szekér (Budapest: Hungarian Review Books, 2013). No one has been able to identify the name Homokos. The officer's status as major may reflect the fact that the reference is to one of the officers named by Soos. It is not clear, furthermore, when Soos might have become acquainted with Koszorús. The included letter of 1947 refers to several years. This could mean that they knew of each other at the time of the crucial events of early July or even before. It is very unlikely that they had any contact between July 1944 and 1947.

July 2nd 1944

Ferenc Koszorús, lieutenant colonel of the Hungarian 1st armored division, learns about the Regent Horthy's critical situation:

"On the evening of July 2nd I had a chance encounter on the bank of the Danube in the center of Budapest with Lieutenant-General Károly Lázár, the head of Horthy's personal guard unit. During the 1920s we had worked together closely. Our friendship remained close over the years. We could rely on each other as true Hungarians.

At that time I was the head of the first armored division of Budapest, and during those weeks I also represented the second armored division, which was still active on the Russian front.

Our discussion was burdened by the woeful and disgraceful condition of the country. Lieutenant-General Lázár confided that we were now in the sad situation that the commands of Admiral Horthy were no longer heeded. He told me that men of the Arrow Cross [i.e., Nazi] Party attempted to have István Bárczy killed at his home. The assassination failed, and the investigation revealed that the planning and ordering of the attempt could be traced to the undersecretary of the Ministry of Internal Affairs, László Baky. Admiral Horthy demanded his immediate removal.

Lázár revealed that Baky, encouraged by the Germans, intended to overthrow the government to establish an Arrow Cross state, and for that he would recruit, organize, and prepare needed forces with German support. Baky intended to organize a violent coup d'état. Regent Horthy gave an order, to affect the range of internal, police and military affairs, for the immediate removal and disbanding of the aforementioned provincial police battalions. Nobody paid attention to this order of the Regent, however. On the contrary, an increasing number of troops were brought to Budapest. Undoubtedly, they were intending to complete the deportations, but there is no doubt that their chief goal was the violent Nazi takeover of the government.

Without much reflection and hesitation I asked Lieutenant-General Lázár to urgently inform Regent Horthy that if I receive an appropriate order, I could bring about the compulsory removal of the provincial battalions.

I had no illusions for myself personally about the serious consequences, resulting from my unauthorized actions. In fact, I had no authority for this action since I, as the leader of the armored army corps, had no business conducting action that was beyond the sphere of my limited authority; such action had to be ordered by the responsible division commander. I knew that if this action, which did not seem promising, succeeded, I would be acting against the most cherished interests of the Nazi leadership, for which they would make every effort to get me out of the way. I had to take on this thankless task; I realized that besides me there was hardly anyone else to take it on.

I was fortunate to get to know these outstanding soldiers in extremely difficult circumstances; the troops got to know me, too. We complemented these units with fresh forces. The Nazis did not know of the existence of our division."

July 3rd 1944

Koszorús continues:

"On the following day, July 3rd, I received from Lieutenant-General Lázár Regent Horthy's order to prepare carrying out of the proposed maneuver as soon as possible.

I shared this matter only with my chief of staff, Major István Beleznay. I lost no time in making the necessary preparations. First of all, I traced all the areas in which Baky's battalions were placed. I talked personally with the men in these battalions. I determined that the basic framework of the battalions (commissioned and noncommissioned officers) was in poor condition, made up of reserve officers, untrained, immature youngsters, armed chiefly with light weapons and a healthy supply of machineguns. But heavy armaments were lacking. I learned also that at this time the German military presence was made up of three police (*Gestapo*) battalions, possessing, however, only light weapons. For transportation their motorbikes were available. On the late afternoon of July 3rd, I went to the troops of the first armored division, directly to Esztergom, where I notified and spoke with the tank and reconnaissance officers, especially with their outstanding commanding officers, Major Zoltán Balló and Lieutenant-Colonel Imre Németh.

On the basis of information from Lieutenant-General Lázár, I told my officers that we had to bring into line those who resisted the highest order of the land, an order for which we are now expecting renewed confirmation. I reminded them the "Hungarian military oath" before God they took asserted that an honest soldier could not disregard it even at the risk of death and this is the oath that we reconfirmed, being aware that he who for some reason violated this. I stressed that with the national oath we accepted "unconditional loyalty" that we would defend Hungary's frontiers, its independence, and constitution against every enemy, "whoever it might be." Today there are those who disregard all these considerations, who are attempting, with the aid of a foreign power, to overthrow the Hungarian constitution, its legally established state, and to deliver for the sake of a foreign power's arbitrary interests thousands of Hungarian citizens. The national oath and the Hungarian honor demands of us that we prevent this traitorous infamy. This is what I consider the path of honor, and on this path I intend to embark. Who is willing to join me in this endeavor? Without hesitation, the officers immediately indicated their unanimous willingness.

On the same evening I outlined and distributed a detailed, written plan for encircling and taking control of Budapest. I gave the instruction that the initiation and execution of these plans were to commence with the repetition of a radio signal that I would send from Budapest. Only the chief officers of armored regiment and the reconnaissance battalion received my written instructions. The next morning I made arrangements for supplying the necessary live ammunition and supplies. By the mediation of Lieutenant-General Lázár I informed Regent Horthy that I was prepared to carry out his order."

Ferenc Koszorús, *Emlékiratai és Tanulmányainak Gyüjteménye* [Collection of Memoirs and Essays], published by the Universe Publishing Company, Englewood, N.J., 1987. (Written in Washington on November 17, 1961), pp. 55–58. Cf. Tsvi Erez, "Hungary – Six Days in July 1944" in: Randolph Braham (ed.), *Holocaust and Genocide Studies 3* (1988): 51. While Koszorús focused on his personal actions as soldier, he neglected to explain that the initiative to activate his unit did not originate as his own idea, but actually was proposed to him by the MFM, by his close associates, Major Károly Chemez and Major László Beleznay, and, most significantly, by Géza Soos. Koszorús described his meeting of July 2nd with Lázár as a chance encounter. But that is not the whole story! In a letter of October 11, 1949, Soos wrote that he had known Koszorús for several years (in other words, perhaps as early as July 1944). Soos wrote in 1949: "Being a high-ranking officer in the Hungarian army he (Koszorús) took part in the Hungarian resistance movement and through his very efficient courageous help, the so-called Baky-putsch was frustrated in July 1944, the Regent, and the Jews of Budapest were saved."

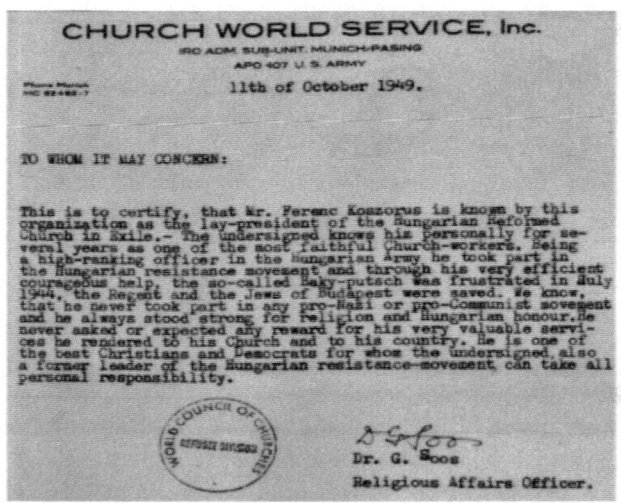

Zsuzsa Hantó and Nóra Szekér (eds.), *Pácélosokkal az életért: "Koszorús Ferenc, a holokauszt hőse"* (Budapest: Kiskapu Kiadó, 2014), p. 191.

The above letter, in which Soos wrote generously about his friend, is an indication that Soos and Koszorús probably knew each, as early as the July crisis, because of their Calvinist associations.

The motivation of a rescue mission, which it turned out to be, can be attributed primarily to Soos. The efforts to save Jews was a motivation that is more significantly to be that of Soos, less so for Koszorús. Soos had become aware of the dangers of the Nazi attacks on Jews when he attended the Evian conference in Geneva in 1938. As an eighteen-year-old student Soos concluded his his analysis of Hungary's crisis: "It is clear that the only reasonable path is that of the helping hand. For this path personal sacrifice is necessary." Bálint Török, *Farkas esz meg, medve esz meg . . . Szent-Iványi Domokos és a Magyar Függetlenségi Mozgalom* [The Germans and Then Russians Devour Us . . . Szent-Iványi Domokos and the Hungarian Independence Movement] (Basel and Budapest: Európai Protestáns Magyar Szabadegyetem, 2004), p. 97–98.

> **July 4th 1944**

General János Vörös, chief of the Hungarian general staff, writes in his diary for July 4th about his discussion with Regent Horthy. As a friend of the German, Vörös attempts to prevent Horthy from stopping the deportations:

"His majesty informed me that it was his intention to prevent the further deportation of Jews; he wants the Jews to remain, at least those in and around Budapest. He will give instructions to the competent authorities in the ministry of interior. I noted that we must be especially cautious in this matter. It is only right that those Jews who became Christian long ago and those who received decorations in the war [World War I] not be deported. But I think we must avoid at all cost the political friction which would result from a delay in the solution of the Jewish question."

<small>Vörös diary for June 29, Mario D. Fenyo, "The War Diary of the Chief of the Hungarian General Staff in 1944," *East European Quarterly* 2 (1968): 315–333, here pp. 323–324.</small>

Acting Foreign Minister Mihály Arnóthy-Jungerth reports to Regent Horthy that the Germans in Switzerland are showing a propaganda film that displays the brutality of the Hungarian provincial police.

<small>Miklós Mester, *Arcképek két tragikus kor árnyékában* [Portraits in the Shadows of Two Tragic Periods], pp. 76–77. For the probable date of this report see p. 40, note 71 above.</small>

July 5th 1944

July 5th: Telegram of Per Anger, chief administrative officer at the Swedish embassy in Budapest, to Christian Günther, the minister for foreign affairs of Sweden in Stockholm. Horthy reveals that he was not totally opposed to the deportation of Jews from the provinces:

"During our conversation the Regent openly admitted that, unfortunately, he has very little opportunity to prevent what is happening with the Jews today. Since the occupation, Hungary is no longer a sovereign nation . . . The Regent said that he knows that the eastern part of Hungary is a war zone, where most of the Jews had been deported for work. In no way does he want to defend the deportations, but he understands, nevertheless, that authorities consider it important to transfer the Jews from that part of Hungary. That is because among the Jews there are countless communists. They arrived during the past decades, and they have nothing in common with the Hungarian nation."

Péter Bajtay (ed. and transl.), *Emberirtás; Embermentés. Svéd követjelentése 1944-ből. Az Auschwitzi Jegyzőnyv* [Extermination (and) Rescue: Swedish Diplomatic Reports of 1944. The Auschwitz Protocol] (Budapest, 1994), pp. 88–89. In this way Horthy expressed a sentiment that is generally recognized about him, that he tended to make a distinction between Budapest Jews and those in the provinces. He had friends among the Budapest Jews whom he wished to protect.

Dr. Géza Soos recalls the actions of Horthy to stop the deportations, but it is not clear precisely when the actions he ascribes to the regent took place. It appears, in retrospect, that Horthy probably took decisive steps on the 5th of July to stop the deportations:

"Koszorús then reported to the Regent that these units would be able to cope with any forces the Germans and Hungarian Nazis might be able to collect. Horthy called General Faragho, commander-in-chief of the provincial police, and General Lázár, commander of the bodyguard, and, in a highly dramatic manner, put to them a series of questions. Had the officers taken a military oath of allegiance? If so, to whom? Were they willing to live up to their oaths? On receiving affirmative answers, the Regent ordered the two gendarme battalions returned to their stations, appointed Faragho commander-in-chief of all forces in Budapest, and instructed him to take all measures necessary to prevent the deportation of the Budapest Jews and to protect the security of the country. All Hungarian forces in the capital were alerted, along with the combat tank units, posted at strategic positions. This caused great excitement in the next days as no one—including the Germans, the prime minister, chief of the Hungarian general staff or the *minister* of war—knew what was happening. The German units in and around Budapest were prepared for action."

Soos reporting his recollections to the OSS, in: *Raday Gyüjtemény Évkönyve, IV–V (Budapest, 1985)*, p. 255.

July 5th 1944

Mihály Arnóthy-Jungerth reports for the Ministry of Foreign Affairs at the meeting of the Council of Ministers, claiming that the deported Jews are being killed at the rate of 6,000 per day. Plans for retaliation by the Allies entail the bombing of Budapest and the destruction of governmental buildings.

The number 6,000 and the reference to bombing Budapest suggest that this report was based at least partly on the Lichtheim-Wiskemann telegram that had been decoded by Hungarian intelligence services. (See above discussion.) Elek Karsai and Ilona Benoschofsky (eds.), *Vádirat a nácismus ellen. Dokumentumok a magyarországi zsidóüldözés történetéhez* [Indictment of Nacism in the context of the history of Jewish Persecution in Budapest] (Budapest: Balássi Kiadó, 2017), III, document no. 27.

General János Vörös, chief of the Hungarian general staff, writing in his diary for July 5th:

"General Lázár, the commander of the Regent's bodyguard, sounded alarm at 2300 hours. Units from Esztergom occupied the northern sector of Budapest."

<small>Vörös diary for June 29, Mario D. Fenyo, "The War Diary of the Chief of the Hungarian General Staff in 1944," *East European Quarterly* 2 (1968): 315–333, here p. 325. Cf. Erez, "Hungary – Six Days in July 1944," p. 48.</small>

Major Ernő Bangha, the royal guard serving at the palace under Lázár, reports:

"Lieutenant-General Lázár oriented us confidentially. Cars appeared at the entrance of the palace door. Officers of the provincial police with the typical rooster-feather hats got out. They crowded around a single person in civilian attire: this was Baky, the secretary of state for internal affairs. . . . During the subsequent audience the Regent ordered that those provincial police units that had come to Budapest had to return to their home bases without delay. If this did not occur, the Regent would draw on the army to make sure that his order was obeyed. Without any sign of protest, Baky took note of the order and promised to have it carried out completely."

<small>The precise date of this statement is uncertain, but it corresponds best with the events here with the following texts. *Magyar Hírlap*, July 5, 1993, Quoted from János Sebők, *A titkos alku. Zsidókat a függetlenségért. Horthy-mítosz és a holocaust* [The Secret Bargain: The Jews for Independence; Horthy-myth and the Holocaust] (Budapest 2004), pp. 191–192.) See Bangha's more complete text on p. 33 above.</small>

Night of July 5th and July 6th: Ernő Munkácsi, member of the Jewish Council, reports:

"That night saw a series of dramatic events take place. Colonels Tölgyesi and Paksy-Kiss, the anointed executioners of the Jewry, were staying at the Pannonia Hotel on Rákoczi Avenue, coincidentally just a stone's throw away from the center of Jewish life in Budapest and the headquarters of the Jewish council on Síp Street. Around two o'clock in the morning, a car from the office of the Regent pulled up in front of the hotel. A high-ranking officer got out and brought Tölgyessi to the royal castle, where he had to report to Lieutenant General Lázár, commander-in-chief of the royal guards. Lázár handed him orders made out specifically in his name, to the effect that the command of the consolidated law enforcement troops in Budapest had been transferred to Lázár by the Regent. Around four in the morning, the car from the Regent's office returned to the hotel and took Paksy-Kiss to the castle. In both cases, the vehicle was escorted by sidecar motorcycles armed with submachine guns. Paksy-Kiss was also given his personalized orders by Lázár. According to Ferenczy's testimony, around three o'clock in the morning. . . . The deportation did not happen—not because anyone directly gave orders for it to halt, but simply because the gendarmerie was no longer there to implement it. When the presiding judge of the people's court asked Ferenczy whether the Germans alone would have been capable of carrying out the deportations, he replied: 'The Germans would not have been able to pull it off, because it was scheduled for the sixth.'"

Ernő Munkácsi, *How it Happened*, 2018, pp. 210–211. Cf. Hungarian text *Hogyan Történt?* (Budapest, 1947), pp. 177–179. Braham also believes that this event occurred on July 5th. In addition, he states that the armored regiment from Esztergom was asked to come into Budapest at this time. Braham, *The Politics of Genocide*, II, p. 880. At his trial in 1945 Ferenczy remembers these same events in very similar terms, also for July 5th. Judit Molnár, *Csendőrtiszt a Markóban. Ferenczy László czendör alezredes a népbíróság elött* (Budapest: Scolar, 2014), p. 112. Szent-Iványi relates the same events, but dates them for July 7th. Domokos Szent-Iványi, *Visszatekintés,* [Taking a Look Back] p. 153. Cf. *The Hungarian Independence Movement 1939–1946* Edited by Gyula Kodolányi and Nóra Szekér (Budapest: Hungarian Review Books, 2013).

Historian Kristián Ungváry writing about the night of July 5th:

"During the night of July 5th, on Horthy's order, tanks under the leadership of Ferenc Koszorús entered the capital."

Ungváry maintains that the reason for this order was not the stopping of the deportations for the sake of the Jews, but rather the fear that a coup d'état was being planned against Horthy. Krisztián Ungváry, *Horthy Miklós—a kormányzó felelősége 1920–1944* [Miklós Horthy—the Regent's Responsibility] (Budapest: Jaffa Kiadó, 2020), pp. 193–194.

(Koszorús continues his report):

"On the evening of July 5th, I was having dinner in Irányi Street with my uncle. We had hardly finished our dinner when at 22:30 my bodyguard appeared and reported that Regent Horthy is calling me urgently. After a car trip of a few minutes I appeared at the royal palace. Regent Horthy received me in the presence of Lieutenant-General Károly Lázár and informed me that Baky and his co-conspirators were planning a coup d'état, the violent takeover of the government, for July 6th. After listening to the outline of my plans, Regent Horthy personally handed me the order to take those parts of the first division that I had placed in readiness to remove Baky's provincial police battalions from Budapest immediately, by force if necessary, thus preventing the coup d'état. After receiving this order I reported to the Regent the instructions that I had already given to my troops, along with the specific arrangements for their implementation. Regent Horthy took note and approved my plan.

I was taken by car immediately to the office of the first armored division, and at 23:30 I gave the order to carry out the planned maneuver. I called my chief of staff, Major István Beleznay, and after I became convinced by means of radio contacts that our maneuver was in progress, on July 6th at 2:20 I drove out to Óbuda, to the front line of my troops. I stayed here, and I led the campaign from here."

July 6th 1944

During that same morning, Horthy takes further steps to make sure that the provincial police leave the city. At 11:00 a.m. on July 6th Colonel István Láday, chief officer of the Galánta battalion, confirms that his battalion is being forced to leave:

"The Regent spoke to us in a harsh manner: 'You have betrayed my confidence and become political playthings, perhaps against your will. I order all provincial police units to leave the capital today by 4:00 p.m. I do not wish to see any rooster feathered police officer in Budapest. In order to ensure calm, I have summoned army units to the capital.'"

Attila Bonhardt, "The Role of Colonel Ferenc Koszorús in the Prevention of the Deportation of the Jews of Budapest," in: Géza Jeszenszky (ed.), July 1944: *Deportation of the Jews of Budapest Foiled* (Reno, Nevada: Helena History Press, 2017), pp. 203–218, here pp. 215–216. Cf. Zsuzsa Hantó and Nóra Szekér (eds.), *Páncélosokkal az életért* [Saving Lives with Tanks. "Ferenc Koszorús, "the Hero of the Holocaust."] (Budapest: Kiskapu, 2015), pp. 38–39. About the identity of Láday see note 54 above.

July 6th 1944

Koszorús reports on his further actions:

"On July 6th at 5:00 a.m. all parts of the armored regiment and the reconnaissance battalion had arrived at the points I had assigned, and north of Budapest, at Óbuda, all roads leading to the capital were sealed off.

After reviewing my troops and speaking with my officers, at 7 o'clock, I sent a patrol officer to László Baky. He delivered to Baky my message that I was here, prepared to carry out the order from the highest authority, with the troops of the first division, and with the newly granted authority I ordered them to clear the provincial police out of Budapest within twenty-four hours, and I expected to make sure that this order would be carried out. Inasmuch as there was resistance to the carrying out of the order I would take care of the clearing out by force. At 9 o'clock the returning patrol officer reported that the course of events and the order that I had sent caught Baky's people by surprise, resulting in bewilderment, running around, and a lot of telephoning. It was evident that Baky was counting on the help of the Germans. A few minutes before 9 o'clock, after all the running around and telephoning, Baky had my patrol officer report to me that he would clear out of the city with his provincial police."

Historian István Deák also writes about the motivation behind the military intervention:

"[Horthy] found out in good time what Auschwitz signified, but preferred to ignore it. That did not, however, hold for the Jews of Budapest! When it was their turn in June/July 1944, he ordered military action against the gendarmes, who, as he feared, were also planning a coup against him."

Europäische Rundscahu, 94/2, pp. 82 and 85. Quoted in Paul Lendvai, *The Hungarians: A Thousand Years of Victory in Defeat* (Princeton: University Press, 2003), p. 423.

Lieutenant-General Károly Lázár, commander-in-chief of the royal guards, sums up the events of the preceding days:

After the Regent's office received very reliable information that the Jews were to be deported under the leadership of László Baky, the Regent, seeing that his orders had been ignored, appointed me to be in charge of the weaponized forces of Budapest with the assignment to remove all provincial police units from the city. I proceeded to do the following things: I alerted Colonel Csikós and the bodyguard to prepare for action; I ordered the tank division under Colonel Koszorús to deploy immediately to Budapest. That division did indeed arrive here at daybreak. I sent part of the provincial police out of Budapest; I arrested its officers, Colonel Tölgyesi and Colonel Paksy-Kiss, and forced them to appear in the royal headquarters.

Domokos Szent-Iványi, *Visszatekintés* [Taking a Look Back], p. 153. Cf. *The Hungarian Independence Movement 1939–1946* Edited by Gyula Kodolányi and Nóra Szekér (Budapest: Hungarian Review Books, 2013).

Veesenmayer's telegram to Foreign Minister Joachim von Ribbentrop, July 6th, reporting on his conversation with Prime Minister Sztójay presented five reasons why Horthy decided to stop the deportations. The fifth reason listed for the halting of the deportations is significant and is the focus of the English translation. The information transmitted is missing in the telegram sent by Lichtheim; it was evidently added in Bern to produce the most unsettling impact on those Hungarian and German leaders who promoted the deportations:

NG-5523

Persönlichkeiten im eigenen Lande selbst.

5. Streng vertraulich las mir Sztojay ferner drei von ungarischer Abwehr entzifferte Geheimtelegramme des englischen und des amerikanischen Gesandten in Bern an ihre Regierungen vor. Dieselben enthalten eine detaillierte Darstellung, was mit den Juden, die aus Ungarn deportiert werden, geschieht. Es wird darin erwähnt, daß dort bereits 1 1/2 Millionen Juden vernichtet worden seien und derzeit laufend der grösste Teil der abtransportierten Juden das gleiche Schicksal erleiden. In denselben Telegrammen wird dann folgender Vorschlag gemacht: Bombardierung und Vernichtung des Bestimmungsortes, wohin die Juden kommen, ferner Zerstörung der Bahnen, die Ungarn mit diesem Ort verbinden. Ziel Bombardierungen aller ungarischen und deutschen Dienststellen mit genauen, zutreffenden Strassen und Nummern-Angaben in Budapest die in dieser Sache mitwirken und zuletzt großaufgezogene Propaganda unter über die ganze Welt und die Darstellung des genauen Sachverhalts. In einem weiteren Telegramm sid 70 ungarische und deutsche Persönlichkeiten namentlich genannt, die Hauptverantwortliche darstellen.

Sztojay erklärte mir, daß ihn persönlich diese Drohung kalt lassen, da er im Falle unseres Sieges die Sache als uninteressant betrachte, im anderen Falle sowi

110653

The translation of the fifth segment (pp. 3-4) in Veesenmayer's report to Berlin on the 6th of July follows here:

"I have just learned from Sztójay on telephone that the Regent, with apparent agreement of the government, stopped the deportation . . . . Moreover, in strict confidence, Sztójay read aloud three secret telegrams that the English and American ambassadors in Bern sent to their governments, decoded by the Hungarian intelligence agency. These describe in detail what happens to Jews deported from

Hungary. The telegrams mention that 1.5 million Jews have already been exterminated there, and the same fate awaits the majority of Jews who are being deported now. The following suggestions are made in these telegrams: bombing and destroying the destination of the Jewish transports, and. In addition, destroying the railroad lines connecting Hungary to this location. Targeted for precision bombing there are precise Budapest street addresses given for every Hungarian and German offices that played a role in the deportations, along with large-scale propaganda to let the whole world know exactly what is happening. A further telegram names seventy prominent Hungarians and Germans who carry the primary responsibility.

Sztójay told me that he is personally unmoved by these threats because, in the event of our victory, the whole issue will become uninteresting, and in the alternative scenario, his life will definitely be over. Despite all this, it was clear that these telegrams had made a strong impression on him. I have heard in the meantime that the Council of Ministers has also been informed about these telegrams and that they had a similar effect. . . . The consequences of the most recent bombings—some of which have been extremely severe and damaged residential areas as well—have been rather unpleasant, and there is widespread worry that after the removal of the Jews, Budapest will perish."

The original German text is found in Braham, *The Destruction of Hungarian Jewry: A Documentary Account* (New York: Pro Arte, 1963), II, pp. 425–429. The English translation of the entire telegram is found in Jeszenszky (ed.), *July 1944*, pp. 286-289. This text is also available in Hungarian translation in: Zsuzsa Hantó and Nóra Szekér (eds.). *Páncélosokkal az életért.* "*Koszorús Ferenc, a holocaust hőse,*" pp. 278–279. Cf. *The London Times*, January 27, 2005. Martin Gilbert was the first scholar to point out the potential significance of the decoded telegram from Switzerland. Because Gilbert did not have reliable information about the events in Hungary, his narrative contains mistakes. For example, it is not true that Veesenmayer ordered the end to the deportations. Sztójay, as the following telegram explains, was presenting the reasons why Horthy, not Veesenmayer, decided to stop the deportations. Although the deportations were halted in Budapest, Eichmann succeeded in having deportations outside Budapest. Cf. Braham, *The Politics of Genocide*, II, pp. 890-893.

July 6th: Expelled from Budapest, Láday reports about his battalion experiencing the forced departure at Óbuda:

"The battalion set out on foot. We removed our decorative rooster feathers. The mood was tense and nervous. The unit proceeded quietly down Hungarian Boulevard. In front of the Andrássy army barracks the soldiers [of the Esztergom armored division] were in readiness, keeping their eyes on us, the withdrawing unit. Armored units followed our battalion until our train had left the station."

Bonhardt, p. 216. This narrative is supported by recollections of Beleznay. Jenő Lévai, *Zsidósors Magyarországon* [The Fate of Jews in Hungary] (Budapest: Magyar Téka, 1948), p. 229.

Historian Kristián Ungváry insists that the assignment of the armored units was clearly not the rescue of Jews:

"During the morning of July 6th the first armored division units 6th occupied most points in Budapest, but in the suburbs (for example, Újpest, Óbuda, and Budakalász) no one in the world prevented the provincial police from deporting Jews for another three days. . . . At this time the Jews of the mentioned areas were languishing in masses at the brick factories of Békásmegyer and Budakalász. The campaign was not intended for the sake of their rescue. Therefore, the Koszorús mission that the regent had ordered did not have as its goal the halting of future deportations, even if that was its actual result."

Krisztián Ungváry, *Horthy Miklós—a kormányzó felelősége* [Miklós Horthy—the Regent's Responsibility] (Budapest: Jaffa Kiadó, 2020), p. 194. Ungváry's assumptions about any intent to save Jews outside of Budapest are debatable. If Horthy had the intention to save Jews, that effort (considering the resources available to him) had to be restricted to Budapest.

July 6th: Similarly, Ferenc Szálasi, the leader of the Hungarian Nazis, notes this event in his diary:

"Armored units arrived around Óbuda and took up places on the streets and squares, concealed with green branches. In some of the streets the guns were put in a firing position, and news spread that Major-General Lázár, the commander of the royal guard, had taken over command of the armed forces."

Elek, Karsai, *Szálasi naplója. A nyilasmozgalom a II. világháború idején* [The Diary of Szálasi. The Arrow Cross movement during the Second World War] (Budapest: Kossuth Könyvkiadó, 1978), p. 254. Bonhardt, *July 1944*, p. 215.

July 7th 1944

Koszorús report continues:

"On the following day, July 7th, Baky began the retreat from Budapest. It appears that the German invading authorities realized that it would be better to act in this fashion. The removal was completed by mid-day July 8. When I was convinced that this actually happened, I proceeded to have my excellent troops return to their stations, and I informed the office of the Regent about the completion of our task.

It was obvious, as far as I was concerned, that the Germans would never forgive me for their shameful helplessness, and, as was their custom, they would certainly send a Nazi officer to my apartment to get rid of me. They were terribly annoyed by this fiasco; after all, right under their noses my action saved the legal Hungarian government. Despite the invasion the Hungarian form of government prevailed, my action saved about 300,000 persons, who had been destined to be deported to German death camps; it also delayed the power-grab by the Nazis by three and a half months. The invaders needed to prepare and organize the violent October coup d'état. These three and a half months saved the lives of quite a few people because during the second half of October the situation made it impossible to carry out the deportations in a manner that would have been possible in July. In this way, compared to its neighboring countries, Hungary gained a highly superior distinction."

If Koszorús reflects about saving Jewish lives many years after the war, that does not mean that his primary intent for his actions in 1944 had that particular aim. Moreover, the figure of those saved may have been closer to about 200,000. To be sure, this was before the Arrow Cross Party, which took over after October 15, caused the death of about 76,000 Jews. The Hungarian Statistical Department gave the number of Jews to have resided in Budapest before the German invasions was 231,453. Today the estimated number of Jews still remaining in the capital after the atrocities of the Arrow Cross regime was between 120,000 and 140,000. Tamás Stark, "Facts about the Number Shoah Victims in Hungary," in: Géza Jeszenszky, *July 1944: Deportation of the Jews of Budapest Foiled,* p 195. The figure of about 200,000 as an estimate is supported by the following assessment of the situation of the Jews of Budapest at the time of the Arrow Cross Party's takeover: "As the first step of the concentration of the Jews of the capital, the mayor of Budapest issued several decrees in June of 1944 in order to designate so-called "yellow-star houses." These house were established in all 14 districts of Budapest, and from 24 June 1944, the more than 200,000 Jews of Budapest were compelled to live in some 2,000 buildings designated by virtue of the fact that 50 percent or more occupants were Jewish." Kinga Frojimovics, "The Special Characteristicks of the Holocaust in Hungary," in: Jonathan C. Friedman (ed.), *The Routledge History of the Holocaust* (New York: Routledge, 2011), pp. 248–263, here 257. Such estimates cannot take into account the many who were in hiding.

Sirens sound throughout Budapest from 9:00 a.m. until midday of July 7th. Fülöp Freudiger, member of the Jewish Council, reports:

"At the time the operations were to begin, General Lázár, commander of the Regent's bodyguard, gave the order—in agreement with other similar minded high officials—for the air-raid alarm to be given. During the alarm, which lasted several hours, they posted tanks and armored divisions at strategically important points of the city. . . . and the insurrection was immediately squashed."

Randolph L. Braham (ed.), *Hungarian-Jewish Studies* (New York: World Federation of Hungarian Jews, 1973), 127. Cf. Jenő Lévai, *Zsidósors Magyarországon* [The Fate of Jews in Hungary], pp. 228–229. Mária Schmidt, *Kollaboráció vagy kooperáció. A budapesti Zsidó Tanács* [Collaboration or Cooperation: The Jewish Council of Budapest] (Budapest: Minerva, 1990), p. 302.

The End of Deportations from Budapest. Regent Horthy remembers:

"Baky and Endre had planned a surprise action to arrest and deport the Budapest Jews. As soon as news of this reached my ears, I ordered the armored division stationed at Esztergom to be transferred to Budapest, and I instructed the chief of the Budapest police to assist in preventing the forcible removal of Jews."

Miklós Horthy, *Memoirs*, (London: Hutchison, 1956), p. 220.

July 8th, 1944

July 8th: German Ambassador to Hungary Edmund Veesenmayer reporting to the German foreign office:

"The coup d'état story involving Baky, which apparently the Regent believes, is a story that people with evil intentions put into his head to cause trouble for Germany. The actual cause for this movement is the fear that Germany is losing the war. That is the reason why these people are making a desperate effort to create an alibi for their future."

Braham, *The Destruction of Hungarian Jewry: A Documentary Account* (New York: Pro Arte, 1963), II, p. 438.

July 8th: Telegram of Per Anger, chief administrative officer at the Swedish embassy in Budapest, to Christian Günther, the minister for foreign affairs of Sweden in Stockholm:

"We have information that the Hungarian government, because of its attempts to halt the deportations, is in the midst of a crisis. It appears that in response, Baky and Endre, with the aid of the provincial police, have attempted a coup d'état. At the last possible moment the Hungarian army, with the aid of tank units arrived in Budapest and prevented this threat. [I myself was witness of the forceful movement of tank units in the eastern and southern sides of the city.]* According to German sources, Ambassador Veesenmayer left the city for talks with Hitler about these events."

Anger reports to the Swedish foreign ministry. Péter Bajtay (ed. and transl.), *Emberirtás; Embermentés. Svéd követjelentése 1944–ből. Az Auschwitzi Jegyzőkönyv* (Budapest, 1994), p. 98.
* Anger also reports about his personal observation to Erik von Postnak, also of the foreign ministry, on July 18. Bajtay, p. 111. Contrary to what Anger claims, there is no record that Veesemeyer left Budapest at this time.

Samu Stern, the head of the Jewish Council, recalls:

"The plan (to kill Bárczy) came to light, and the assassination attempt failed. The Regent had the Esztergom armored regiment come to Budapest with lightning speed to squelch the coup d'état attempt."

Mária Schmidt, *Kollaboráció vagy kooperáció. A budapesti Zsidó Tanács* [Collaboration or Cooperation: The Jewish Council of Budapest] (Budapest: Minerva, 1990), p. 83. Another member of the Jewish Council, Otto Komoly, recalls: "On July 7th–8th Horthy resolved to take strong action for the first time since the German occupation. He ordered the 3,000-man Gendarmerie force posted by Baky in Budapest to proceed to the provinces, and he assembled an armored division under reliable command. These steps foiled not only the plot, but for reasons which we shall not discuss here, the deportation plans as well." Bela Vago, "Budapest Jewry in the Summer of 1944: Otto Komoly's Diaries," in: *Yad Vashem Studies* 8 (1970): 81–105, here 85.

Rezső (Rudolf) Kasztner (Kastner), a prominent member of the Jewish Council, states:

"Eichmann conspired with Baky, Endre, and the clique of provincial police officers conducting the deportations to take over the government. But the Regent's supporters learned of the plan. The Hungarian army was alerted in the entire country to the plans of the provincial police. With great speed an infantry regiment was brought from the provinces into the city. At the same time, the provincial police received the order to leave the city. Soon after the ultimatum message from Roosevelt, combined with the subsequent, horrendous July 2nd US bombing attack on Budapest, impelled Horthy's stand against the coup attempt."

Rudolf Kastner, *Kastner-Bericht über Eichmanns Menschenhandel in Ungarn* (München: Kindler, 1961), p. 135).

On July 8th, Eichmann hears with dismay that the Regent had stopped the deportations. A deportation train destined for Auschwitz was forced to return on Horthy's order.

"In all my long experience, such a thing has never happened to me before. . . . that won't do. . . . this is contrary to our agreement. It cannot be tolerated!"

Jenő Lévai, *Eichmann in Hungary: Documents* (Budapest: Pannonia Press, 1961), p. 126.

Eichmann continues his efforts to carry out deportations. For the 14th of July Ernő Munkácsi, member of the Jewish Council, reports that 1,500 Jews had been forced to board trains at Kistarcsa, about 20 kilometers northeast of Budapest, destined for Auschwitz:

"Horthy issued orders to stop the train [from the town of Kistarcsa] and return the detainees to their respective internment camps. The command caught up with the train near the town of Hatvan, and the Jewish prisoners were back in Kistarcsa before the day's end."

Munkácsi, *How It Happened,* p. 231. Zone VI, outside Budapest, housed 24,128 Jews, who were deported on July 6–8. Braham described the "Kistarcsa Tragedy." Despite the halting of the deportations in Budapest, Eichmann worked with deceptive means to carry out more deportations from the provinces. He succeeded on July 19th with a transport of about 1,300 Jews from Sárvár and additional transports on July 24th and on August 4th to 5th about 1,500 Jews from Kistarcsa also to Auschwitz. Braham, *The Politics of Genocide,* II, p. 769, 779 and 890–893.

Géza Soos reporting to the American intelligence services (OSS) after his escape to Italy in December 1944:

"Almost immediately after the July crisis the Germans began to make their preparations. They managed to have the Hungarian armored units returned to Esztergom, from where they were eventually dispatched to the [Russian] front. Two German panzer divisions were brought into the Budapest area."

Karsai, Elek. "Soos Géza és Hadnagy Domokos tájékoztatása a magyarországi helyzetről és a Magyar Függetlenségi Mozgalomról 1944" [Report of Géza Soos and Domokos Hadnagy about the Hungarian Situation and the Hungarian Independence Movement in December 1944], in: *Raday Gyüjtemény Évkönyve*, IV–V (Budapest, 1986), p. 259.

July 9th, 1944

July 9th: With the support of the United States War Refugee Board, Raoul Wallenberg arrives in Budapest from Sweden to commence his rescue work. On July 11 he meets with Dr. Soos. Wallenberg's first reports of the situation of Jews to the foreign ministry in Stockholm reflect information that he could have received from Dr. Soos.
Dr Géza Soos recalls his meeting with Wallenberg:

"The MFM assigned Kálmán Saláta and me to make contact with the oppressed... That is how I made the acquaintance of the legendary Raoul Wallenberg; I was one of the first persons he looked up. Then I spent a long evening of discussion with him and his friend Anger."

[Mrs. Géza Soos] (ed.), *Evangéliumot Magyarországnak. Soos Géza Emlékkönyv* (Budapest: Bulla, 1999), p. 142.

July 29th, 1944

Wallenberg reports on July 29, 1944:

"The Regent's position with respect to the Jews is reflected by a series of minor interventions and especially by the fact that he ordered a halt to the deportations. It is a fact, moreover, that on two occasions trains filled with deported passengers were ordered to return before reaching the country's border."

Péter Bajtay (ed. and transl.), *Emberirtás; Embermentés. Svéd követjelentések 1944–ből*, p. 118. Wallenberg also lists Soos as one of his confidential sources in a note written on July 18th. That is the date of a report by Wallenberg to Sweden. Bajtay, pp. 106 and 121.

* * *

Events of early July assured the relative safety for the Jewish population in Budapest. Later actions by Eichmann and the Nazi Arrow Cross Party should not detract from their significance.

"Never before had any army unit successfully challenged a German occupation force, the SS, and the *Gestapo*."

Israeli historian Tsvi Erez, quoted by János Sebők, *A titkos alku. Zsidókat a függetlenségért. Horthy-mítosz és a holocaust* [The Secret Bargain: The Jews for Independence; Horthy-Myth and the Holocaust] (Budapest 2004), p.194.

"The courageous escape [of Vrba and Wetzler] proved a life-saving one for a whole community [i.e., of Budapest]. . . one of the most remarkable acts of saving lives in the Second World War."

Martin Gilbert in: Alfred Wetzler, *Escape from Hell: The True Story of the Auschwitz Protocol* (New York: Berghan, 2007), p. viii.

Appendix A: The OSS Interrogations of Géza Soos

22 January 1945

Subject:　　　　　　　SOOS, Dr. Geza

1. About 26. Judge. Attached to the Foreign Ministry. Has wide contacts in Protestant circles. On list of Budapest residents who were recommended by a Hungarian (now in British service) as reliable, pro-Allied individual in key positions and knowledgeable on Hungarian current affairs and personalities.

JBX–002–1023

BB/007

10/23/44

2. "About December 1st, Dr. Geza SOOS, former Deputy Chief International Cultural Relations Hungarian Foreign Ministry, left Budapest with party including Major Dome, HADNAGY, Engineer Corps Hungarian Army recently dismissed for anti-Nazism from important post Aviation Section Ministry National Defense, Baron John ZENTINCK / or BENTINCK/ a Dutch POW, Arpad TOPERCER/sic/, WT operator István RAKOVITS (qqv), mechanic and HADNAGY's wife and daughter ....

"SOOS was contact of Andor GELLERT (qv), SICE Hungarian Section. Latter sent him WT set from Stockholm last summer, never received. SOOS came to Italy as result GELLERT's word torm /sic/ from Stockholm he was leaving for

Italy and hoped SOOS could escape to meet him here. SOOS brought childishly insecure cipher and crude signal plane /sic/ for communication his staff in Budapest…

"SOOS claims leadership MFM, Hungarian independence movement consisting (qv-MFM) … "

16 December 1944

3. Subject, "ex-Deputy Chief in the Hungarian Foreign Ministry's Department of International Cultural Relations, reached Italy by plane on the 9th of this month, having flown there from Hungary with a small group of his compatriots. He asserts that he is the head of the MFM (Magyar Fuggetlen[sé]gi Mozgalom), an organization of 2700 white-collar workers, which is non-political in character, but devoted to the independence of Hungary and interested in the direction of resistance in that country."

Subject asked that a message be transmitted to the Soviet Union. The message is contained in document, is all operational regarding attempts of the MFM to contact the Russians and work with their approval. Director states that preliminary findings on subject are favorable and suggests that message be transmitted.

2/29/44

4. Connected with Hungarian anti-German circles in Stockholm. (Addendum to this statement: "Reliability doubtful; SEE xx–5795")

JBX–0021204
Crabbe, Source 1 & 2
10/23/44

5. Born Budapest 1912. Protestant Youth leader. 16 October 1944 resigned post of secretary, Hungarian Foreign Office. Alias G. Pal GYULAKUTI; SALZER; SCHULTZE; Gizi NENI; PALI.

.....Caserta, 12/1944

6. Subject is listed among a group of democratic, anti Nazi Hungarian journalists in Budapest. He is editor of the Soli Deo Gloria Hirado, was born in 1912, and his address in Budapest XI Mohai u. 32.

JHK–79; B–2

November 10, 1944

7. See document JBX–002–1228a, 1/9/45. Here subject's trip from Budapest to Italy 9/44 called a peace mission for HORTHY, not a flight (see below).

8. Aliases: see above, also Pal G. Suba. Subject's father a prominent Hungarian jurist. Subject has a wife and three children in Hungary. He carries a Hungarian diplomatic passport. Until 1936, subject employed in the Ministry of Justice, and late[r] transferred to the Cultural Relations Division of the Foreign Office because of his familiarity with Protestant youth movements. He attended the YMCA World Congress in Cleveland in 1939 / Dealing al ... with refugee problems, he came in contact with the Polish Underground Movement. Through the diplomatic pouch he kept London in touch with the Polish refugees in Hungary, the messages being sent to Stockholm and forwarded from there. He was also administrator of the funds sent by London to the Polish refugees in Hungary. During this time he was in contact with the British legation at Berne, his Polish and Red Cross connection gaining him access to Switzerland.

Periodic reports on the Hungarian political situation were sent to Stockholm after 3/19/44 and then turned over to the American Legation there. When this channel became unsafe, a radio set was sent to subject from Stockholm, but he never received it. But he did receive instructions from his contact in Stockholm (before latter's departure for Italy) to try to organize a Hungarian resistance movement in Hungary.

Subject's flight from Budapest to Italy commenced on 12/3[0/44.] The party, including subject, Major HADNAGY (pilot of plane and head of Tech. Sect. of Hung. Air Corps) and his wife and child, a Hungarian lieutenant and wt operator, TOPERCZER Arpad, a Dutch lieutenant and ex-POW Baron Johannes ADOLF BENTINCK, and a Hungarian sergeant and mechanic Istvan RAKOVITS,

was taken by car to Papa. Here there was plane which was supposed to take Gen. HELLEBRONTH to Germany for a conference with Hitler. On Dec. 9 they left Papa in this plane and headed for Rome, but they were grounded by bad weather in San Severo. At present the party is being held in custody by OSS, Bari for interrogation.

JBX–002–1226

Bari, C–3, 12/25/44

9. Chief secretary of Secretariat, which is the control group of the MFM (qv). Subject used alias Schultze when in contact with Sweden both by telephone and in writing; SALTZER for contacts in Switzerland; GIZI NENI (Aunt Gizi) when in contact with Hungarians in Switzerland; PALI within the underground movement and Pal G. GYULAKUTI used other than in the underground, and it is by this name that he is known and sought by the German Secret Police. As representative of the Protestants in Hungary, subject contacted DULLES, U.S. rep., who was contacted through Rev. Visser 't HOOFT, a Dutch minister in Zurich and Elisabeth Wis[k]eman[n], Balkan Desk Genf.* Of the British Embassy. (The latter are in Switzerland). In Sweden

subject was in contact with ULLEIN-REVICZKY, former Hungarian ambassador in Stockholm; in U.S.A. with Istvan SZABO, Domokos KOSARY, Peter KOVACS, Dr. Sandor TARICS, Tibor ECKHARDT and Prince ODERSCALCHI, Lt. Tibor BERENYI and Janos PIRHY.

JBX–002–103

AE/oo5, Bari, 1/3/4[5]

* Note (FB): Wiskemann was press attaché at the British legation in Bern, not Geneva.

10. Subject is one of X–2 Balkans' valuable sources of info.; Hungarian national who arrived in Bari, Italy from Hungary in early Dec. 1944. Although an SI body, he furnished much good information to X–2, of counter-intelligence interest. Since being released by OSS, Dr. SOOS has been in Rome, and he continues to voluntarily furnish X–2 favors. He is considered by the Saint Balkans Desk as a reliable source of information for the post-war set-up. Is very much concerned about the welfare of his family. Request our representative in State Dept. in Budapest investigate regarding them.

JBX–002–716

16 July 1945

11. Subject is source of document on Activities of Hungarian Red Cross in Rome.

JBX–160, 6/29/45

12. Report of Geza SOOS.

JBX–003–1809

JZK–5045 9/25/45

13. Personnel form on subject.

JBX–003–918   9/18/45

14. Subject assigned a symbol.

JBX–003–919

9/19/45

15. Memorandum to A.C of S., G–2, RAAC from 276 FSS RAAC containing accusation by Ladislaus (Laszlo) HORVATH against subject. Note: Soos denies having any official connection with the "Free Hungarian Movement."
J X–212 9/19/45

Source for the above OSS reports: National Archives: RG 226 Entry 214 Box 4 file 24600 Location 250/64/33/2

***

An additional OSS report elaborates and adds information about Soos meeting Aradi and Perczel. I am grateful to Duncan Bare for making me aware of the following important item:

5. January 1945; Saint Bari-Saint Washington (JBX 002–103); Contacts of the Hungarian Resistance Movement (Magyar Fugget[len]segi Mo[z]galom) Baky Laszlo, So[os] in the ministry, considered f[r]iendly towa[r]ds MFM and bitter enemy of Szalasi. Appears to be of good character and is probably an outstanding personality. Talented and zealous. The MFM of which Dr. Soos is a leader, appears

to be an official underground movement of the Horthy regime. From an American pov [i.e., point of view], Soos is an exponent of the Horthy regime and is trying to save or at least salvage it with the aid of the U.S. Tibo[r] Eckha[r]d[t,], Oderscalchi P[r]inc[e], playboy. Szentivanyi Sando[r] ev. Had a W/T in his house, has an American wife. Kemeny Gyo[r]gy, Budapest, Zionist, offered W/T communications with London, Kallay Kristof, son of PM, Apor Gabor, Horthy kept his W/T set in his p[r]ivate [r]ooms. Soos met Apor's representatives Aradi and Perczel at the Hungarian consulate in Bern, May-June 1943. Toth K Janos, Hungarian FM, Ba[r]anyai Lipot, Heuer Janos, has had contacts under the following aliases, Schultze, Saltzer, Gizi Neni, Pali, Gyalakuti Pal G. Dulles in Switzerland, th[r]ough ev. Visser't Hooft, a Dutch minister in Bern. Wis[k]eman[n] Elisabeth, Balkan Desk Genf. Of the British embassy. Ullein [R]eviczky, Sweden, Szabo Istvan Rev. (US) carried a special cipher, Kosa[r]ly Domokos, ev, Kovacs Peter, Tarics Sandor. Imgs. Source: RG 226, Entry 211, Box 44, WN 20413–20417.

* * *

OSS Interrogation Summary

Elek Karsai edited and published the final OSS summary that resulted from the above interrogations. Karsai asserted that he was able to examine the summary of the interrogations at the National Archives in Washington.*

Soos and Hadnagy challenged the interrogation summary's accuracy. Despite the fact that they objected to mistakes in this text, there is no evidence that their criticisms were taken into account in the final version of the report. There are numerous obvious mistakes, especially in the spelling of names and mistakes in dating events.**

*Elek Karsai (ed.), "Soos Géza és Hadnagy Domokos tájékoztatása a magyarországi helyzetről és a Magyar Függetlenségi Mozgalomról 1944 decemberében (Az Amerikai központi hírszerző hivatal által készitett összefoglaló jelentés)" [Report of Géza Soos and Domokos Hadnagy about the Hungarian Situation and the Hungarian Independence Movement in December 1944. - The summarizing report prepared by the American central intelligence agency], in: *Raday Gyüjtemény Évkönyve,* IV-V (Budapest, 1986), pp. 238–287, here p. 244.

**The detailed criticism by Soos and Hadnagy has been published in Ilona Tüdős (ed.), *Evangéliumot Magyarországnak,* pp. 154–157. Cf. pp. 54–55 above.

Although the summary provides valuable information, one must keep in mind that the OSS recordings may be responsible for a lack of precision and even misunderstandings of the original statements by Soos and Hadnagy. This caution may relate to the following texts in the above *Chronology and Documentation*:

a) Statements attributed to Bishop László Ravasz, p. 69.
b) Statements attributed to Géza Soos about the revelations of the drunk Galánta officer, pp. 82–84.
c) Statements attributed to Soos about Koszorús, pp. 93–94.

Appendix B: The Auschwitz Report (OSS Translation)

HEADQUARTERS
2677th Regiment
OFFICE OF STRATEGIC SERVICES (PROV)
APO 512, U.S. Army

1 May 1945

H Analysis No. 20

SOURCE   : Sullivan, Henie, and Louis
SUB-SOURCE   : As stated
DATE OF INFO: 7 April 1944
TO   : Commanding Officer, 2677th Regiment.
                  (Attn: Chief SICE, Hq 2677th Regiment.)
FROM   : A. G. FLUES, Major AC
                  Commanding BDPTCU
SUBJECT   : Testimony of two escapees from Auschwitz-Birkenau
                  Extermination Camps at Oswiecim, Poland.

The accompanying text is the translation of a document brought to Italy by Dr. G. Soos, secretary of the Hungarian underground movement MFM, in microfilm form. The film is a reproduction of the original document hidden by Dr. Soos with other papers deposited with trustees of the Hungarian underground and remains in his possession at Rome. The original, written in Hungarian, was transmitted to him by Dr. Jozsef Elias, a protestant pastor of Jewish ancestry who is the head of "Te'Pasztox Bizottsag," and an organizer of Jewish resistance in Hungary.

Two young Slovak Jews escaped from the Birkenau-Auschwitz concentration camps at Oswiecim, Poland, on 7 April 1944 and reached Hungary, Dr. Soos believes, at the end of June or early July. They were interrogated by Dr. Elias and this document is the result of the interrogation. The identity of the two men was not revealed to Dr. Soos, in order not to endanger their personal security. He heard, however, that the Jewish underground made arrangements to send them to a neutral country, presumably to

Switzerland, in order to preserve them for ultimate testimony. Dr. Soos believes that the first escapee originates from Sered u/V., Slovakia, while the second escapee comes from Nagyszombat, Slovakia.

The first escapee was sent from the collecting camp of Sered u/V. to the Auschwitz camp on 13 April 1942 and from there to the adjoining Birkenau camp the same day; the other was sent from the camp at Navaky on 14 June 1942 to the Maidenek concentration camp at Lublin; then to the Auschwitz camp on 27 June 1942; and finally to the Birkenau camp in September or October 1942, where he joined his fellow escapee.

The original report, translated without alteration here, is compiled in three parts; the first describes the experiences of the first escapee from the time of his deportation from Sered until January 1943, mostly spent at Birkenau. Part II describes chiefly the experiences of the first escapee but also contains testimony and data given by the second escapee, who arrived at Auschwitz 30 June 1942 but did not meet his companion at Birkenau until September or October 1942. This part covers the period from early 1942 until their escape in April 1944. The third part describes the experiences of the second escapee from the time he left Novaky on 14 June 1942 until he was transferred from Auschwitz to Birkenau in September or October 1942.

Within each part the story is told in rough chronological order; owing to the disorganization of the text, titles have been added by the editors to facilitate reading.

EXTERMINATION CAMPS, OSWIECIM, POLAND

Part I. Testimony of the First Escapee.
    1. Arrival of 640 Slovak Jews at Auschwitz Camp (Oswiecim, Poland), mid-April 1942.
    2. Description of Auschwitz Camp.
    3. Arrival at Birkenau Camp, mid-April 1942.
    4. Description of Birkenau Camp.
    5. Arrival of 12,000 Russian POWs and 1300 French Jews previous to April 1942.
    6. Experiences at Birkenau April-May 1942.
    7. Experiences at Birkenau May 1942-January 1943.

Part II. Testimony of Both the First and Second Escapees.
    8. Transport arrivals at Auschwitz-Birkenau, early 1942-December 1942.
    9. Description of the extermination crew.
    10. Transport arrivals at Auschwitz-Birkenau, January-February 1943.
    11. Description of the new Birkenau crematoria and gas chambers, February 1943.
    12. Transport arrivals at Auschwitz-Birkenau, March-September 1943.
    13. Treatment of the Theresienstadt Czechs, September 1943-March 1944.
    14. Transport arrivals, September 1943-April 1944.
    15. Organization and population of the Birkenau camp, April 1944.

-iv- SECRET

Part III. Testimony of the Second Escapee.
    16. Internment at Maidenek camp at Lublin, June 1942.
    17. Internment at Auschwitz, 30 June 1942-September or October 1942.

Part IV. Estimate of Jews Exterminated at Birkenau, April 1942-1944.

I. TESTIMONY OF THE FIRST ESCAPEE

1. Arrival at Auschwitz Camp (Oswiecim, Poland)

On 13 April 1942, some one thousand of us were loaded into closed freight cars at the reception center at Sered. The doors of the cars were sealed so that we could not learn the route taken. When the doors were opened after a long journey, we were astonished to see that we had left Slovakia and were at the railway station of Zward, in Poland. The guard, which heretofore had consisted of members of the Slovak Hlinka Guard, was replaced by German Waffen-SS personnel. After some cars were left behind, we proceeded to Auschwitz, where we arrived at night and were shunted onto a siding. The cars left behind had supposedly been dropped because of difficulties in billeting; they followed us in a few days. When we arrived, we were lined up in rows of five and counted. The number of arrivals was 640. We reached the Auschwitz camp after 20 minutes' march, carrying our heavy luggage--we had left Slovakia well equipped.

In Auschwitz we were brought at once into a large barracks. We had to deposit our parcels on one side of the building; on the other side we had to strip naked and to hand in our clothes and valuables. We went naked into a neighboring barracks where our heads and bodies were shaved and disinfected with lysol. As we left this barracks everyone was given a number. The numbers began at 28,600.[1/] Holding our numbers in our hands, we were driven into

---

[1/] Note the statement on page 9 that women were designated by a separate numbering system. The summary of 1942 transport arrivals is given on page 13ff. Some prisoners were exterminated on arrival, without being numbered.

a third barracks where the admission proper was made. This consisted of our numbers being tatooed on the left breast in an extremely brutal manner. Many of us passed out during the process. Our personal data were also taken. We were sent from here to a cellar in groups of 100, then into a barracks where we were issued prison uniforms and wooden shoes. The whole procedure lasted until about 10 a.m. That same afternoon our uniforms were taken away and in their place we received second-hand Russian uniforms, or rather rags. Thus equipped, we were led to Birkenau.

2. Description of the Auschwitz camp.

Auschwitz is actually a reception center for political prisoners, for those "in protective custody." [2] In April 1942, at the time of my assignment there, there were about 15,000 prisoners, mostly Poles, German nationals [3], and Russian civilians. [4] A few of the inmates were criminals or hoboes.

The Birkenau labor camp, as well as the agricultural settlement at Harmansee, are subordinate to the Auschwitz camp command. All prisoners come first to Auschwitz, where they are provided with appropriate numbers; they are either kept there or are sent to Birkenau; only a few go to Harmansee. Prisoners are allotted numbers in the order of their admittance. Numbers are used only once, so that the last number shows the total number of prisoners admitted up to that date. At the time of our escape from Birkenau,

---

[2] Schutzhaeftlinge
[3] Reichsdeutsche
[4] Schutzrussen

at the beginning of April 1944, this /highest/ number was about 180,000. Numbers were at first tatooed on the left breast, but later, as these numbers because illegible, on the left arm above the wrist.

All categories of prisoners receive the same treatment, regardless of nationality. But for ease of control they are distinguished by different-colored triangles located on the left side of the upper garment, under the prison number. The nationality of the prisoner is indicated by initial letters (i.e., P for Pole, etc.) placed inside the triangle. The colors of the triangles indicating the various categories are:

   red - political protective custody
   green - incorrigible criminal
   black - work derelict (mostly Russians)
   pink - homosexuals
   purple - member of the sect of Bible Researchers

The markings of Jewish prisoners differ from the insignia described above only in that the triangle, which is red in most cases, is converted into a Star of David by the addition of a small yellow triangle.

There are several factories and workshops in the vicinity of the Auschwitz camp, among others a DAW,[5] one Krupp, one Siemens plant, and a complex called "Buna," several kilometers long, in process of construction, which is outside the camp area proper. These plants are manned by prisoners.

---

[5] Deutsche Aufruestungswerke, or German Armament Works.

The dwelling-area of the camp, that is, the actual concentration camp, covers an area approximately 500 by 500 meters in size. This zone is fenced off by two rows of concrete columns about 3 meters high. The columns are connected with each other by high-tension wires supported by insulators. Between these two fences, about 150 meters apart, there are watch towers about 5 meters high, equipped with machine guns and searchlights. In front of the inner row of high-tension columns there is a barbed-wire fence. Touching this ordinary fence is answered by machine gun fire from the watch towers.

The camp itself consists of 3 rows of buildings. The camp road runs between the first and second row of buildings. There was previously a wall between the second and third rows of buildings, and until August 1942 Jewish girls from Slovakia, who had been deported in March and April 1942, were billeted in the structures behind this wall. There were about 7,000 of these girls. After they were taken to Birkenau, the wall was pulled down. At the entrance of the camp was the following sign in big letters: "Arbeit macht frei." [6]

Within a radius of about 2,000 meters the whole camp is surrounded by watch towers at a distance of 150 meters from each other. In contrast to the guard installations called Kleine Postenkette, which are described above, this system is called the Grosse Postenkette. [7] The various factories and shops are located

---

[6] "Work liberates."

[7] Respectively, small and large guard belts.

Plan of the AUSCHWITZ CAMP
Plan I

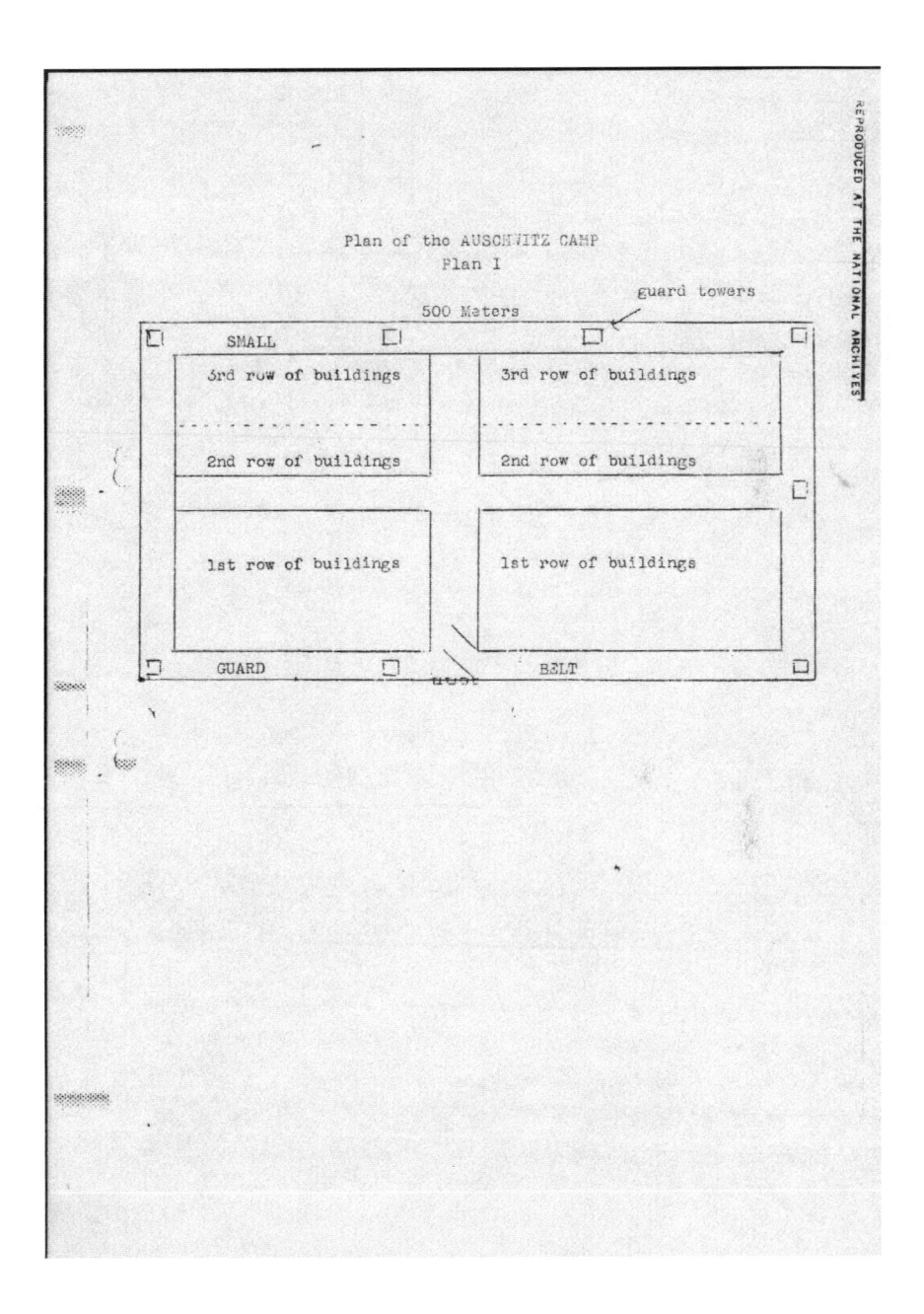

500 Meters   guard towers

SMALL

3rd row of buildings | 3rd row of buildings

2nd row of buildings | 2nd row of buildings

1st row of buildings | 1st row of buildings

GUARD   BELT

between these two guard belts.

Watch towers of the small (inner) belt are manned only at night, at which time the double fence is also charged with electric current. Sentries of the small belt are relieved in the morning and the towers of the large belt are manned. Escape through these two sentry belts is nearly impossible. To get through the inner belt during the night is out of the question, since the towers of the large belt are so close to one another (only 150 m., with each tower guarding a radius of 75 meters) that one cannot approach the belt without being observed. Anyone approaching is shot without warning. Relief of the guards in the big belt takes place at night only after the roster has been checked in the small belt zone, and it is ascertained that all prisoners are within that area. If, at the roll call, any prisoner is found missing, an alarm is given by sirens.

When a prisoner is missing, the guards of the outer belt remain in their towers and the guards of the inner belt also take up their posts. Hundreds of SS men with bloodhounds search the area between the two guard belts. The sirens alert the whole region, so that even after miraculously breaking through the two guard belts the escaping prisoner faces the danger of falling into the hands of numerous German police and SS patrols. Escaping prisoners are greatly handicapped by their shaved heads and marked clothes (rags painted red). The population of the area is so intimidated that, at best, it is passive to escaping prisoners. Death is immediately meted out to all those giving any aid to an escaped prisoner, even to those who fail to report instantly the location of such a person.

If a prisoner is not caught after three days, the guards of the outer belt leave their posts, since it is assumed that the prisoner was successful in breaking through both guard belts. If the escaped prisoner is caught alive, he is hanged in the presence of the entire camp. If he is found dead, his body is exposed at the gates of the camp. In its hands is placed a sign which reads: "Hier bin ich." [8]

During our two years imprisonment many attempted to escape, but with the exception of two or three all were brought back dead or alive. We do not know if those not brought back succeeded in escaping, but we do know that we are the only Jews brought from Slovakia to Auschwitz or Birkenau who did escape.

3. Arrival of the First Escapee at Birkenau.

As I said before, we were sent to Birkenau on the first day of our arrival in Auschwitz [mid-April 1942]. There is in reality no community called Birkenau; this is a new name probably originating from the near-by beechwood "Birke." The area known as Birkenau is called "Rajska" by the local population. The center of the Birkenau camp is four kilometers from Auschwitz, the outer guard belts of the two camps being separated by a railroad track only. At that time we knew nothing about Neuberaun, a town about 30 to 40 kilometers from Birkenau which for unknown reasons was given as our mailing address.

4. Description of Birkenau camp.

When we arrived at Birkenau, one large kitchen, capable of

---

[8] "Here I am."

SECRET

handling 15,000 people, and two other buildings had already been completed and one additional house was under construction. All these buildings were enclosed by ordinary wire fence. The last-mentioned buildings were used for the reception of prisoners and were built according to the same plan. Each was about thirty meters long and eight to ten meters wide. The walls were scarcely more than two meters high, the roof reaching the disproportionate height of five meters. Such a building resembles a stable with a hayloft perched on top. Since there is no ceiling, the inside height is about seven meters. An inside wall, with a door in the center, divides each house lengthwise into two parts. The house-walls and the dividing wall support balconies running lengthwise at a height of 80 centimeters above each other. These balconies are divided into small cells with three persons to each cell. There are layers of cells on each wall. The dimensions given /sic./ show that the cell is not long enough to permit a person to lie down stretched out and is just high enough to enable him to sit up. Since the height of a cell is 80 centimeters, it is impossible to stand up in it. Approximately 400 to 500 persons are billeted in each house or, as they call it, block.

The Birkenau camp at this time covered an area of 850x1600 meters. Like Auschwitz, a small or inner guard belt surrounds it. Beyond this inner belt a new, much larger camp was under construction. Upon completion, it was to be incorporated in the camp already functioning. We do not know the purpose of these large-scale preparations. As at Auschwitz, the Birkenau camp is surrounded at a distance of 2 kilometers by an outer belt of guard-posts. The

SECRET

guard system is similar to that of Auschwitz.

5. **Arrival of 12,000 Russian POWs and 1300 French Jews Previous to April 1942.**

The buildings that we found in Birkenau upon our arrival had been built by 12,000 Russian POWs who were brought there in December 1941. They worked under such inhuman conditions during the extraordinarily cold weather that nearly all had died by the time we arrived. They had been given numbers from 1-12,000, but this was outside the numbering system for other inmates. When additional Russian POWs arrived, they did not receive subsequent numbers like other prisoners, but were allotted numbers between 1 and 12,000 vacated by deceased Russian POWs. It was impossible, therefore, to estimate by means of this numbering system the total number of Russian POWs received at the camp. Russian POWs were assigned to Auschwitz and Birkenau for punishment only.

We found the surviving Russians in a terrible state of degradation and neglect. They were billeted in the unfinished buildings, were exposed to the weather, and died in great numbers. Their corpses were superficially buried by hundreds and thousands. Later we had to dig up these corpses and bury [burn?] them.

The first French male transport also reached Auschwitz before ourselves. It contained 1,300 naturalized French Jews. The numbering of these French Jews began at about 27,500. As I mentioned before, our numbers began with 28,600, therefore, no male transport had arrived in Auschwitz between the French and ourselves.

9/ See page 13 for list of transport arrivals from early 1942 to December 1942.

(Women were processed separately and were numbered parallel with men; the girls from Slovakia who arrived before us were given numbers 1000-8000). We found the survivors of the French Jewish transport in Birkenau, about 700 men in a state of total exhaustion. The remainder died within one week.

6. **Experiences at Birkenau April-May 1942**

The following were billeted in the 3 completed blocks:

(a) The so-called "prominents," i.e., professional criminals and older Polish political prisoners who were entrusted with the leadership of the camp;

(b) Survivors of the French Jews (about 700);

(c) Jews from Slovakia, 634 at first,[10/] to which were added a few days later those who had stayed behind in Zward;

(d) Surviving Russians who were living in the half-completed houses or had no shelter at all, and whose numbers diminished so rapidly that they did not constitute a group to be accounted for.

We Jews from Slovakia had to work with the Russian survivors. French Jews worked separately. After three days I was sent with 200 Slovak Jews to work in the Auschwitz Deutsche Aufrustungswerke. We were billeted at Birkenau and went out to work early in the morning. Food was given us twice daily, one liter of carrot soup at noon and thirty dekagrams of bad bread in the evening. Working conditions were hard beyond imagination, so that most of us could not stand it. Weakened as we were from starvation and the inedible

---

10/ 640? See description of the author's own transport on page 1.

food, the death-rate took on frightening proportions; in our working group of 200, from 30-35 died each day. Many were simply beaten to death by the work supervisors and the so-called "*capos*." The daily shortage caused by deaths was made good from the groups staying in Birkenau.

Returning from work at night was difficult and dangerous for us. We had to carry home, a distance of 5 kilometers, our tools, firewood, heavy cooking bowls, and the corpses of our comrades who had died or had been beaten to death during the day. We had to march in military formation with this heavy load. The *capo* punished what he considered unmilitary marching with cruel beatings or even by beating the culprits to death. By the time the second transport arrived, 14 days later, only about 150 of us were alive. We were counted off every night. Corpses were loaded on small carts and taken to the near-by birchwood, where they were burned in holes several meters deep and 15 meters long.

Every morning on our way to work we met 300 Jewish girls from Slovakia who were in a labor gang known as a *Kommando*, and worked in the vicinity at some kind of digging. These girls were dressed in old rags of Russian uniforms and wore wooden clogs. Their heads were shaven. Unfortunately we could never talk to them.

7. Experiences at Birkenau May 1942 - January 1943.

By the middle of May 1942 a total of four Jewish male transports had reached Birkenau from Slovakia. All received the same treatment as ourselves. From the first and second transports, 120 of us were sent to Auschwitz on orders of the Auschwitz camp command, which had asked for doctors, dentists, university students, and professional administrators and clerks. After one week at Auschwitz 18 doctors and nurses, as well as three clerks, were selected from the 120 professionals. The doctors were assigned to the Auschwitz hospital and the three clerks, including myself, were sent back to Birkenau. Two of my companions, Laszlo Braun from from Nagyszombat and Grosz from Verbo, both of whom have since died, went to the Slovak block. I went to the French block, where we were given administrative work. The remaining 99 persons were sent to work in the Auschwitz quarry where they perished within a short time.

Shortly afterwards a so-called hospital (Krankenbau) was established in one of the buildings. This was the notorious Block No. 7. I was assigned there as head-nurse at first; later I became the manager. The head of the hospital was Victor Mordarki, No. 3550, a Polish political. This hospital was nothing other than an assembly point for those awaiting death. All prisoners unable to work were sent here. Naturally, there could be no question of medical treatment or nursing. Every day about 150 people died and their corpses were sent to the Auschwitz crematorium.

At the same time, the so-called "selection" was started. The number of prisoners who were to be gassed and their bodies burned was determined twice weekly, on Monday and Thursday, by the camp doctor (Standortarzt). Selectees were loaded on a truck and taken to the birchwood. Those who reached there alive were gassed in the big barrack built for the purpose and located next to the hole for burning bodies, and then were cremated in that hole. Approximately 2000 from Block No. 7 died each week, of which about 1200 deaths

-12- SECRET

resulted from "natural causes" and about 800 from "selection." Death reports on those dying from natural causes were made out and sent to camp HQ at Oranienburg. Selectees were marked up in a book labelled SB.[11]/ I was manager of Block No. 7 until 15 January 1943, during which time I could observe what was going on. About 50,000 prisoners were destroyed during that period, either from "natural causes" or through "selections."

---

[11]/ Sonderbehandlung, or "special treatment."

-13-   SECRET

II. TESTIMONY OF BOTH THE FIRST AND SECOND ESCAPEES

8. <u>Transport Arrivals at Auschwitz-Birkenau, Early 1942 - December 1942</u>.

In view of the fact that prisoners were given consecutive numbers, as we said before, we are in a position to determine with considerable exactness the order of arrival and fate of the various transports. The order of arrival ran as follows:

Numbers	Transports
c. 27,400-28,600	First transport of naturalized French Jews.
c. 28,600-29,600	First Jews from Slovakia, our own transport. /arrived mid-April 1942-ed./
c. 29,600-29,700	100 Gentile men from various transit camps.
c. 29,700-32,700	Three complete Slovak Jewish transports, 3000 men.
c. 32,700-33,100	400 habitual criminals (Gentiles) from Warsaw.
c. 33,100-35,000	Approximately 2000 Jews from Cracow.
c. 35,000-36,000	Gentile Poles, political prisoners in protective custody.
c. 36,000-37,300	1330 Slovak Jews arriving from Lublin-Maidenek in May 1942.
c. 37,300-37,900	600 Gentile Poles, with few Jews, coming from Radom.
c. 37,900-38,000	100 Gentile Poles arriving from the Dachau reception center.
c. 38,000-38,400	400 naturalized French Jews with their families, the entire transport numbering about 1600 people. Of these only about 400 men and 200 women were assigned to the camp. The remaining thousand, including women and older

-14- SECRET

men, were sent directly to the birchwood, where they were gassed and cremated without being entered on the records and assigned numbers.

After this time, all incoming Jewish transports were handled like the French transport. About ten percent of the men and five percent of the women were assigned to the camp, the remaining being immediately exterminated. Polish Jews had been handled this way even earlier. Trucks from the various Polish ghettos arrived continually for months, going directly to the birchwood, where these Jews were gassed and cremated by the thousands.

c. 38,400-39,200	800 naturalized French Jews, a great many of whom were destroyed in the way described above.
c. 39,200-40,000	800 Gentile Poles, political prisoners in protective custody.
c. 40,000-40,150	150 Slovak Jews with their families. With the exception of 50 women, who were sent to the women's camp, the majority of the transport was gassed in the birchwood. Among the 150 men were Zucker and Vilmos Sonnenschein, both from Eastern Slovakia.
c. 40,150-43,800	Almost 4000 naturalized French Jews, mostly intellectuals. About 1000 women of this transport went to the camp and 3000 persons were gassed in the birchwood.
c. 43,800-44,200	400 Slovak Jews from the Lublin camp, including Matyas Klein and Meilech Laufer, both from Eastern Slovakia. 12/ This transport arrived on 30 June 1942.
c. 44,200-45,000	This transport contained 1000 persons,

12/ This is evidently the transport of the second escapee, see page 38.

-15-   SECRET

	A few women were sent to the women's camp and all others went to the birchwood. Among the men sent to the camp were Jozsef Zelmanovies, from Snina; Adolf Kahan, from Bratislava; Walter Reichmann, from Sucany; and Eszter Kahan from Bratislava. I had occasion to speak with the latter on 1 April 1944. She is block-inspector in the women's camp.
c. 45,000-47,000	2000 French Gentiles, including communists and other political prisoners, among them the brothers of Thorez and Leon Blum. The latter were specially tortured, and then gassed and cremated.
c. 47,000-47,500	500 Dutch Jews, among them many German emigres. About 250 persons from this transport went to the birchwood.
c. 47,500-47,800	About 300 Russian civilians (Schutzrussen).
c. 48;300 (sic) - 48,620	320 Slovak Jews. About 70 women went to the camp and the remainder of the transport of 650 persons were sent to the birchwood. This transport contained 80 persons who were deported to Sered n/V. by the Hungarian police. In this group were:
	Dr. Zoltan Mandel of Presov, who later died;
	Holz (first name unknown), a butcher from Pistany who was later sent to Warsaw;
	Miklos Engel of Zilina;
	Chaim Katz of Snina, whose wife and six children have been gassed, and who at the present time works at the morgue.
c. 49,000-64,800	15,000 naturalized French, Belgian, and Dutch Jews. This number accounts for no more than ten percent of the transports arriving between 1 June and 15 September 1942. Most of these were large family transports, many of their members being sent directly to the

-16- SECRET

birchwood. The Sonderkommando [13]
which did the gassing and cremating
worked day and night shifts. At this
time Jews were gassed and burned by
hundreds of thousands.

c. 64,800-65,000 About 200 Slovak Jews. Some 100
women were sent to the women's camp,
the others going to the birchwoods.
Among those coming to the camp were:

Lajos Katz from Zilina;
Avri Burger (his wife died) from
  Bratislava-Poprad;
Miklos Steiner, from Bystrica n/V.;
Gyorgy Fried, from Trencin;
Buchwald (?);
Jozsef Rosenwasser, from Eastern
  Slovakia;
Gyula Neumann, from Bardejov;
Sandor and Mihaly Wertheimer, from
  Verbo; and
Bela Blau, from Zilina.

c. 65,000-68,000 Naturalized French, Belgian, and Dutch
Jews. About 1000 women were sent to
the women's camp and a minimum of
3000 persons were gassed.

c. 68,000-70,500 2500 German Jews from the Sachsenhaus
reception-center.

c. 71,000-80,000 Naturalized French, Belgian, and Dutch
Jews. Not more than ten percent of
those arriving were sent to the camp.
The number exterminated is conserva-
tively estimated at 65,000-70,000.

9. Description of the Extermination Crew.

On 17 December 1942, 200 young Slovak Jews were executed
in Birkenau. They had been engaged as Sonderkommandos in the
gassing and cremating crews. Their plan to revolt and escape was
betrayed and the executions followed. Among those executed were:

---

[13] Labor gangs with special assignments. See below.

-17-   SECRET

Sandor Weisz
Oszkar Steiner
Aladar Spitzer
Ferenc Wagner
Dezso Wetzler
Bela Weisz

All these men came from Nagyzombat. Two hundred Polish Jews, who had just arrived from Makow, replaced the executed Sonderkommandos.

We lost our direct contact with this "working place" after the elimination of the Slovak Jewish Sonderkommandos, and this brought a deterioration in our supply situation. Transports arriving at the birchwood brought with them, although they had to leave their luggage in Auschwitz, large amounts of foreign currency, mostly dollars in banknotes or gold, tremendous quantities of gold and precious stones, and even foodstuffs. Although these valuables had to be handed in, it was unavoidable that a great deal, especially gold dollars, went into the pockets of the boys who were working in the extermination crews and had to go through the clothes of those who had been gassed.

In this way a considerable amount of wealth and foodstuffs got into the camp. One could buy nothing for money in the camp officially, of course. But one could make a deal with the SS men and with civilian workers who were employed in the camp at various skilled jobs and so could smuggle in some food and cigarettes. Prices were naturally abnormal; a few hundred cigarettes cost twenty dollars in gold. Barter also flourished. But the high prices did not disturb us since we had more than enough money. We obtained clothing from the Sonderkommandos and so were able to change our rags for good clothes which had belonged to those gassed. For instance, the coat I am now wearing belonged to a Dutch Jew.[14/]

The Sonderkommandos were segregated. We did not associate with them because of the horrid smell they spread. They were always filthy, in rags, totally brutalized, and became violent savages. It was no rarity for one to club another to death. Such an occurance was nothing sensational among other prisoners as well, since the murder of a prisoner is not considered a crime. It is simply recorded that prisoner number so and so died; the cause of death is immaterial. I was present when a young Polish Jew named Jossel explained the fine art of "expert murder" to an SS man and, to demonstrate his point, killed another Jew with his bare hands, without using any weapon.

10. Transport Arrivals at Auschwitz-Birkenau, January - February 1943.

At about the number 80,000, the systematic extermination of those from the Polish ghettos began.

Numbers	Transports
c. 80,000-85,000	About 5000 Jews from various Polish ghettos, including Mljawa, Makow, Zichenow, Lomzsa, Grodno, Byalistok. Transports arrived continuously for thirty days. Only 5000 persons were assigned to camp; the remainder was gassed immediately. The Sonderkommandos worked feverishly in two shifts twenty-four hours a day, but they could hardly cope with the task of gassing and burning. It can be estimated without exaggeration that between 80,000 and 90,000 persons were exterminated. These transports

---

14/ Apparently the interrogator examined the coat at this point, since the original text notes that the coat carried the trade-mark of an Amsterdam tailor.

	brought with them particularly large sums of [Polish?] money, foreign currency, and precious stones.
c. 85,000-92,000	6000 Jews from Grodno, Byalistok, and Cracow, and an additional 1000 Gentile Poles. The large majority of the Jews went to the birchwood directly. An average of 4000 Jews were driven into the gas chamber daily.
	In the middle of January 1943, three transports of 2000 persons each arrived from Teresin [Theresienstadt Czechoslovakia] The markings of these transports were, "CU", "CR", and "R", which were incomprehensible to us. All parcels belonging to these transports were similarly marked. Of these 6000 persons, only 600 men and 300 women were sent to the camp, the remainder being gassed.
c. 99,000 (sic) - 100,000	Large Dutch and French Jewish transports arrived at the end of January 1943. Only a fraction went to the camp, the remainder being gassed.
c. 100,000-102,000	2000 Gentile Poles, mostly intellectuals, arrived in February 1943.
c. 102,000-103,000	700 Gentile Czechs, the survivors of whom were later sent to Buchenwald.
c. 103,000-108,000	3000 French and Dutch Jews and 2000 Gentile Poles.

An average of two transports of Polish, French, and Dutch Jews arrived daily during February 1943. In most cases entire transports were gassed. The number of those gassed in this month alone can be estimated at about 90,000.

11. The New Birkenau Crematoria and Gas Chambers.

At the end of February 1943 the newly-built crematoria and

SECRET

gas chambers were opened in Birkenau.[15/] The practice of gassing and burning corpses in the birchwood was stopped and bodies were taken to the four new crematoria built for the purpose. Ashes had been utilized as fertilizer previously on the Harmansee Estate, so that it is difficult to find traces of the mass murders.

There are four crematoria at work in Birkenau at the present time, two larger ones (models I and II) and two smaller (models III and IV). Models I and II consist of a waiting hall, gas chambers, and incinerators. The large waiting hall, which is equipped to resemble the hall of a bath, can accommodate 2000 persons. There is reported to be another waiting hall, equally large, below this one. A few steps lead from the big hall (on the ground level) into a very long and narrow gas chamber. False showers are built into the walls of the gas chamber so as to give the impression of a very large washroom. Three skylights in the ceiling of the chamber can be hermetically sealed by valves. A narrow-gauge track runs from the gas chambers through the waiting hall to the incinerators.

There is a high smoke-stack in the center of the hall where the incinerators are located. Nine incinerators are built around it, each having four doors. Each door will admit three average corpses at one time. Each incinerator will burn twelve bodies in one and a half hours, giving a total capacity of approximately 2000 corpses each twenty-four hours.

[15/] This confirms information as to the date the Birkenau crematorium and gas chamber complex went into operation, obtained in POW interrogation, PWB Report No.____.

−21−   SECRET

The victims are first led to the waiting hall, where they are told they will go to the bathhouse. They undress and, in order to support their delusion that they are going to bathe, two attendants clad in white distribute a towel and a piece of soap to each. Then they are squeezed into the gas chamber. Two thousand persons will pack the chamber to such an extent that all must stand up. The attendants often fire into the chamber to force those inside to make room for others. When everybody is in the chamber, the doors are sealed from the outside. There is a short wait, presumably to allow the temperature inside to rise to a certain degree. Then SS men with gasmasks go up on the roof, open the valves on the windows, and pour a powderlike substance into the chamber. The cans containing this substance carry the inscription: "Cyklon zur Schaedlingsbekaempfung"[16/] and the trademark of a Hamburg factory. These cans evidently contain a cyanide preparation that gassifies when the temperature rises to a certain degree. Everyone in the chamber dies within three minutes. Up to the present, there has been no case of anyone showing signs of life when the chamber was opened--a phenomena not so rare in the birchwood, where the procedure was more primitive. The chamber is ventilated after being opened and the Sonderkommandos move the corpses to the incinerators on flat cars. The crematoria designated models III and IV operate in about the same manner, but their turnover is only about half as large. The total capacity of the four crematoria, therefore, is 6000 corpses per day.

16/ Cyclon for exterminating criminals.

-22-   SECRET

In principle only Jews are gassed. Gentiles are usually shot, being gassed only in exceptional cases. Before the establishment of the crematoria, Gentiles were executed in the birchwood and their bodies burned there. Later, however, such executions were carried out in the hall of the crematoria, which was especially equipped for the purpose, by shooting in the nape of the neck.

Inauguration of the first crematorium occurred in March 1943 and was celebrated by the gassing and cremation of 8000 Jews from Cracow. Prominent guests from Berlin, including high-ranking officers and civilian personalities, attended and expressed their highest satisfaction with the performance of 'the gas chamber. They diligently used the spyhole in the door of the gas chamber.

12. Transport Arrivals March - September 1943

Number	Transport
c. 109,000- (sic) 119,000	Early in March 1943, 45,000 Jews arrived from Salonika. Ten thousand men and a much smaller number of women were sent to the camp. The remainder, at least 30,000 people, were sent to the crematoria. Of the 10,000 men in the camp, nearly everyone, perhaps all, died shortly afterwards. Most of them fell victims to an epidemic disease similar to malaria, many died of typhus, and others could not stand the hard conditions in the camp.

In view of the great mortality among the Greek Jews, resulting from malaria and typhus, selections were temporarily halted. Sick Greek Jews were told to report. We warned them not to do so, but many reported nevertheless. All were killed by intercordial injections of phenol. Such injections were administered by a medical noncommissioned officer who was assisted by

149

two Czech doctors, Cespira Honza and Zdenedk Stich, both of Prague. These doctors are at present in the Buchenwald reception center. Both doctors did everything they could to help the unfortunates, and when they could do nothing else, eased their pain.

Approximately 1000 survivors of the 10,000 Greek Jews were sent with another 500 Jews to build fortifications in Warsaw. A few hundred of these returned several weeks later in a hopeless condition and were immediately gassed. Four hundred Greeks suffering from malaria were sent to Lublin for "further treatment," following the suppression of the phenol injections. We received news of their arrival in Lublin, but we know nothing about their fate. It is certain that not one of the 10,000 remains in the camp.

Following the suppression of the "selection" system, the murder of prisoners was also forbidden. The following Reichsgermans were flogged for multiple murder:

```
          Alexander Neumann, professional criminal
                   Zimmer, professional criminal
          Albert Haemmerle,      "         "
          Rudolf Osteringer,     "         "
          Alfred Klein, political prisoner
          Alois Stahler,     "         "
```

These notorious murderers also had to sign a statement admitting the killing of a certain number of their fellow-prisoners.

Early in 1943, 50,000 discharge forms were received by the Auschwitz political department. This news caused great joy among us, as we hoped that some of us at least might be released. But these forms were filled in with the personal data of those gassed and were placed in the archives.

Numbers	Transports
c. 119,000-120,000	1000 Gentile Poles from the Pawiak prison in Warsaw.
c. 120,000-123,000	3000 Greek Jews, part of whom were sent to Warsaw to replace their dead compatriots. Those who stayed behind died off quickly.
c. 123,000-124,000	1000 Gentile Poles from Radom and Tarnow.
c. 124,000-126,000	2000 men from various Gentile transports.

In the meantime, Polish, Belgian, and French Jewish transports arrived continually, and their members were gassed without even a fraction going to the camp. One of these consisted of 1000 Polish Jews coming from Lublin-Maidenek. Among them were three Slovaks, including one named Spira from Stropko or Varanno.

At the end of July 1943, transports abruptly stopped coming. There was a short respite while the crematoria were thoroughly cleaned and prepared for further activities. The work started again on 3 August. Transports of Jews from Benzburg and Sossnowitz came first, and were followed by others without interruption during the whole month of August.

c. 132,000 (sic)-136,000	Jews from Benzburg and Sossnowitz. Only 4000 men and few women went to the camp. Over 35,000 were taken to the crematoria directly. Most of these died in the so-called quarantine camp from exceptionally inhuman treatment, starvation, various diseases, and last but not least, murders in their own ranks. Those chiefly responsible for the crimes committed against them are Tlyn, a professional criminal of German nationality who came here from the Sachsenhausen reception center, and

-25- SECRET

Mieczislaw Katerzinski, a Polish
political prisoner from Warsaw.

At this time "selections" were started again on a particularly large scale in the women's camp. The camp doctor, an SS Sturmfuehrer and son or nephew of the Berlin police director, acted with a brutality which stood out even in this camp. The practice of "selection" was carried out without respite from this time until our escape.

c. 137,000 (sic) - 138,000	1000 Gentile Poles from the Pawiak prison in Warsaw and about 80 Greek Jews arrived at the end of August.
c. 138,000-142,000	3000 Gentiles from various transports.
c. 142,000-145,000	3000 Jews from various Polish labor camps and a group of Russian POWs arrived at the beginning of September 1943.
c. 148,000 (sic)- 152,000	Family transports from Teresin (Theresienstadt), which arrived during the week following 7 September 1943.

13. <u>Treatment of the Theresienstadt Czechs, September 1943 - March 1944.</u>

For some reason unknown to us, the Theresienstadt transport enjoyed exceptional treatment. Nobody was gassed or even shaved, members kept their belongings and were billeted by families in a separate section of the camp. The men did not have to work, members were allowed to send mail to relatives, and a special school for the children was permitted under the leadership of Fredy Hirsch, at one time youth leader of the Makabi of Prague. 17/

17/ The largest Jewish sports club in Czechoslovakia.

However, members of these transports had to endure the sadistic tortures of a "camp inspector" named Arno Boehm, a professional criminal of German nationality who was, by the way, one of the most abject individuals in the entire camp. Our astonishment increased when we had an occasion to see the official roster of the transport. This roster bore the peculiar title, "Specially treated Czech Jews for six months' quarantine." [18/] We knew very well what the "SB" marking meant, but we could not find an explanation for the exceptional treatment and the extraordinarily long quarantine. According to our experience up to that time, the quarantine never lasted longer than three weeks. We became suspicious as the end of the six months' quarantine period approached, and were convinced that these Jews would also end up in the gas chamber. Looking for an opportunity to make contact with the leaders of the group, we explained their situation and did not leave them in any doubt as to their fate. A few of them, especially Fredy Hirsch, who obviously enjoyed the full confidence of his companions, told us that they would resist if our suspicions should materialize. Men of the <u>Sonderkommandos</u> promised that they would join immediately if the Czech Jews put up active resistance. Many hoped that a general uprising could be instigated in the camp.

We learned on 6 March 1944 that the crematoria had been put into condition for the Czech Jews. I went to see Fredy Hirsch without delay to inform him, and appealed to him to act immediately.

18/ "S/onders/B/ehandlung/-Transport tschechische Juden mit 6-monatlicher Quarantaene."

-27-   SECRET

He replied, "I know what my duty is." I sneaked to the Czech camp again before dawn and heard that Fredy Hirsch was dying. He had poisoned himself with luminol. The following day, 7 March 1944, he was transferred in a state of coma, with 3791 of his companions with whom he arrived in Birkenau after 7 September 1943, to the crematorium, on trucks where all were gassed.[19] The youths went to their death singing. The resistance did not come off. Determined men of the Sonderkommando had waited in vain.

About 500 elderly Czechs died during the six months' quarantine period. Of the whole group, the only ones left alive were eleven sets of twins taken to Auschwitz for biological experiments. When we left Birkenau these children were still alive. Rozsi Fuerst, a girl from Sered n/V., was among those executed. All were forced to inform their relatives that they were all right one week before their execution, that is, during the first days of March. The letters had to be dated 23 or 25 March. They were also told to ask for parcels from relatives abroad.

14. Transport Arrivals, September 1943 - April 1944.

c. 153,000 (sic)-154,000	1000 Gentile Poles from the Warsaw Pawiak prison.
c. 155,000 (sic)-159,000	4000 men from various prisons, Jews who had been in hiding and were captured around Benzburg, and a group of Russians (Schutzrussen) arrived in October 1943. At the same time, Russian POWs also came in and received numbers 1-12,000.
c. 160,000 (sic)-165,000	About 5000 men, mostly Dutch and Belgian Jews, and the first transport

---

[19] March 7, the day chosen by the Germans for this execution, is an outstanding Czechoslovak national holiday, the birthday of President Masaryk.

-28- SECRET

of Italian Jews came from Fiume, Trieste, and Rome. Not less than 30,000 persons from these transports were taken directly to the gas chamber.

Mortality among the Jews assigned to camp was particularly high. The method of selection took its toll at an increased rate. Selection reached its peak between 10-24 January 1944, when the strongest and healthiest Jews were taken regardless of their labor assignment or profession. Only doctors were spared. Everyone had to line up for the "selection," and a close check was made to ascertain that all were present. The "selection" was then made by the camp doctor (the son or nephew of the police chief of Berlin) and by the Birkenau camp commandant, SS Untersturmfuehrer Schwarzhuber. All Jews transferred from Block No. 7 to the "hospital" (Krankenbau), which was located in another part of the camp, were gassed without exception. In addition to these, another 2500 men and 6000 women were sent to the gas chamber through "selection."

c. 165,000-168,000	3000 Jews arrived from Teresin on 20 December 1943. This roster had the same title as the one which had come in September.[20] They were billeted with the September arrivals and enjoyed the same privileges. Twenty-four hours before the extermination of the first group the later arrivals were segregated in an adjoining part of the camp which happened to be empty. They are still living in this quarter. In view of their knowledge of the fate of the first group, they are already preparing to resist. Resistance has been organized

20/ See footnote 18.

                                    -29-   SECRET

                           by Ruzenka Laufer and Hugo Langsfeld,
                           both of Prague. They are collecting
                           easily inflammable material and want
                           to set their blocks on fire. Their
                           quarantine will be over on 20 June
                           1944.

  c. 169,000 (sic)-   1000 persons, including Poles,
     170,000   Russians, and Jews in smaller groups.

  c. 170,000-171,000   1000 Gentile Poles and Russians, and
                           a smaller number of Yugoslavs.

  c. 171,000-174,000   3000 Dutch, Belgian, and native
                           French Jews arrived in late February
                           and early March 1944. This was the
                           first shipment of native as distin-
                           guished from naturalized French Jews.
                           They came from the unoccupied zone.
                           An overwhelming majority of these
                           were immediately gassed.

In the middle of March 1944 a smaller group of Benzburg Jews, who had been found in hiding, arrived. We learned from them that many Polish Jews had escaped to Slovakia and from there to Hungary, and that these had been helped by Jews still living in Slovakia.

After the extermination of the Teresin Jews, no reinforcements arrived until 15 March. As a consequence, the number at the camp was substantially reduced, for which reason all men arriving in later transports, mostly Dutch Jews, were assigned to the camp. We had just learned of the arrival of large Greek Jewish transports when we left the camp on 7 April 1944. [21]

15. Organization and Population of the Birkenau Camp, April 1944.

The Birkenau camp consists of three sections (see plan

---

[21] A Reuter's dispatch of 20 March 1945, date-lined Athens, tells of the return from the Oswiecim camp of a Greek Jew, Leon Vatis, whose story and prison number tallies with the information given herein.

-30- SECRET

no. 3). At the present time, only sections I and II are surrounded by the inner guard belt, as section III is still in the process of building and is not inhabited.

When we left Birkenau at the beginning of April 1944, the number of inmates of the camp was as follows:

Place	Slovak Jews	Other Jews	Gentiles	Remarks
I Section Women's reception centers Ia and Ib	c.300	c.7000	c.6000	In addition to 300 Slovak girls, 100 girls are employed in the staff building.
II Section				
a. Quarantine camp	2	c. 200	c. 800	Dr. Endre Mueller from Podolinec, one of the two Slovak Jews, is block-inspector.
b. Camp of the	c.3500			With six months quarantine.
c. Not occupied at present				
d. Staff camp	c. 58	c.4000	c.6000	
e. Gypsy camp			c.4500	Remnant of 16,000 Gypsies. They are not performing labor and are dying out quickly.
f. Hospital	6	c.1000	c.500	The six Slovak Jews are engaged in hospital administration.*

g. /Shown on plan, but not accounted for./

* Number	Name	Place of Origin	Duties
36;832	Walter Spitzer	Nemsova	Block inspector
29;867	Josef Neumann	Snina	"Capo" of corpses
44;989	Josef Zelmanovics	Snina	Personnel
32;407	Lajos Eisenstaedter	Korompa	Tattooer
30,049	Lajos Solmann	Kezmarok	Clerk
	Chaim Katz	Snina	Personnel

157

Plan II

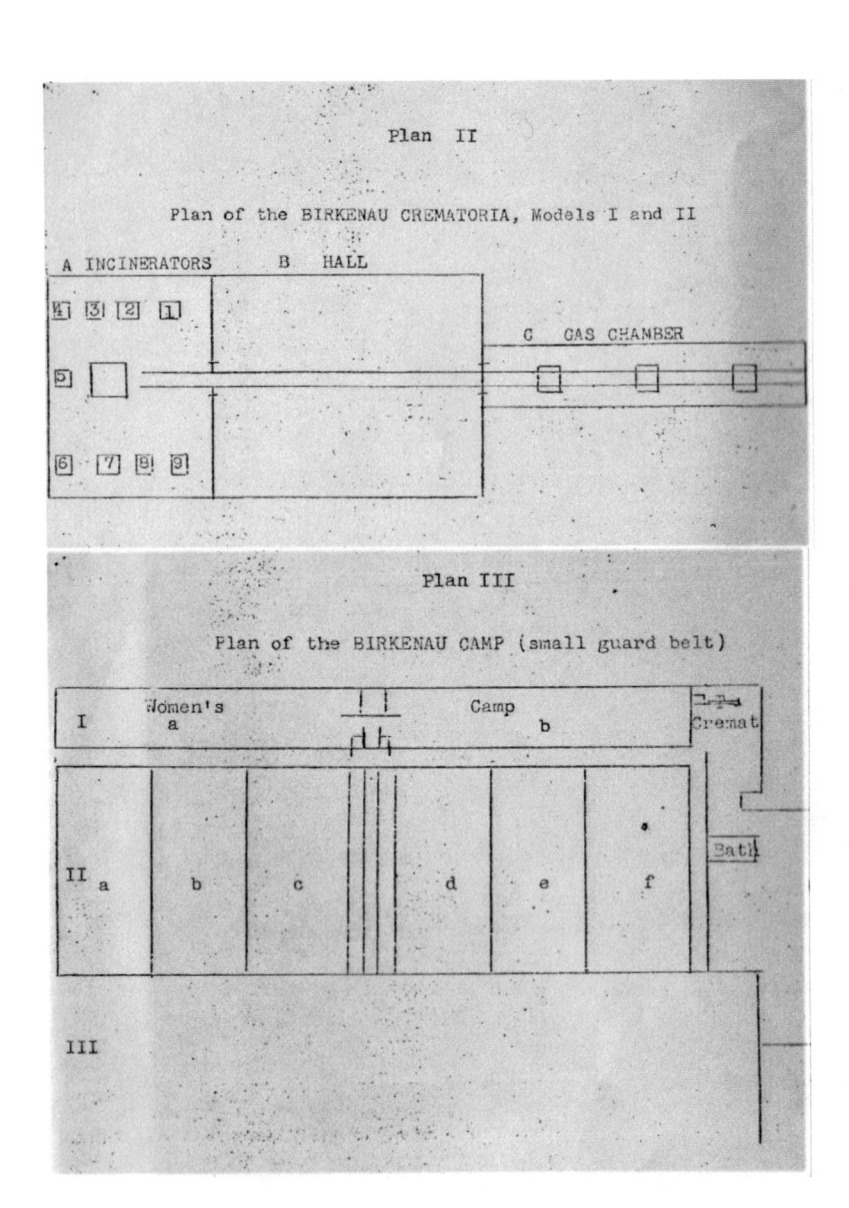

Plan of the BIRKENAU CREMATORIA, Models I and II

A INCINERATORS   B HALL

[4] [3] [2] [1]

C GAS CHAMBER

[5]

[6] [7] [8] [9]

Plan III

Plan of the BIRKENAU CAMP (small guard belt)

I	Women's a		Camp b	Cremat
II a	b	c	d e	f Bath
III				

-31- SECRET

The internal administration of the Birkenau camp is carried out by prisoners assigned to that work. Prisoners are not billeted by nationality, but by their labor assignment, that is, by Kommandos. Each block has five functionaries:

    1 Block Inspector (Blockaeltester)
    1 Block Clerk (Blockschreiber)
    1 Block Nurse
    2 Block Handymen

The block inspector wears on his left arm a white band showing the number of his block. He is responsible for order in his block, where he is, so to speak, master of life and death. Up to February 1944 almost half of all block inspectors were Jews. At that time an order from Berlin prohibited filling this office with Jews, following which the Jews were relieved from duty. Three Slovak Jews, however, are carrying on to this day. They are:

Name	Place of Origin	Duties
Ernest Rosim	Zilina	Inspector, Block No. 25, (cleaning crews, plus artisans from Benzburg)
Dr. Endre Mueller	Podolinec	Inspector, Block No. 15, quarantine camp
Walter Spitzer	Nemsova	Inspector, Block No. 14, hospital area

The block clerk is the executive assistant of the block inspector. He does all clerical work, keeps the roster up to date, and is in charge of a large file. His work is loaded with great responsibility since the roster has to be kept in order in a painstaking manner. Prisoners are recorded by their numbers only, not by their names, and consequently an error is easily made. Mistakes of this kind may be fatal. If by mistake the clerk reports an individual number dead by mistake, which can easily occur in view of the high mortality rate--and has in fact happened--such a mistake is simply corrected by executing the wearer of the number later. Once a report is forwarded, it cannot be corrected, and the reported roll must agree with the actual roster. The post of clerk confers great power within the block. Unfortunately there are often abuses.

The <u>nurse</u> and <u>handymen</u> perform manual work around the block. Naturally there can be no question of any nursing.

The <u>camp inspector</u> (<u>Lageraeltester</u>) is over the whole camp. He is also a prisoner. The present camp inspector is Franz Danisch, No. 11,182, a political prisoner from Koenigshuette, Upper Silesia. The camp inspector is absolute master of the entire camp. He is entitled to appoint and remove block inspectors and clerks, and can also assign men to labor crews, etc. Danisch is fair even to Jews; he is objective and incorruptible.

The <u>camp</u> <u>clerk</u>, who actually has the greatest power in the camp, is assigned to the camp inspector. He is the only man in direct contact with the camp command, receiving orders and handing in reports. As a result, he has a certain amount of influence with the camp command. Block clerks are his direct subordinates and make their reports to him. The present camp clerk is Casimir Gork, No. 30,029, a Polish political prisoner who was formerly a bank clerk. Although Gork has anti-semitic views, he does not molest the Jews.

Principal supervision of the blocks is exercised by six to eight SS <u>block</u> <u>leaders</u>. They call the roll nightly and report to the commander, Untersturmfuehrer Schwarzhuber, a Tyrolean whose title is camp leader (Lagerfuehrer). Schwarzhuber is a drunkard and a sadist.

The camp commandant is the superior of camp leaders of the Birkenau and Auschwitz camps, as well as the leader of the Auschwitz reception center. The name of the present camp commandant is Hoess.

The capo heads each labor detachment (Arbeitskommando); larger detachments have several capos. A capo can dispose of the prisoners at will during working hours, and he often beats them to death. In the past, Jews were often capos, but this was forbidden by the order from Berlin already mentioned (February 1944). One Jew, a mechanic named Roth from Nagymihaly, still holds such an office.

Supreme control of the work is entrusted to German experts.

III. TESTIMONY OF THE SECOND ESCAPEE

16. Internment at Maidenek camp at Lublin, June 1942.

We left Novaky on 14 June 1942, passed through Zilina, and arrived at Zwardon at 5 p.m. Here we detrained and were counted. The transport was taken over by SS men, who expressed loudly their indignation at the fact that we were travelling without any water. "Those Slovak barbarians would not even furnish water," they said. We continued and arrived at Lublin in two days. As soon as the train stopped, the following order was given. "Those between 15-50 years old who are fit for work will leave the train; children and old people will stay in the cars." We got out. The station was surrounded by Lithuanian SS men armed with machine pistols. The railroad cars containing the children and old people were sealed and the train started off. We do not know where the train went or what happened to the passengers.

An SS Schaarfuehrer took over command at the station and told us that we have a long trip ahead. Those who wished to take their parcels with them could do so; those who thought they could not carry them might load their parcels on a truck ready for the purpose. This truck would arrive without fail. Some of my companions took their luggage with them while others loaded theirs on the truck. We found a factory which bore the sign "Bekleidungswerke"[22]/ just behind the town. There were about a thousand

---

[22]/ Clothing factory.

persons, dressed in dirty striped prisoners' uniforms, lined up in the factory court. They were obviously waiting for dinner. This spectacle was not very encouraging, as we recognized the people as Jews. When we reached the hill, we suddenly saw the very large camp of Maidenek, surrounded by a barbed wire fence three meters high.

As soon as I entered the gate of the camp, I saw Maco Winkler, who is from Nagyszombat (Trnava). He warned me that all my parcels and clothes would be taken away. Slovak Jews who had arrived earlier surrounded us. They were dressed in rags of prisoners' uniforms, had shaven heads, were barefoot or in wooden clogs, and many had swollen legs. They begged for food or other small items. We distributed almost anything we had, since we knew that anything we kept would be taken away anyhow. We were then led to the warehouse where we had to hand in all our belongings. Then we were driven on the double to another barracks where we stripped, had our heads shaved, were put under a shower, and finally received our underwear and prisoners' uniforms, a pair of wooden shoes, and a cap.

I was attached to the so-called Labor Section II. The whole camp consisted of three such labor sections, separated from each other by wire fences. Slovak and Czech Jews billeted in Labor Section II. We were trained for two days how to lift our cap when we met a German, and were drilled for hours in the soaking rain. Barracks installations were very peculiar; our furniture consisted of three very long tables on top of one another. Prisoners had to sleep under and on the tables.

                                    -36-   SECRET

      We received soup in the morning. It was so thick that we had to eat it with our hands. A similar soup was served at noon, and in the evening we had so-called "tea" with 30 dekagrams of indigestible bread and two or three dekagrams of marmalade or synthetic fat, both of the worst quality.

      In the early days we were taught to sing the camp hymn in an excellent manner, and had to stand around for hours and practice. The hymn is as follows:

Aus ganz Europa kamen Wir Juden nach Lublin. Viel Arbeit gibt's zu leisten Und dies ist der Beginn.	From all of Europe came We Jews to Lublin. There is much work to do, And this is the beginning.
Um diese Pflicht zu meistern Vergiss Vergangenheit Denn in der Pflichterfuellung Liegt die Gemeinsamkeit.	In order to master this duty Forget the past, For in the fulfillment of duty Lies community feeling.
Drum ruestig an die Arbeit Ein jeder halte mit Gemeinsam wollen wir schaffen Im gleichen Arbeitsschritt.	So actively at work, Let each one hold his own, Together we want to labor At the same work-pace.
Nicht alle wollen begreifen Wozu in Reihen wir stehen. Die muessen wir dann zwingen Dies alles zu verstehen.	Not all want to understand Why we stand in ranks. We must then force them To understand all this.
Die neue Zeit muss alle Uns alle stets belehren Dass wir schon nur die Arbeit Der Arbeit angehoeren.	The new era must teach us - All of us - forever That we now only to labor, Only to labor belong.
Drum ruestig an die Arbeit Ein jeder halte mit Gemeinsam wollen wir schaffen Im gleichen Arbeitsschritt.	So actively at work, Let each one hold his own, Together we want to labor At the same work-pace.

      Billeting was as follows: Labor Section I, Slovak Jews; Labor Section II, Slovak and Czech Jews; Labor Section III, partisans. Sections IV and V were being constructed by those billeted in sections I and II. Partisans billeted in section III were shut up in their barracks. They did not work and were not allowed to leave their quarters; their food was thrown down in front of the door and taken inside from there. The guards shot at them whenever possible.

The capos were Reichsgermans and Czechs. The former treated prisoners brutally, while the Czechs tried to assist them whenever possible. A gypsy named Galbavy from Holics, was camp inspector, and his substitute was a Jew named Mittler from Sered n/V. Mittler evidently obtained his position as a result of his brutality, since he used his power to torture his fellow-Jews, who were already suffering enough indignities. He never missed an opportunity to commit some mean act.

We were mistreated by SS men every night when the Order of the Day was read. After the day's hard work, we had to stand for hours and sing the camp hymn. This singing was led by an old Jewish conductor from the roof of a near-by building, while the SS men had their fun using their sticks and whips. Rabbi Eckstein of Sered n/V. died in tragic circumstances. On one occasion he arrived a little late for the reading of the Order of the Day, as he was ill in the latrine. The Schaarfuehrer thereupon had him dipped into the latrine twice suspended by his feet, drenched him with cold water, and finally shot him.

The crematorium was located between the first and second labor section. Corpses were burned here. The mortality rate per section of 6000 to 8000 was about 30 daily, but this number increased five and sixfold shortly afterwards. Later ten to twelve sickmen were taken daily to the crematorium, from whence they never returned. The crematorium had electric heating installations which were handled by Russian prisoners.

Bad nourishment and unbearable conditions caused various diseases among us. Grave stomach ailments were the most widespread, and an incurable disease that resulted in swollen feet also took its toll. People's legs were so swollen that they could not move them at all. More and more of these were taken to the crematorium, where they were murdered by methods unknown to me. When on 26 June 1942 the number of these unfortunates had been reduced to 70, I decided to take the first opportunity and to volunteer for transfer to Auschwitz.

17. Internment at Auschwitz, 30 June 1942-September or October 1942.

I handed in my prisoner's uniform on 27 June 1942, received civilian clothes, and travelled in a transport to Auschwitz. We travelled forty-eight hours in sealed boxcars, without water or food, and arrived at Auschwitz half dead. There we were greeted by the sign over the gate, "Arbeit macht frei."[23] The court was clean and neat, and the brick buildings and the lawns made a good impression on us after the primitive and dirty barracks at Lublin-Maidenek. We thought that we had made a good change. First we were led to a cellar where we received tea and bread. Next day they took away our clothes, shaved us, tattooed our number on the left arm over the wrist and issued prisoners' uniforms similar to those we had had at Lublin. After our personal data were taken, we became regular political prisoners of the Auschwitz reception center.

---

[23] See footnote No. 6.

We were billeted in Block No. 17, where we slept on the ground. Slovak girls were quartered in the next row of buildings, separated from us by a wall. They had been deported from Slovakia in March and April 1942. We were put to work on the construction of the enormous "Buna" plant. Work began at 3 a.m. Food consisted of potato or carrot soup at noon and 30 dekagrams of bread in the evening. We were cruelly beaten during work. Since our place of work was situated outside the outer guard belt, the area was divided into squares 10 meters by ten meters. Each square was guarded by one SS man, and anyone crossing the borders of his square during work was instantly shot as "attempting to escape." It often happened that an SS man ordered a prisoner to fetch some object from outside his square. If the prisoner obeyed and stepped over the line, he was shot. The work was very hard. We were scarcely permitted to rest and had to march back to the camp in military order. Whoever did not keep in step or broke ranks was cruelly beaten or sometimes shot. When I joined this labor crew, about 3000 men were working, of whom 2000 were Slovak Jews. Very few of us could stand the hard work because of the poor food. Many attempted to escape, although they had no hope to success. We witnessed several hangings each week.

After a few weeks of painful labor, a typhus epidemic broke out in camp. The weak prisoners died off by the hundreds. Construction on the "Buna" plant stopped and the camp was closed. Those who remained alive at their place of work were sent to the quarry at the end of July 1942. Work here was even more difficult, if that was possible, than at the "Buna" plant. We could never accomplish as much as was wanted by our supervisors since we were too weak. Most of us had swollen legs. Our labor gang was reported for laziness and negligence, and a commission came to examine each one of us thoroughly. All those with swollen legs or whom the commission found to be unfit were segregated. Although my legs hurt badly, I mastered my pain and stepped out smartly when called before the commission. I was found fit. About 200 of the 300 persons were declared ill. They were immediately sent to Birkenau where they were gassed.

After this I was detailed to work at the DAW.[24] My job was painting ski boards. We had to finish a minimum of 110 pieces per day; anyone who could not complete that amount was flogged in the evening. We had to work very hard to avoid the evening punishment. Another group manufactured boxes for shells. One one occasion 15,000 such boxes when finished were found to be a few centimeters shorter than ordered. Thereupon several Jewish prisoners, among them one Erdelyi (who was said to have relatives in Trencin-Ban), were shot for sabotage.

The Jewish girls from Slovakia who lived beyond our wall had been transferred to Birkenau in August 1942. I had occasion to talk to them briefly. They were starved, dressed in old rags of Russian uniforms, and were barefoot or wore wooden shoes. Their hair was shorn and they were completely neglected.

We underwent a very severe physical examination on the same day (sic). All those suspected of typhus were sent to the birchwood, while we who had been declared fit were sent starknaked into the evacuated and disinfected barracks. We were again

---

[24] See footnote No. 5.

shaved, bathed, and given new clothes. I learned by accident that there was a vacancy in the cleaning squad (Aufräumungskommando), volunteered, and received the assignment.

A hundred prisoners, all Jews, worked in this cleaning squad. We worked in a completely isolated part of the camp where mountains of luggage, consisting of rucksacks, suitcases, and other such pieces were stacked in warehouses. Our job was to open this luggage and to sort the objects found. We filled suitcases with combs, mirrors, sugar, cans of food, chocolate, drugs, and so forth. The suitcases were stored according to their contents. Clothes and underwear were taken to a large barrack where they were sorted and packed by the Slovak Jewish girls. These goods were then loaded into railroad cars and shipped out. Unusable clothing was sent to a textile factory in Memel, while good garments were sent to a Berlin welfare association. Valuables, such as money, gold, foreign currency, and precious stones, were supposed to be handed in to the political division. SS supervisors stole a substantial part of these valuables, and much was also taken by the prisoners working there. The boss of this assortment detail, who is recognized as an expert in the field, is Albert Davidovics, from Iglo (Jihlava?). He occupies the same post to this day.

SS Sturmfuehrer Wikleff, commander of this detachment, was a brute who often beat the girls. These girls came daily from Birkenau to work. They told us unbelievable stories about conditions prevailing there. They were beaten and tortured. Mortality was higher among them than it was among the men.

"Selections" were made twice weekly, and there were new girls daily to replace those who had been "selected" or who had died in some other way.

On my first nightshift I had occasion to see how transports coming to Auschwitz were treated. A transport consisting of Polish Jews arrived. They had travelled without water and about a hundred were dead on their arrival. When the doors of the cars were opened, the Jews, completely weakened by the long journey and privations, were driven out wailing. Quick beating by SS men speeded up the unloading. Then the unfortunates were lined up in rows of five. Our task was to remove the corpses, those half dead, and parcels from the railroad cars. We placed the bodies at a collecting point. All those unable to stand on their feet were declared dead. Parcels were thrown into one stack. The cars had to be thoroughly cleaned so that no trace of the transport remained. A commission of the political division then selected ten percent of the men and five percent of the women, who were assigned to camp. The remainder was loaded on trucks and taken to the birchwood, where they were gassed. Corpses and those half dead were also loaded on trucks. These were burned in the birchwood without being gassed first. Small children were often thrown on the truck with the corpses. Parcels were moved by truck to the warehouses, where they were sorted as as described above.

Typhus raged during July and September 1942 in the Birkenau and Auschwitz camps, especially among the women. Those who were ill were not treated at all. At first typhus suspects were killed by means of phenol injections, later they were gassed in large numbers. Within two months 15-20,000 prisoners perished, most of them Jews. The women's camp suffered particularly. They had no sanitary installations at all and the girls were full of lice. Big "selections" were held weekly. Regardless of the weather, the girls were forced to line up naked for these "selections," and to wait in deadly fear to see whether they would be "selected" on that occasion or would have a week's grace.

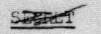

Many men and women committed suicide. They simply touched the high-tension wire of the inner guard belt. So many women perished that not more than five percent /sic/ of the original number survived. There are 400 girls at Auschwitz and Birkenau at this time, the remainder of the original 7000. The majority of these have secured camp administration jobs for themselves. One of them named Kata (I do not know her family name), from Bystrica n/V., fills the high position of camp clerk. About a hundred Slovak girls are employed in the Auschwitz staff building. They do clerical work for both camps and interpret for interrogators who interview prisoners. Some of the girls work in the kitchen and laundry of the staff building. Lately the Slovak girls are better dressed, as they have been able to complete their wardrobe from the stocks of the Aufraumungskommando. Many even wear silk stockings. They are now letting their hair grow and altogether are much better off than in the past. This does not apply, of course, to the several thousand other prisoners

-44-

in the women's camp. The Slovak Jewish girls are the oldest inmates of the women's camp and thus have a somewhat privileged position.

I soon lost my comparatively comfortable job [October 1942?] with the Aufraumungskommando, and as punishment was transferred to Birkenau, where I spent one and a half years. On 7 April 1944 I succeeded in escaping with my companion.

-45-

A CONSERVATIVE ESTIMATE OF THE NUMBER OF JEWS EXTERMINATED AT BIRKENAU FROM APRIL 1942 TO APRIL 1944, ACCORDING TO COUNTRIES OF ORIGIN (by the two escapees):

Poland (shipped by trucks)	c. 300,000
Poland (shipped by trains)	600,000
Holland	100,000
Greece	45,000
France	150,000
Belgium	50,000
Germany	60,000
Yugoslavia, Italy, Norway	50,000
Lithuania	50,000
Bohemia, Moravia, Austria	30,000
Slovakia	30,000
Various camps of foreign Jews in Poland	300,000
TOTAL	c. 1,765,000

The Camps of Auschwitz and Birkenau

Weissmandl and Vrba

Numerous copies of the Vrba-Wetzler Report circulated. But a diagram of the extensive Auschwitz-Birkenau complex can be found attached only to certain copies, and not in the OSS English translation above. Perhaps the most detailed one is the one that found its way from Bratislava to Switzerland, first to Nathan Schwalb, and then passed on at an unknown date to the War Refugee Board. Responsible for the Yiddish notations was evidently Rabbi Michael Dov Weissmandl, also the one to smuggle the report to Schwalb. See reference to this copy of the Auschwitz Report on p. 10, note 23 above.

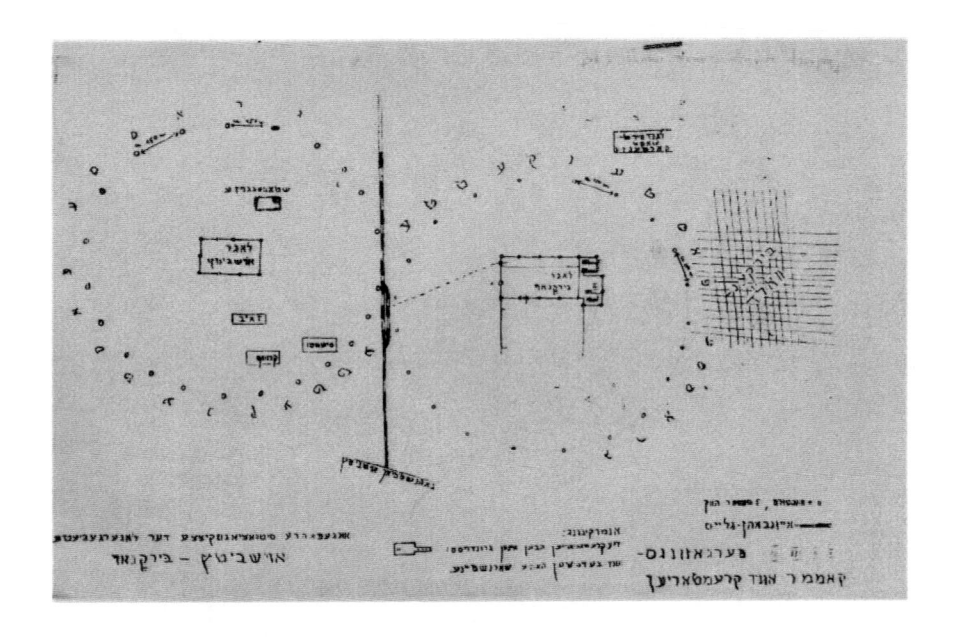

Below is the diagram that Rudolf Vrba published. Vrba recalls his meeting with Weissmandl about the report. See his *I Cannot Forgive* (Vancouver: Regent College Publishing, 1997), See pp. 258-260 and 317.

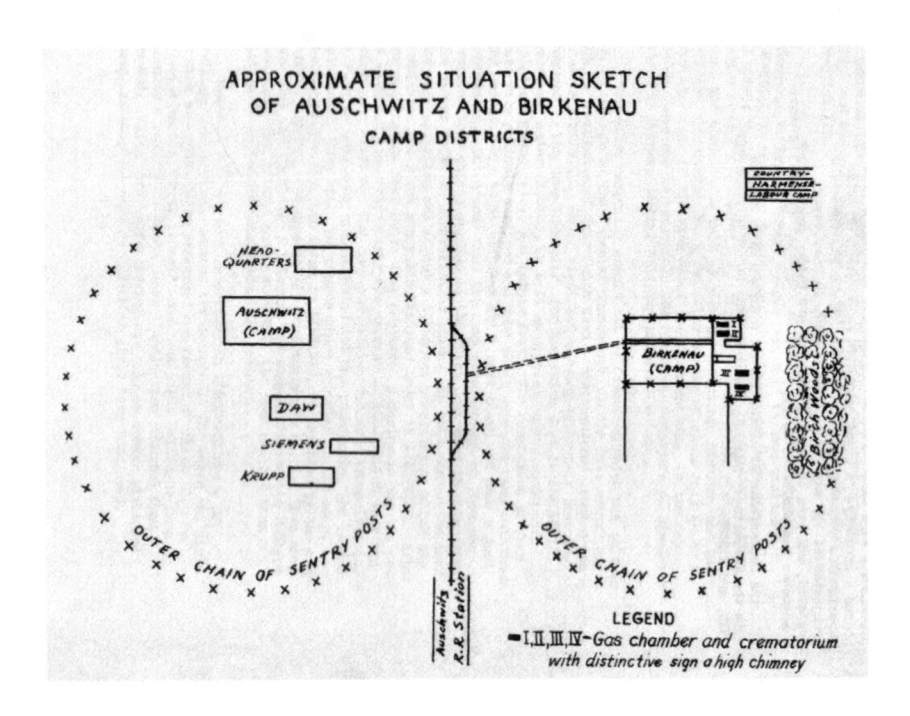

VI. Appendix C: Sándor Szenes, *The Auschwitz Interviews*

Introduction: Sándor Szenes[109]

When and how did the Auschwitz Report get to Hungary? In the historical works available there are as many uncertainties and contradictions as there are questions. Randolph L. Braham carefully studied and compared the eleven reports and reminiscences of eight individuals (the two escapees, the two individuals who helped them in Žilina, and the four prominent Jewish leaders in Hungary during the summer of 1944), but he has found so many contradictions that he was forced to admit that we cannot determine with certainty when the transmission took place, and only in the second half of June did the Jewish leaders in Hungary begin to send the report to influential government circles, church leaders, and their friends in other countries.[110]

Other studies about the question of how and when are no less contradictory. Jenő Lévai mentions a 16–page report in Hebrew sent from Bratislava, supposedly reaching Budapest about June.[111] Dezső Schön, editor of the *Új Kelet,* a Hungarian journal appearing in Israel, writes in his book about the Eichmann trial that the report arrived in Budapest about the middle of May.[112] Elek Karsai writes: "... In the

---

[109] Sándor Szenes introduces his interviews in: " . . . akkor már minden egyházfő asztalán ott volt az Auschwitzi Jegyzőkönyv . . . " *Valóság* 10 (October 1983): 75–90. The slightly abbreviated text appears in Frank Baron's translation. The complete interviews are in the book by Szenes, *Befejezetlen múlt* [The Unfinished Past] (Budapest, 1994, 2nd ed.).
[110] Randolph L. Braham , *The Politics of Genocide*, II, pp. 709–724.
[111] Jenő Lévai, *Szürke Könyv* [Gray Book] (Budapest: Officina, 1946), p. 59.
[112] Dezső Schön, *A jeruzsálemi per* [The Jerusalem Trial] (Tel Aviv, 1946).

middle of June people were aware of the Auschwitz death camps in Budapest; they knew its layout and operation."[113] Péter Bokor simply mentions in his narrative that "shortly" after the completion of the report its contents were known in the east and the west. Archbishop Gennaro Verolino, the former advisor to the papal ambassador in Budapest, made the following assertion in an interview in Rome: "The middle of June . . . This was the time at which the Auschwitz Report reached the world, even Budapest and, what is more, Buda (i.e., at the royal residence)"[114]

In the following montage of interviews, prepared in 1981 and 1982, about the relationship of the churches to the Jewish population, the speakers are four contemporary witnesses, and in the following excerpts they speak about the Auschwitz Report: József Éliás, a retired Calvinist pastor; Mrs. László Küllői-Rhorer (née Mária Székely), translator and interpreter; Dr. András Zakar, a retired Catholic priest and the former secretary of Cardinal Justinian Serédi; and the author Sándor Török.

In response to the question how and when, József Éliás, the former secretary of the *Jó Pásztor Bizottság* (Good Shepherd Mission) asserts, in contrast to the publications cited above, that he received a German copy of the report "directly from people associated closely with the escapees on the last days of April or the first days of May." His coworker of those days, Mária Székely, the translator of the report, remembers the first encounter with the German text in the following way: "It could have been about the end of April, or, more likely, the first days of May. This memory belongs to one of those most agonizing experiences that I simply cannot

---

[113] Péter Bokor, "Miért nem bombázták az amerikaiak a náci haláltáborokat?" [Why Did the Americans Not Bomb the Nazi Death Camps?] *Historia* 1 (1981).

[114] With the emphasis on Buda the author clearly wished to emphasize that even Admiral Horthy, whose residence was in Buda, was aware of the report. Elek Karsai, *Végjáték a Duna mentén* [The End Game on the Shores of the Danube] (Budapest, 1982), pp. 115–126.

forget." Éliás reports, moreover: Mária Székely "brought six copies of the typed Hungarian text in seven or eight days. Éliás could begin the distribution of the Hungarian copies on about the 10th of May or shortly thereafter. The addressees were primarily the religious leaders of the major churches in Hungary: Catholic, Calvinist, and Lutheran. But Török's interview shows that the report also reached hands at the highest government circles.

A binding rule in the authentication of historical facts dictates that the whole or part of reminiscences can be viewed as reliable only if verified by independent sources. Éliás's report was first and most immediately confirmed by Mrs. Küllői-Rhorer. Sándor Török, one of the persons entrusted with passing on the report, also represents confirmation; unfortunately, no other members of his select group are now available to be interviewed. András Zakar, the former secretary of the cardinal, represents an indirect but convincing witness. Finally, authentication is provided by a letter of May 17, 1944, by the representatives of the Calvinist Church to Prime Minister Döme Sztójay, who actually promoted the deportations. In this letter there is an unmistakable warning: We know that deportation means the "final solution" (*Endlösung*). As it becomes evident from the Éliás interview, this assertion was written with the awareness of the Auschwitz Report.

Further confirmation by historians and archivists enables me to state as a fact that the Auschwitz Report was in Budapest at the end of April or at the beginning of May, and by the time the deportations of Jews began from the countryside the report was "on the desk of every church leader," as József Éliás maintains at the conclusion of his interview.[115] Unfortunately, church histories of this period and the diaries of church leaders overlook this fact.

---

[115] Cf. Jean de Bavier of the Red Cross, confirmed the availability of this information on May 12th. Arieh Ben-Tov: *Facing the Holocaust in Budapest. The International Committee of the Red Cross and the Jews in Hungary, 1943–1945* (Dordrecht: Kluwer Publishing Company, 1988), p. 126.

1. József Éliás

"Cardinal Dr. Jusztinián Serédi was the first addressee."

I first became acquainted with the name of József Éliás, a retired Calvinist pastor, during the early sixties when I lived in Debrecen for a few years in the capacity of reporter for the newspaper *Népszabadság* [Freedom for the People] in the counties of Hajdu-Bihar and Szabolcs-Szatmár.

We became personally acquainted in about 1973, at a difficult time for him. He had been suspended by his superiors and brought before a church court, where he defended himself. Having been assigned by my newspaper to cover the case, I became convinced that his cause was honorable, and I followed his trial with special attention.

Few people are aware, even in Debrecen, that József Éliás received extraordinary international recognition. The International Hebrew Christian Alliance (IHCA), which considers its chief task the struggle against racial and sectarian prejudice, established a prize during the Second World War and voted to award 800 British pounds to church representatives able to contribute the most in saving lives in countries occupied by Germany. At its 1948 congress in London, the IHCA honored József Éliás with its award.

The year 1942 brought about great changes in the young Éliás. In the summer he had been deputy pastor in Cegléd, where he joined the subversive organization named after former Prime Minister Teleki*, the predecessor of the organization formed after the German occupation, Magyar Függetlenségi Mozgalom (MFM) [Hungarian Independence Movement]. He had been recruited by an old friend, Dr. Géza Soós, the secretary of the Calvinist international student organization Soli Deo Gloria and consultant of the Foreign Office. Bishop László Ravasz called him to Budapest as early as December of that year. From that time on he was spiritual advisor and later director of the Calvinist Church's Good Shepherd Mission, an organization dedicated to the spiritual life and defense of Christians of Jewish origin. He did not accept this post immediately or eagerly. But he made the decision when he learned that before him five clergymen had refused this position.

His tenure as spiritual advisor began in the winter of 1942–1943. The months represented a decisive turning point in the war: As the Germans at Stalingrad and the Hungarian army at the River Don suffered catastrophic defeats, the nation became more involved in the war. József Éliás reports: "From the beginning the difficult tasks of saving lives was the major concern of the Good Shepherd Mission's work. For me the tasks of the Church and the movement converged." In the spring of 1944 Elias received an extraordinary responsibility from Géza Soós, his contact in the movement: that he should translate the Auschwitz Report from German into Hungarian and organize the secret delivery to designated addresses.

* Pál Teleki, professor of geography and later prime minister (1939-1941), committed suicide and thus dramatically protested against Hungary's participation in Germany's invasion of Yugoslavia. For information on Dr. Géza Soos see p. 3 above.

JÓZSEF ÉLIÁS: In 1944, on one of the last days of April or on one of the first days of May, Géza Soós invited me to meet with him. He indicated in advance that he wished to discuss an important matter at length. As I recall, we met in the café of the National Museum. Géza, who was a person of great energy but otherwise calm and collected, seemed on this occasion to vibrate with excitement. I sensed that he had something extraordinary to communicate. He said that a secret organization of prisoners in a concentration camp of the Germans in Poland was successful in bringing about the escape of two young Jews. The escape bordered on the miraculous. These men had the task of informing the world about what was going on in Auschwitz. Having reached a place of safety, the escapees prepared a detailed report about Auschwitz, which they supplemented with drawings. They referred to it as a kind of official record in order to emphasize its factuality and reliability. A representative of our opposition movement on the border of Slovakia received one of the German copies of the report; the messenger had arrived with it in Budapest on the morning of our meeting. The leaders of the movement decided that I should be responsible for the tasks that the report required.

SZENES: What were these tasks?

ÉLIÁS: We needed, first of all, an accurate, clear, and speedy translation from German into Hungarian; second, six typed copies of the Hungarian text; third, five copies to persons designated by Géza transmitted in such a way that the persons involved should not even suspect from where and through whom they received the report. Fourth, we had to return the sixth copy and the original German copy we had to return to Géza in a manner to be indicated at a later time. Finally, the Hungarian copies should not be copied on the office typewriters of Good Shepherd. During our conversation there was an empty chair between us, and we put our briefcases on it. I can still visualize how Géza slipped the report into mine. After he listed the addresses (among them those of the highest ranking church leaders), he added, "The government officials must not learn that the report is in our hands. It is not necessary to enlighten them because," he emphasized, "the head of the government and most of the ministers under him know about Auschwitz and its function. The opposition movement wants to orient the church leaders, above all, so that the government will not mislead them and so that these influential individuals can exert pressure on the government to prevent the tragedy awaiting the Jews." Géza said that the movement would find a way to get the report into the hands of Hungarians and others living in Switzerland. Finally, he stressed that those whom I involved in this undertaking as translator and messenger must be loyal, capable, and reliable people. We discussed who might be the right persons for delivering the report. As far as the translation was concerned, we agreed on choosing Mária Székely, my most loyal, well-educated, and tested colleague.

SZENES: Did you know about Auschwitz when you worked for the Good Shepherd organization?

ELIÁS: When I received the report, I was already informed about almost all essential aspects. My colleagues had heard only all kinds of unconfirmable rumors about German concentration camps.

SZENES: How did you get information about almost everything?

ÉLIÁS: At that time an exceptionally good relationship developed between the Calvinist Good Shepherd Mission and the Catholic Holy Cross Society [Magyar Szent Kereszt Egyesület, MSZKE]. This organization was concerned with the protection of the spiritual and secular interests of Catholics of Jewish origin. In 1944, it carried out its mission under the protection of Baron Vilmos Apor, bishop of Györ. Two outstanding persons were in charge: as president of the international organization Professor József Cavallier and József Jánosi, a Jesuit priest and the spiritual leader of the organization. Professor Cavallier, descendant of an old French Catholic family, and I shared a strong interest in ecumenical Christianity. For him religious faith related to all suffering humanity. He was an extraordinary colleague; he supported my work fully. A few days after the German occupation he asked me to visit him in the office of MSZKE in the Muzeum Street. I went, and he reported to me then what he had heard from the papal legation on the basis of confidential information from Vatican sources: the entire German timetable relating to the Hungarian Jews. As in other countries, it would also begin here with the revocation of rights, then the wearing of the yellow star, the establishment of a ghetto, and, finally, deportation, the gas chamber, and the crematorium. From Cavallier I heard for the first time about Auschwitz and similar camps. After his shocking revelations he made me promise not to tell anyone what I had heard. He thought that it was essential that I know what was about to happen, but he believed (and I agreed) that for the time being we should not divulge widely what we knew because we could cause a panic in Jewish circles, and we could undermine the opportunities of the organization to help. Later we were not so secretive. As soon as I received the report I informed Géza. But at the time Cavallier told me everything, it was still only about March 21 or 22, the third or fourth day of the German occupation. There was no yellow star, no ghetto; the Sztójay government had just taken control. We could still harbor hope that everything would turn out otherwise than it did. Two days later, at the end of the first week of occupation, Dr. Lajos Kemény, a high-ranking Protestant pastor in Budapest, one of the best and most aggressive supporters of Good Shepherd, asked me for an interview, and on the basis of German sources he told me precisely the same thing that I had learned from Cavallier. At that time I was still young and could sleep well, but in those days my nights changed into sleepless ones . . .

SZENES: Let's return to the fact that Géza Soós put the report's German text into your briefcase. What happened then?

ÉLIÁS: I went back to my office at 5 Lázár Street. There was a larger room with eighteen fellow workers, and I had an adjoining small room, separated by a glass wall, for confidential conversations. From time to time others worked here, mainly translators. I called in Mária Székely and asked her to read the German text of the report, to discuss the contents with me, and to let me know whether she could do the translation. Just a few hours later she returned in a terrible state of shock, but exercising self-discipline, she was able to tell to me what she had read. As I listened to her I had the impression that she was not well, and I was quite concerned that she might not have the strength to do the translation. But being a strong person, she accepted the assignment. While she did not feel that she could perform the work in the office, she indicated that her apartment would be suitable. We discussed the form that the completed text should take.

SZENES: How long did the translation take?

ÉLIÁS: In seven or eight days she returned with the Hungarian text in six typed copies. Although by this time I was somewhat acquainted with the contents of the report, I read one copy immediately. The closely typed text extended to about thirty-five to forty pages, and, unless my memory fails me, there were also a few simple, roughly sketched drawings of the camp, the crematorium, and the organization of security. The text reported precisely about the functioning of the organized destruction of human beings and provided facts about the masses of people from various countries deported and killed. It was shocking. While the translations were being prepared, Géza got in touch with me and asked me to have Mária Székely take the sixth Hungarian copy, along with the German original, to him at the Foreign Ministry. Only now, thirty-seven years after the events, did I learn that Géza had entrusted Maria to do an English translation as well.

SZENES: You were in the possession of five copies of the report. To whom were they addressed and who delivered them?

ÉLIÁS: Cardinal Dr. Jusztinián Serédi was one of the addressees. Upon my request József Cavallier took responsibility for delivery. I took the report to him, and we had a private discussion of the matter. Earlier he had been the international secretary of the council of bishops and the chief editor of the Catholic daily newspaper, and his close relationship with Serédi allowed him, for all practical purposes, to gain access without knocking. Although he thought it advisable not to make the delivery personally, he guaranteed that he would get the report into the hands of the cardinal. He did, in fact, succeed in this. The second addressee was Bishop Dr. László Ravasz, President of the Universal Congregation of Calvinist Churches, to whom Albert Bereczky, the Pastor at Pozsonyi Street in Budapest, took the report.

SZENES: Had Bereczky heard of Auschwitz before?

ÉLIÁS: I do not know, but it is certain that he knew a lot. He suffered a great deal from all sorts of illnesses, but in the terrible months of 1944 he was prepared to do everything with his time, strength, mind, and courage. He was outspoken, not always diplomatic when he was preaching, and if it was necessary, he was even willing to insult others; in saving lives he was more ingenious and inventive than any of us. At the beginning of the German occupation he hid from the Gestapo the leader of the Small Landholder Party, later president of the the republic, Zoltán Tildy, in the church on Pozsonyi Street and in the central office of the Scottish Mission, and elsewhere he hid Gyula Kállai (a leader of the Communist Party), the daughter of Arpád Szakasits (left-wing leader of the Social Democratic Party), and many others. The third copy of the report was addressed to Lutheran Bishop Dr. Sándor Raffay. At my request Pastor Dr. Lajos Kemény, the self-sacrificing supporter of Good Shepherd, took it to him. The fourth copy was directed to the engineer Ottó Komoly, one of the leaders of Jewish public life in our country and of the Hungarian Zionists. After the German occupation he served as director of an assistance group in the Budapest delegation of the International Red Cross; in December 1944 the fascists captured and executed him. At the time of the distribution of the report I knew little about him, and I was cautious in dealing with him. I asked my trusted friend, Judge Dr. Géza Kárpáty, to take the report to him.

I was careful to choose a person who was not known in church or public life. My friend Géza put on the clothes of the gardener of his villa on Gellért hill–he looked like a laborer of those days. He went to Ottó Komoly like this, without introducing himself at all, and he turned over the mail without any explanation. Later I learned that Ottó Komoly was in contact with the opposition movement, and he reported the reception of the document from an unknown source to Géza Soós. When he learned that it had come to him through the movement, he asked for permission to make copies of the report. I learned from Géza that he was asked to wait for a time, that later copies could be made and distributed. My assumption is justified that in this way one or two copies of the report could have reached the general public to some degree. There was even the somewhat humorous circumstance that a man who was sympathetic with me and my work came to me and brought me a copy (I have no idea how many times it had been copied) in order to provide me with confidential information. Géza said that he himself would take care of the fifth copy of the report at an appropriate time. The time came when Sándor Török, a distinguished journalist in the early forties, escaped from internment.

SZENES: This sounds mysterious; please explain.

ÉLIÁS: The Germans interned Török together with many other intellectuals, but he escaped in mid-May.* A government decree at that time brought the organization of Hungarian Jews [Magyarországi Zsidók Szövetsége] into existence. Török was selected to be a representative of Christian Jews in the administrative committee of this organization. He reported to Cavallier and to me, and he asked for our help. I learned from Géza Soós that the opposition movement took notice of him, and it took steps to help him gain access to the royal residence, to the circle of the deputy regent's widow, Mrs. István Horthy (née Countess Ilona Edelsheim Gyulai), the recipient of the fifth copy of the report, and Sándor Török delivered it to her.

SZENES: Why was the countess the addressee?

ÉLIÁS: One of the leaders of the movement, Domokos Szent-Iványi had been a coworker of Miklós, the Regent Horthy's younger son; he had good connections to the family of the regent as well as to the countess, who was convinced that the Germans had caused the airplane accident involving her husband. For this and other reasons she was favorably inclined toward being drawn by Szent-Iványi into the opposition movement. Török was chosen for the task of informing the countess and through her, others about the situation of those being persecuted. He was assigned to be the contact person for information from the royal residence.

SZENES: Did you get any indication about how the addressees reacted to the report?

ÉLIÁS: The reaction of Cardinal Serédi did not come to my attention. I heard that of Ottó Komoly only in the sense that he asked for permission to make more copies. Bishop Raffay asked only Pastor Lajos Kemény where this text had originated. Török told me that the widow of István Horthy had not inquired about the origins and had had no doubts about its contents. I learned the most about László Ravasz; there is even written confirmation of this. Albert Berecky took the report to the bishop on May 12 or 14. The bishop was residing at Leányfalu and was seriously ill. On May 15, the first deportation trains left for Auschwitz from the southern region of the Carpathian Mountains. News about this could not have reached László Ravasz unexpectedly: Baron Zsigmond Perényi, president of the upper chamber of the legislature, visited the bishop as early as the end of April and informed him that the rounding up of the Jews from the Carpathian Mountains and Western Hungary was in progress. They were not being taken to work in Germany; their fate would be the same as that of the Polish and Slovakian Jews. This fact motivated László Ravasz finally on May 17 to send a petition to Prime Minister Sztójay in the name of the Calvinist Universal Congregation. In the last paragraph he wrote: "It is necessary to draw your Excellency's attention to the sad events that transformed the deportation of Jews in other countries into a final solution . . . . " It was the first occasion that a Hungarian church leader wrote to the prime minister that deportation was equivalent to a "final solution," or *Endlösung.* as the Germans called the mass killing, the genocide.

I have no doubt that Bishop Ravasz composed the petition of the congregation; he knew exactly how to present the facts to the other side so that no one could have doubts that it was getting the message in a suitable manner. Bereczky showed me the text of the petition even before it was sent, and he was very happy that in his text the influence of the report was apparent. He said that the government could not mislead the churches by saying that the Germans were taking the deportees for work assignments. On the other hand, I was happy that with the cooperation of the Good Shepherd Mission the opposition movement was able to achieve its goals through the acquisition of the report, its translation, and delivery. When on May 15th, 1944, the first deporting train left the borders, the Auschwitz Report, a credible account about their destination, was on the desk of every church leader.

* In fact, the Hungarian government released Török and allowed him to represent the interests of Christian Jews. Braham, *The Politics of Genocide*, I, p. 451.
** Concerning the airplane accident that had caused the death of Deputy Regent István Horthy see Konrad Matthaeidesz, "Egy legenda valósága" [The Truth about a Legend]. In: *Historia* 2 (1982).

* * *

2. Mária Székely

"... the report is exempt from feeling; the text is dry . . . inexpressibly dreadful."

Mária Székely. Deaconess. Her photograph on a somewhat yellowed identification card dated April 7, 1944, with a circular stamp shows a young woman with an attractive face and a serious countenance. The daughter of a prominent dental surgeon, Mária Székely, who spoke several languages and who held a position as bank clerk in 1943 became a volunteer of the Good Shepherd Mission, after the German occupation accepted a position there. Actually, she was never a deaconess, but with this official church designation she could live securely and conceal her real activities. She saved persecuted people; she participated in the organization of homes for children in need of protection and concealment. She forged documents that could save lives; she served as interpreter for the spiritual advisor of the Good Shepherd Mission, and for the International Red Cross delegates she was engaged in difficult negotiations in which the lives of adults as well as children were at stake. She translated from Hungarian and into Hungarian texts and documents that had to be kept secret.

* * *

MÁRIA SZÉKELY: I remember the first reading of the report in the Good Shepherd office in Lázár Street. This is one of those agonizing experiences that I can never forget. This event could have taken place during the last days of April or, more likely, in the early days of May 1944. After so many years I am unable to give the precise date.

SZENES: Many who heard news of Auschwitz in the spring or summer, possibly on the basis of the report, did not want to believe that what was happening there was actually possible. Did you believe it?

SZÉKELY: This first-hand report was so shocking and staggering that it is impossible to express it in words. Not the least doubt could arise about its truthfulness, but I am not surprised that there were those who did not want to believe it. I felt that I could not succumb to doubts caused by shock and despair. However great the difficulty, I had to concentrate on the translation so that I could complete it as soon as possible. The task that I accepted responsibility for required a total commitment. For six to eight days I worked day and night, and I can say that this work cannot be compared to any other translation assignment that I have ever taken on. In contrast to the trickling news items available, the report revealed the total and terrible reality of the extermination of human beings, organized methodically and pedantically, planned as a crime of massive proportions. I have not been able to blot this out, nor the brutal fact that people who planned and carried this out could sink to such low depths.

SZENES: I have seen two contemporary and identical copies of the report. They extend to about forty pages. The translation was certainly a formidable task. Where did you work? After all, this was a prohibited and perilous undertaking, not only for the translator but also for those close to the translator.

SZÉKELY: About one month after the German occupation I was able to move to the house of Károly Szladits on Érmelléki Street. This was special for me because in this way I lived only a few minutes away from the office of the Hungarian Delegation to the International Red Cross, where I worked in the summer of 1944. The Szladits family gave me a room in the attic, and this was an ideal place in every respect. I was able to complete the translation work without any interruption. Even dictionaries were available, and Károly Szladits was a great help and supporter with his kindness. He knew that I was working on something important, but he was sensitive and intelligent; he did not expect me to inform him. In this way I was able to type the Hungarian text with my own small typewriter under secure circumstances. I prepared six copies.

SZENES: Did the Szladits family not realize that you were occupied with this very distressing matter?

SZÉKELY: Because of the dreadfulness of the world around us, my personal feelings probably did not make any impression. Moreover, in that house and in the particular room I occupied many other exciting and distressing events were transpiring; I am thinking of the falsification of documents in an effort to save lives, as well as meetings and discussions with people about such matters. Even if the family noticed something, no one was inquisitive.

SZENES: The authors of the report wrote down the organization of the camp, the method of tattooing and selection, and the operation of the gas chamber and the crematorium. You encountered hitherto unfamiliar notions and concepts. How did you come to terms with all this?

SZÉKELY: It may seem unbelievable, but this report is exempt from feeling; the text is dry, as if the authors simply wrote about how one should bake bread; I can hardly find the appropriate metaphor without the risk of making light of the matter. I am not saying that it was easy to do the translation, but I did not meet many new expressions or concepts. Of course, that which was expressed was inexpressibly dreadful even in the dry mode of presentation.

SZENES: How did you copy the illustrations?

SZÉKELY: As I recall, it was quite difficult to acquire carbon paper and tracing paper, but at last, despite my lack of talent in drawing, I succeeded in copying and pressing the illustrations through the carbons.

SZENES: Cardinal Serédi was the addressee of one copy that you prepared. In the papers of the cardinal archives for the year of 1944 I saw the copy of the Auschwitz Report, and the drawings still show the remains of a purple carbon paper. Is it possible that you used this kind of carbon?

SZÉKELY: Definitely purple! I am sure of it!

SZENES: Then it appears that this copy is the result of your work, but several copies found their way to the cardinal in the course of the summer, and it is impossible to be sure which one ended up in the archives, 1 here is no particular archival designation on it. But how long is it possible to hold such a secret?

SZÉKELY: At the time of the translation only a single person saw the report. My fiancé, who has been my husband since 1945, visited me at the Szladits family whenever his work as surgeon and the bombing raids allowed. I did not keep secrets from him. If I had not told and shown him what I had learned from the report, any sincere communication would have been impossible. I remember that he was deathly pale as he read the text ... As you might expect, my work on the translation was also the cause of dramatic moments, as a result of my own fault, to be sure. It was warm in my room, and I went outside with my papers and dictionary to the ground-level terrace, which was only three to four meters from a loose wire fence. A strong gust of wind came along and caught one page of my German text, including drawings, and it flew against the fence, where it got stuck. On the other side of the fence an armed German soldier was on guard, walking back and forth. On Érmelléki

Street the Germans occupied the houses all around the Szladits's home. I became greatly frightened by the loss of my paper, but by the time I got to it, the guard had reached over the fence; he removed it and returned it politely. I was lucky that he showed no interest in the text or the drawing . . . Of course, I went back to my room in order to continue my work.

SZENES: At last you produced the Hungarian copies of the text. What happened to them?

SZÉKELY: I gave them to József Éliás at his Lázár Street office. He asked me to take a copy of the Hungarian text along with the original German one to Géza Soós in Uri Street near the royal residence. The Foreign Ministry had an office there. The trip was quite adventurous and exciting. I started my trip to the castle from Széna Square, but just then the sirens sounded, indicating an airplane attack. I ran into one of the houses at the square, down into the air-raid shelter. As soon as I started on my way again, there was still another air-raid, but this period in the shelter was short. Finally, up in the castle people were being checked for their papers, and it was certainly a great relief when I finally found Géza Soós and could give him the German and Hungarian texts of the report. He, too, sighed with relief as he took the papers from me ....

SZENES: Did you translate the report into English, too?

SZÉKELY: Géza Soós gave me this task after I had taken the Hungarian text to him. As I recall, the time allotted was even shorter in this case. The German text was returned to me, and again I worked day and night, and I could not allow my eyes to tire . . . This is something I need hardly explain. Later I heard that somehow suddenly there was an opportunity to get the report to Switzerland; this was the reason for the great rush.

SZENES: Did you ever hear what happened to the Hungarian copies?

SZÉKELY: About ten years ago the report was treated in an article of the daily paper *Népszabadság* [The People's Freedom]; my name was mentioned as the translator. From this article I learned that the copies I had translated had been successfully delivered to high-ranking church leaders. In a moving portion of the television series *Századunk* [Our Century] I heard once again about the report. It was startling to see again the drawings and details of the text projected on the screen and to realize what my work had helped to save as the truth. In May 1981 József Éliás telephoned me, recalling the translation of the report. I had not seen Éliás since 1949, nor had I heard much about him, but we conversed as if we had just interrupted our conversation of the day before. It seemed strange, almost perplexing, that Jozsi praised me effusively; I want to ward off this praise since, after all, I did what I had to do. Somehow I have always felt that people have the duty to undertake the particular task that they are capable of at any given moment.

SZENES: You risked your life by taking on this task ... I would like to ask another question. The literature about Auschwitz is very extensive. Have you read about the camp? Have you had the spiritual strength to take up the topic? Have you visited the camp, by any chance?

SZÉKELY: I have read a great deal about Auschwitz and about the Nazi movement in general, from historical and other perspectives. Perhaps I have been interested, above all, because I have been concerned, then as now, about the problem of fascism as a form of spiritual degeneration, a danger that threatens to corrupt man. I have not been to Auschwitz, but at the beginning of the 1960s my husband, children, and I went to Buchenwald. We arrived there from Weimar, and we were struck by the contrast and incompatibility of culture and fascism. My children looked at everything that can be seen there with little comprehension, as if this had happened not on earth but on some other planet.

3. András Zakar

"... the Church must protest at any cost."

Dr. András Zakar, now a retired Catholic clergyman, had an unusual background for one who chose the priesthood for his vocation. Before he began his theological studies, he acquired an engineering degree at the Technical University of Budapest. His career as a priest was unique. He started not a chaplain in a parish but rather as a secretary in the cardinal's residence. Early in the spring 1944, he became the personal secretary of Cardinal Jusztinián Serédi and remained in this position until the cardinal's death, at the end of March 1945. Then for the following three years he became the secretary of the new cardinal, József Mindszenti. Today he is retired in a quiet, small street in a comfortable bachelor's flat among books and manuscripts.

The year during which he served as secretary for Cardinal Serédi was a dramatic one in the life of the country: the German occupation and soon thereafter the liberation by the Red Army took place: The war destroyed the country from east to west. The excerpts from my tape-recorded interview with András Zakar about the events of that year focus on the cardinal's participation in the events of that year, especially on the relationship of the Catholic church to the Jews and the deportations. András Zakar is perhaps the only living witness among those who once worked closely with the cardinal.*

---
* In his review of Szenes's *Befejezetlen múlt* Braham writes about András Zakar: "Rationalizations for Cardinal Serédi's attitude toward the Jews can be found in the interview with Reverend András Zakar, the Cardinal's former secretary. The interview reflects not only his concurrence with the Cardinal's positions, but also his own well-known antipathy toward the Jews. Zakar's anti-Semitic views were fully revealed in his booklet that was published in Switzerland in 1976:

Elhallgatott fejezetek a magyar történelemből [Silenced Chapters from Hungarian History] (Fahrwangen: Duna Könyvkiadó, 1976). In the tradition of the era, Zakar attempted to prove that the Jews and "the talmudists" were responsible for every major tragedy in Hungarian history from the time of the Mohács disaster in 1526 to the peace treaties that were concluded after World War II. He claimed that "Jewish forces" were responsible for guiding Admiral Horthy into adopting pro Hitler policies." Randolph L. Braham, "Sándor Szenes, [Review of] *Befejezetlen múlt."_East European Quarterly* 22 (1988): 122.

DR. ANDRÁS ZAKAR: My main task in the service of Cardinal Serédi was to take care of the matters he entrusted to me and to keep in confidence whatever information he gave me. About his activities I can tell you, of course, only what I experienced and how I see it today: I would like to emphasize that reports and information from many sides came to the office of the cardinal, and I was not at all adequately oriented about all aspects of these matters.

SZENES: As far as you know, were the cardinal, the bishops, and the priests aware—perhaps through the Vatican—of the fate of Jews in Germany and in occupied Austria?

ZAKAR: Without a doubt the bishops and the cardinal at Esztergom were informed about what was happening to the Jews and about the position of the Vatican. In this context we have to regret the fact that the literature on this subject has treated almost exclusively the sufferings of the Jews and the overwhelming agonies and the fateful actions; on the other hand, there is hardly mention the important circular that Pope Pius XII published about the German situation in the spring of 1937, which is generally referred to by its initial words *Mit brennender Sorge* [With the Greatest Possible Alarm]. And this was precisely the alarm signal for the world and above all for Europe to take heed: extraordinary and dangerous events are taking place in Germany. This encyclical was translated into every language. Everywhere, and in our country as well, priests studied and discussed it, held lectures and sermons about it and interpreted it in publications. The encyclical provided a sufficiently correct basic direction for the interpretation of fascism, this new paganism. On the basis of all this we can say that our priests were duly informed about the seriousness of the questions and consequences of the national-socialist ideology and race theory.

SZENES: Did the leaders of the Catholic Church have knowledge, for example, about the church's relationship to anti-fascist resistance in countries occupied by the Germans or about the so-called German solution to the Jewish problem?

ZAKAR: Information about these matters was available. After all, the French resistance movement was especially famous, and there were quite a few reports about it in the Hungarian press. On the other hand, the actions of the Dutch bishops at that time were instructive for the Hungarian situation of 1944. As early as 1944—in other words at a very early stage—the bishops published their letter protesting against the terror and the persecution of the Jews, at a time when the Germans felt very strong and for this reason came down with a drastic strike against the church, which had been spared of persecution up to that time.*

SZENES: Did it occur to the Church leaders and the cardinal that the country could be occupied and that the same fate that befell the Jews in 1940–1942 in other countries could await them here as well?

ZAKAR: I concluded on the basis of the cardinal's speeches in parliament and his other pronouncements that he was forced to realize more and more: We must be prepared for this.

SZENES: I saw a copy of the Auschwitz Report among the papers to 1944 in the archives of Esztergom. Unfortunately, there is no proof of its origin. What do you know about this report?

ZAKAR: Cardinal Serédi himself gave me this report when he stayed at Gerecse to rest and work on tasks of special significance.

SZENES: When was this?

ZAKAR: Well, certainly a month before the distribution of the bishops' pastoral letter of protest, in other words about the end of May 1944.

SZENES: Then the cardinal was acquainted with the report at the end of May. Do you know from whom he received it?

ZAKAR: Those of us close to the cardinal believed that Miklós Esty, the papal representative (chamberlain) brought it to him.

SZENES: When could this have happened?

ZAKAR: Most probably in the middle of May.

SZENES: Between the tenth and twentieth?

ZAKAR: Probably.

SZENES: You are acquainted with the interview segment in which József Éliás, Calvinist minister and the former spiritual advisor of the Good Shepherd Mission, related that upon his request József Cavallier took responsibility for finding a trustworthy person to deliver a copy of the report to the cardinal. Do you think that Cavallier could have assigned such a confidential matter to Miklós Esty?

ZAKAR: Certainly. Miklós Esty was the deputy director of Catholic Action. Cavallier was well acquainted with him, and they could trust each other without any doubt. If Cavallier took responsibility for getting the report to the cardinal, that simply lends credence to the fact that he considered Miklós Esty the right person to deliver it.

SZENES: Did Miklós Esty have the kind of relationship with the cardinal that he could simply give him the document directly?

ZAKAR: As a church official highly decorated by the Vatican he was called upon to assume tasks for the cardinal. Moreover, he was an employee of the National Credit Bank, and he advised the cardinal in matters relating to his estate. He had the opportunity to meet the cardinal privately, either in Esztergom or in Budapest, and to hand the report over to him.

SZENES: Did they not know about the Auschwitz concentration camp at the office of the cardinal before that time?

ZAKAR: Only in the form of rumors, but everybody reacted with skepticism. I remember that I had read the report when I heard the news of the report reaching Switzerland. Those who read it there did not believe it at first and were afraid to print it.

SZENES: Was the content so shocking?

ZAKAR: Yes, that is how unbelievable it seemed. There are limits to the imagination ....

SZENES: About the end of May the cardinal gave you the report that Miklós Esty had given him in the middle of that month.

ZAKAR: Yes. After going for a walk together he gave it to me to read and asked for my reaction to it. On the next day I returned it, and I said that it had moved me greatly and that I believed that the church must protest at any cost. To this the cardinal responded: 'yes, I have already composed the plan of a circular letter that I intend to discuss with the bishops. We will reject this injustice; it has no precedent in the history of the Hungarian nation."

SZENES: In the Esztergom archives I read the pastoral letter in a copy by the cardinal's own hand. The cardinal wrote: "I did not use it; I prepared another one." Is this the draft you are talking about?

ZAKAR: It is probable that this was the first draft. In the preparation of the final draft, which was completed at the end of June, the archbishops, the representative of the Esztergom vicar general, and a number of bishops.[*]

SZENES: When he talked to the bishops, did the cardinal mention the Auschwitz Report?

ZAKAR: No, no. I attribute this to the fact that he was always discreet, even with respect to me, his secretary. His consideration might have been that the Gestapo had an influence on individuals, and by various ways and means could have found out his most guarded secrets. For this reason he concluded that it was safest if he did not talk about them.

SZENES: Would it be correct to conclude that he did not inform the bishops of the contents of the report?

ZAKAR: It is not probable that he sent it to them in the mail. But it is very likely that in the following conference of bishops he read or he had his secretary read it to the bishops. At that time Gyula Mátrai, the cardinal's chief of staff, was the secretary of the bishops' conference.

SZENES: Did he therefore consider the report so important and reliable that he should inform the bishops?

ZAKAR: Because he showed it to me, this is what I consider to be the case. In the entire period of my work there this was the only situation in which he showed such a sign of trust, which surprised and made a great impression on me. In other words, if he showed it to me, then it is certain that he informed Bishop Apor and the others.

---

* Braham provides the following information about Cardinal Serédi's pastoral letter: "Reverend Görgy Kis, the former pastor of Bakonyszentlászló who now lives in Aurach, Austria, notes that in retrospect it was quite fortunate that the pastoral letter was not read in public. In his startlingly frank and extremely informative interview, Reverend Kis states *inter alia* (p. 283): "While the physically and mentally tortured, humiliated, plundered provincial Jews and many tens of thousands of Jewish Christians were removed from the country and pressed into cattle cars and by the time of the pastoral letter's appearance most of them were already killed, Archbishop Serédi divides Hungarian Jewry into two parts: The one part is guilty because it exerted a subversive effect on all aspects of Hungarian life, the other part, in turn, sinned with its silence because it "did not stand up against their coreligionists. What follows from this logically? That both parts, that is all of Jewry, are to be condemned." Cf. Braham, *The Politics of Genocide*, II, pp. 1184 and 1362.

4. Sándor Török

"... the great, dreadful mass murder took place irredeemably ..."

The writer and journalist Sándor Török left Transylvania in the 1920s. He was a laborer; he tried acting; in the course of his life he was an editor or reporter for nine newspapers; he edited radio programs and text books; he published about twenty novels; he wrote children stories about the marvels of Csili-Csala and the adventures of Kököjszi and Bobojsza.

I became acquainted with the painful details of one particular segment of his life through the interview that I prepared, in the course of which we developed a friendship; it was the period of his life between the German occupation and the liberation. In these intense months he was forbidden to continue his work, and he was interned. But then after many complicated efforts in his behalf he was freed and entrusted with an impossible task: he should represent and protect the interests and lives of Christians of Jewish descent against those who intended to kill them. In this particular period he found a great number of people who supported him, sometimes even people he did not know, who helped him to find supportive partners among representatives of the churches and the Red Cross as well as at the royal residence among the members of the regent's family.

What he says is ready to print. He remembers and articulates the way people behaved, the atmosphere, the situations, and the many odd and grim aspects of observed events. After his release from internment in the middle of May* he began his activities for the Association of Hungarian Jews; later he became the vice president of the Association of Christian Jews. At the end of May or the beginning of June he had access to the royal residence thanks to the trust of a number of persons close to Mrs. István Horthy, the deputy regent's widow [i.e., Countess Ilona Edelsheim Gyulai].

* About Török's release from internment see p. 5, note 10 above.

SÁNDOR TÖRÖK: So that I could function at all in the interests of Christian Jews I was greatly dependent on the support of the Holy Cross Fellowship, whose patron was Baron Vilmos Apor, the Catholic bishop of Győr; I also needed the support of the Good Shepherd Mission, which stood under Calvinist Bishop László Ravasz. The Lutheran Bishop Sándor Raffay also supported me. And behind the bishops there were churches, which I believed to have a voice; at least they should have had a voice. At times it appeared that they wanted and were able to help. I express myself with reservation because I took the matter seriously, and at the beginning I was one of those who believed that we could help a lot. In reality we could accomplish very little. What did we accomplish? For a few individuals we obtained identification cards so that they could move about with greater freedom; for others we created the possibility of escaping singly or with their families. But in the last analysis the entire matter--the deportation, the death marches to Germany, the firing squads on the shore of the Danube, and the executions on the highways, the great, dreadful mass murder with several million victims and everything that accompanied it—occurred, occurred irredeemably . . . But we who worked together at that time, believed that we could help. We worked together in various combinations and connections, and from this network of contact a single thin line led to the royal residence in the castle of Buda. By means of this single thread, the Hungarian Red Cross, I became involved in the discussions that Mrs. István [Ilona] Horthy, the widow of the deceased deputy regent, conducted. Gyula Vállay, the director of the

Hungarian Red Cross, and Baroness Gizella Apor, the younger sister of Bishop Apor and voluntary director of nurse's training, enabled me to meet with her.

SZENES: Had you been acquainted with Gyula Vállay and Gizella Apor previously?

TÖRÖK: I did not know either of them. As a result of my charge I immediately went to the Red Cross, and I requested help. That is when I became acquainted with them. The two of them, but especially Gizella Apor, had made visits to the royal residence. After that at the end of May or the beginning of June they took me along and introduced me to Mrs. Horthy [Countess Ilona Edelsheim Gyulai]. While in the outside world the events took their course, here in and about the royal residence a strange situation developed: On the one side there was the residence of Angelo Rotta, who helped us a great deal, and on the other side there was the German embassy surrounded by the different offices of its headquarters; here in the center of the royal residence, in the rooms of the widow of the deputy regent a "conspiratorial" group gathered. I was part of this group, and we discussed and tried to reach a consensus about the news that Mrs. [Ilona] Horthy brought from those close to the regent as well as the news we had brought fro the outside world. Of course, in order to understand what went on, one must imagine, at the same time, the strange situation that was characterized by danger, complexity, lies, attempts to help, attacks, and confusion that affected those who lived in the royal residence and from which they could not isolate themselves. For example, I had the task of calling Mrs. Horthy every day for several weeks on a special phone number, and after introducing myself as the "bookbinder Bardócz" I asked if she had any work for me. If she said that there was a bookbinding job, I could go safely to get the news or to discuss what would have to be done in a certain matter.

SZENES: Who actually belonged to this group?

TÖRÖK: I know of the following individuals: Gizella Apor, Gyula Vallay, József Cavallier, Father Jánosi, and I. I was there four or five times together with Mrs. Horthy, but unless my memory fails me, Jánosi and Cavallier were not present every time. In addition, I went there several time as Bardócz the bookbinder.

SZENES: Who thought up the conspiratorial idea of Bardócz?

TÖRÖK: Gizella Apor, most likely.

SZENES: We are talking about the summer of 1944. What was the atmosphere and mood in the regent's residence? How could you interpret this?

TÖRÖK: What one could see revealed a great deal. At the royal residence, for example, there were two kinds of guards. There were those in full dress, radiant—the Middle Ages—an honor guard with capes, helmets, and halberdiers, performing routine changes of guard. Then there were the more genuine bodyguards, those who stood at the door and in uniforms, decorated with braids. In the inner courtyard, there were guards sitting on benches, and if a general or anyone belonging to the regent's family drove across, then this unit lined up to salute. But on the square directly opposite the court guards, a German tank and a line of German guards stared right back. They observed what was going on at the regent's residence, and I believe that they knew a lot. Gizella Apor, Vállay, and I had to go up into the residence from the side of the Elizabeth Memorial Museum through a small side entrance, and then we saw bodyguards in green uniforms with machine guns posted in what I believe to have been a naively vulnerable position. They protected the residence. . . . The people I met there all knew that the war would end with a German defeat. They were afraid of the Germans and did not respect them, but at the same time they were somehow helpless, hesitating, and paralyzed in their presence. They would have liked most of all to surrender to the British. But where were the British? This was naive dreaming. Horthy and those around him did not know, or did not want to accept, that the Soviet forces would drive the Germans out of Hungary.

SZENES: I can imagine that this must have been a topic of discussion, since the Soviet army was approaching the Carpathian Mountains on the Rumanian border.

TÖRÖK: This topic was hardly treated at all, and if it was, only marginally when there was talk about the news from the eastern front.

SZENES: What was the main topic of your discussions?

TÖRÖK: For the most part we talked about the intentions of the Germans and the defense against them. We talked about the situation of the Jews, the deportations, and the measures that would probably be used against them. These discussions had a serious tone; there were no digressions or jokes. There was no small talk. In general, the ultimate questions had to do with the stand we should take in this or that matter, who would take on which tasks, and who would assume responsibility for how much.

SZENES: What could you tell them?

TÖRÖK: I reported on the situation of the Jews in Pest and about the consequences of the recent decrees. There was a new decree against the Jews every day. I reported about the brutality of the authorities, about its atrocities, and the news I received about the deportations from the countryside. I had a few ideas about how one could ease the misery. I asked for advice, and we discussed who could try to achieve what with the aid of connections.

SZENES: Was it possible to achieve anything?

TÖRÖK: Nothing of great import; only one or two small contributions. For example, we brought an organization of Jewish physicians into being. It consisted of thirty to forty doctors. We were able to get them German identification cards that allowed them to move about even after the usual curfew for Jews. With the aid of forged identification cards a few of them were even able to disappear from the view of the authorities. Among the people, especially among the children packed into houses with Jewish stars, many were sick. There was a great deal of misery among these persecuted people. Almost every kind of work to earn money was either forbidden or severely limited, and the authorities took the men who were capable of working from the families to work camps. Many people needed clothes, food, medication and money. The Holy Cross Society, the Good Shepherd Mission, and the Red Cross were able to help in these areas and had a certain degree of freedom to help, even if only within strictly controlled areas. I was deeply moved by the humanity and behavior of those who met in the circle of Mrs. Horthy. But still do not forget: In the final analysis, what happened to the Jews *did* happen.

SZENES: József Éliás told me that you took one copy of the Auschwitz Report to Mrs. Horthy [Countess Ilona Edelsheim Gyulai].

TÖRÖK: When the Auschwitz Report came into my hands, I took it to the Foreign Ministry and gave it to an official, an under-secretary of state. He was not an important person. I gave it to him and requested that he transmit it to the regent. He looked at it and turned a few pages and said that this was Jewish hysteria. He believed that he understood the reasons for it. The Jews were too sensitive and blew things out of proportion. I could see that from this person the report would not get any further. In agreement with Vállay and Gizella Apor, I communicated to Horthy through Mrs. Horthy.

SZENES: Why did you first go to an insignificant official if you had the chance to get to Horthy immediately?

TÖRÖK: I believed that Horthy would be more likely to put faith in the report if it were sent to him from the foreign ministry. Don't forget that this

official was not the only one who considered the reports about gas chambers and crematoria Jewish scare tactics and rumors.

SZENES: That is true. Accordingly, at the end of May or the beginning of June the Auschwitz Report reached Miklós Horthy by means of the Éliás-Török-Vallay-Baroness Apor-Mrs. Horthy chain.

TÖRÖK: Yes, that's how it happened. Later I heard from Mrs. Horthy about Regent Horthy's reaction to the report: He accepted all of it as the truth.

SZENES: Perhaps you know that Horthy published his memoirs in Buenos Aires in 1953, and in them says: "I learned only in August through secret messengers about the horrible reality of the death camps."

TÖRÖK: I heard about the memoirs. What Horthy writes is not true. At the beginning of the summer those of us who met at the royal residence spoke about matters as if all of us were aware of the Auschwitz Report. What is more, after I had transmitted it to Horthy, I had the impression that this was not the first copy in the hands of the regent and that the Jewish leaders and perhaps even László Ravasz had gotten it to him.

SZENES: This is possible. I imagine that Mrs. István Horthy, Gizella Apor, and Vállay had read the report. Did you discuss it with them?

TÖRÖK: Not in detail. At this time the young Mrs. Horthy and many others were guided by two considerations: compassion and shame. And they also asked themselves what the West would think if we helped the Germans by throwing several hundred thousand people over to them.

SZENES: During that summer you met many representatives of churches as well as people from other countries. Was this your general impression?

TÖRÖK: Yes, I had this impression from almost everyone to whom I turned for help. I visited Calvinist Bishop László Ravasz as well. People often referred to him as a "Calvinist Jesuit." What they meant was that he was very cultured and intelligent. He was seriously ill and was forced to receive me from his sick bed in Leányfalu. I sat next to him. We talked, and suddenly he started to cry. He hid his head in the pillows and cried out: "I did not want this, I did not want this!" I had told him about the situation in the country (of which he was aware of anyway), and I made a reference to the Auschwitz Report, and then he started to cry.

SZENES: Did he have reason to say that he did not want this?

TÖRÖK: He had reason. He belonged to the right-wing church leaders of considerable influence. He not only swam with the current, but for many, especially for the believers, he was, as the highest official of the Calvinist church, an impressive communicator, and influential preacher of the word, the stream itself.*

SZENES: And Cardinal Serédi? I read in a study of church history that you as the administrative chief of the Association of Christian Jews had constant contact with him.

TÖRÖK: This is an exaggeration. But I did actually visit him on two occasions. I had a plan, and I discussed it with József Cavallier and Father Jánosi. The three of us thought that perhaps Cardinal Serédi could do something. Cavallier and Jánosi asked for an audience, and at the appointed time all three of us went to see him.*

SZENES: In Esztergom?

TÖRÖK: No, in the castle at Buda. That was the residence of the highest ranking church leader of Hungary. When I consider with what amazingly serious ceremony the whole event took place, when the cardinal appeared in our circle . . . The three of us stood there in the waiting room, on one side of me the international president of the Holy Cross Society, Cavallier, and on the other side the spiritual leader of the same organization, a Jesuit priest. The highest official of the church entered and held out his ring for a kiss. We lowered ourselves to our knees and kissed the ring. After that the cardinal sat down on a small bench, and Father Jánosi announced that Mr. Török had a proposal, and they, the priest as a representative of his society and Cavallier as a representative of his organization, approved of what I was about to present. The cardinal made a signal, and I proceeded to make my statement. I said that I had information about the measures of the Protestant head of the church against citizens (gendarmes, policemen, public officials, railroad workers, etc.) who aid the Germans in rounding up Jews, members of the Resistance, and leftists would not be allowed to receive the Lord's Supper. For a believing Protestant this is a shockingly severe spiritual punishment. There is an appropriate expression of this in Hungarian church circles: He who does not approach the table of the Lord with pure spirit, "brings about his damnation as he drinks wine and eats bread." I asked the cardinal whether there was a possibility of announcing something like this, for this would have a great impact on Catholics and on others as well. I asked this in the name of those I represented and in the name of mankind, humanity, and God's. The cardinal listened for a long time. There was tension in the air when he finally spoke: "If the pope himself does not undertake anything against Hitler, what can I do in my more restricted circle of influence? Hell!" He tore his little biretta from his head and threw it on the ground. Then he reached down for it slowly, put it back on his head, and said, more quietly: "Please excuse me ..." This was my first meeting with Jusztinián Serédi. He could not accept my petition. He wanted to but could not. This is how he dismissed me.

SZENES: At the end of June the pope requested the cardinal through the Nuncius Angelo Rotta to make a public protest against the persecution of the Jews.

TÖRÖK: Yes, I was aware of this. He had received us before that request came from the pope. Otherwise he would not have said what he did. Later I saw him once more, again with Father Jánosi and József Cavallier. This could have been in the beginning of June. We received news that Jews from Budapest would also be deported. The city was filled with gendarmes from the countryside. The three of us stood again in front of the cardinal, and I asked him to help so that we could at least save the children. I asked him to intervene, to take them into his protection in order to take them to some neutral country, Switzerland or Sweden. He conducted negotiations with the International Red Cross about this, but I wanted to convince him to take some action, to have him intervene and use his influence. The cardinal responded to my pleas: If he could do anything, he would do it, but the Germans would thwart his plans anyway. Then the sirens sounded, which meant that a bombing attack was starting, and we went down into the basement of the cardinal's residence. The cardinal sank down to his knees to his place of prayer in the air-raid shelter with Cavallier and Jánosi behind him, also kneeling to pray. The air raid lasted two hours, and the cardinal prayed during the entire time. This was the last time I saw him . . . On the basis of these meetings I felt that Serédi was a man of good will, but passive. He would have been prepared to help in part strictly on the basis of humanitarian motives and, on the other hand, as a Catholic, but ... in the last analysis, he "cannot do anything."

SZENES: You wrote once that three of you—you, Mrs. [Ilona] Horthy, and Baroness Apor—went to Angelo Rotta's for a secret meeting in the night. What was the urgent reason for this?

TÖRÖK: This happened at the beginning of July, when extremely alarming news reached us: The deportation of the Jews from Budapest was about to begin.

SZENES: What kind of impressions did you have of Rotta?

TÖRÖK: He was an intelligent, sober, and reassuring discussion partner. There was something in Rotta's relationship with me that I also observed with Mrs. Horthy and Baroness Apor. They would have preferred to minimize the tragedy of the Jews for my sake, to conceal the true seriousness of the situation, and they tried to console me: "Things will turn out in the end . . . " But deep down they did not believe this.

SZENES: After the liberation you worked in radio. One of the topics you treated in a program called *Sunday Conversations* was: Do we have to recall these times and events? At a time so close to the horrible crimes of fascism this was a relevant topic. How would you answer this question today?

TÖRÖK: In those *Sunday Conversations* Marcell Benedek was my partner. At that time both of us said that we had to engrave onto our memories everything that happened and the fact that it could happen at all. I believe that today. By means of the propaganda of hate, it is possible to excite the masses to an uninhibited use of force and organized violence. Unfortunately, if the favorable situation exists, somewhere in the world a variant of genocide could occur again.

* Bishop Ravasz's speech in support of anti-Jewish legislation in the Hungarian parliament in 1938 confirms Török's statements about the political views and importance of the Calvinist bishop. Ravasz said at that time: "It is my conviction that this law serves not only the peace and security of our country but also the interests of those who oppose it with fervor (I recognize their full right to do this) ... I would have preferred that the (Jews) themselves could have realized a long time ago that there cannot be a minority within a state that practices the rights of the majority." Szenes, *Befejezetlen múlt*. pp. 94–95.

Bibliography

Actes et Documents. La Saint Siège et les Victims de la Guerre. Janvier 1944 – Juillet 1945 (Libreria Editrice Vaticana, 1981).

Agrell, Wilhelm. *Skuggor runt Wallenberg: Uppdrag i Ungern 1943-1945* (Lund: Historiska Media, 2006).

Agrell, Wilhelm. *The Shadows around Wallenberg: Missions to Hungary, 1943–1945* (Lund: Historiska Media, 2019).

Aronson, Schlomo. *Hitler, the Allies, and the Jews* (New York: Cambridge University Press, 2004).

Aronson, Schlomo. "OSS X-2 and Rescue Efforts during the Holocaust," in: David Bankier, *Secret Intelligence and the Holocaust* (New York: Enigma Books, 2006).

Bajtay, Péter (ed. and transl.). *Emberirtás; Embermentés. Svéd követjelentése 1944– ből. Az Auschwitzi Jegyzőnyv* [Extermination (and) Rescue: Swedish Diplomatic Reports of 1944. The Auschwitz Protocol] (Budapest: Katalizátor Iroda, 1994).

[Bangha, Ernő]. *Magyar Hírlap*, July 5, 1993.

Bare, Duncan. "Hungarian affairs of the US-Office of Strategic Services in the Mediterranean Theater of Operations from June 1944 until September 1945," master thesis presented at the University of Graz, 2015.

Bare, Duncan. "Angleton's Hungarians. A Case Study of Central European Counterintelligence in Rome1945/46," in: *Journal for Intelligence, Propaganda and Security Studies* 9/1 (2015): 8–24.

Baron, Frank. "The 'Myth' and Reality of Rescue from the Holocaust: The Karski– Koestler and Vrba-Wetzler Reports." *The Yearbook of the Research Centre for German and Austrian Exile Studies* 2 (2000): 171–208.

Bauer, Yehuda. *Rethinking of the Holocaust* (New Haven: Yale University Press, 2002).

Ben-Tov, Arieh. *Facing the Holocaust in Budapest. The International Committee of the Red Cross and the Jews in Hungary, 1943–1945* (Dordrecht: Kluwer Academic Publishers, 1988).

Bokor, Péter. "Miért nem bombázták az amerikaiak a náci haláltáborokat?" [Why did the Americans Not Bomb the Nazi Death Camps?] *Historia* 1 (1981).

Bokor, Péter. "Interjú Alfred Wetzlerrel." [Interview with Alfred Wetzler] In: *Látóhatár* (1981): 161–190.

Bonhardt, Attila. "The Role of Colonel Ferenc Koszorús in the Prevention of the Deportation of the Jews of Budapest," in: Géza Jeszenszky (ed.), *July 1944: Deportation of the Jews of Budapest Foiled* (Reno, Nevada: Helena History Press, 2017), pp. 203–218.

Braham, Randolph L. (ed.) "Statement by Ernő Pető." In: *Hungarian-Jewish Studies* New York: World Federation of Hungarian Jews, 1973), pp. 49–74.

Braham, Randolph L. "Sándor Szenes, [review of his] *Befejezetlen múlt.*" [The Unfinished Past] *East European Quarterly* 22 (1988), 122.
Braham, Randolph L. *The Politics of Genocide: The Holocaust in Hungary* (New York: Columbia University Press, 1994. Vols I and II.
Braham, Randolph L. *Destruction of Hungarian Jewry. A Documentary Account* (New York: Pro Arte, 1963).
Braham, Randolph L. *"The Nazis' Last Victims: The Holocaust in Hungary* (Detroit: Wayne State University Press, 1998).
Braham, Randolph L. "Assault on Historical Memory: Hungarian Nationalists and the Holocaust," in: Paul A. Shapiro and Robert M. Ehrenreich (eds.) *Hungary and the Holocaust Confrontation with the Past. Symposium Proceedings* (Washington D.C.: Holocaust Memorial Museum, 2001), pp. 45–75.
ttps://www.ushmm.org/m/pdfs/Publication_OP_2001-01.pdf
Accessed on August 5, 2020.
Braham, Randolph L. and William J. vanden Heuvel (eds.). *The Auschwitz Reports and the Holocaust in Hungary* (New York: Columbia University Press, 2011).
Breitman, Richard, Norman J. W. Goda, Timothy Naftali, and Robert Wolfe (eds.). *U.S. Intelligence and the Nazis* (New York: Cambridge University Press, 2005).
Carlberg, Ingrid. *Raoul Wallenberg: The Biography* (London: MacLehose Press, 2016).
Cesarani, David. *Genocide and Rescue: The Holocaust in Hungary 1944* (Oxford: Berg, 1997).
Cesarani, David. *Final Solution: The Fate of the Jews 1933–1949* (London: Macmillan, 2016).
Cole, R. Taylor. *Recollections of R. Taylor Cole: Educator, Emissary, Development Planner* (Durham: Duke University Press, 1983).
Cornwell, John. *Hitler's Pope: The Secret History of Pius XII* (New York: Viking, 1999).
Csicsery-Rónay, István. "A Magyar függetlenségi mozgalom története." [The History of the Hungarian Independence Movement] *Magyar Szemle*, new series 28, nos. 9–10 (1999).
Csicsery-Rónay, István. *Első Életem* [My First Life] (Budapest, 2002).
Davis, Richard G. *Bombing the European Axis Powers: A Historical Digest of the Combined Bomber Offensive 1939–1945* (Maxwell Air Force Base: Air University Press, 2006).
Davis, Richard G. "The Bombing of Auschwitz: Comments on a Historical Speculation," in: Michael J. Neufeld and Michael Berenbaum (eds.), *The Bombing of Auschwitz: Should the Allies Have Attempted It?* (Lawrence, KS: University of Kansas Press, 2003).
Dési, János. *Lévai Jenő és a zsidósors* (Budapest: Mazsök, 2017).

Edelsheim Gyulai, Gróf Ilona [Horthy]. *Becsület és Kötelesség* [Integrity and Responsibility] (Budapest: Európa, 2001).

Erbelding, Rebecca. *Rescue Board: The Untold Story of America's Efforts to Save the Jews of Europe* (New York: Doubleday, 2018).

Erbelding, Rebecca. "The United States War Refugee Board, the Neutral Nations and the Holocaust in Hungary," in: *Bystanders, Rescuers, or Perpetrators? The Neutral Countries and the Shoah* (Berlin: Metropol Verlag, 2016), pp. 183–197.

Erez, Tsvi (Zwi). "Hungary – Six Days in July 1944" in: Randolph Braham (ed.), *Holocaust and Genocide Studies* 3 (1988): 37–53.

Erez, Tsvi (Zwi). "Horthy and the Jews of Budapest." In: Michael R. Marrus (ed.), *The "Final Solution" Outside German,* II. In: *The Nazi Holocaust* (London: Meckler, 1989), IV, pp. 616–642.

Fatran, Gila. "The 'Working Group,'" in: *Holocaust and Genocide Studies* 8/1 (1994): 164–201.

Favez, Jean-Claude. *Warum Schwieg das Rote Kreuz? Eine Internationale Organisation und das Dritte Reich* (Munich: Deutscher Taschenbuch Verlag, 1994).

Fenyo, Mario D. *Hitler, Horthy, and Hungary: German-Hungarian Relations, 1941–1944* (New Haven: Yale University Press, 1972).

Fenyo, Mario D. "The War Diary of the Chief of the Hungarian General Staff in 1944," *East European Quarterly* 2 (1968): 315–333.

Fleming, Michael. "British Narratives of the Holocaust in Hungary," *Twentieth Century British History* 27/4 (2016): 555–577.

Fleming, Michael. "Jan Karski, Auschwitz and News of the Holocaust." In: W Lonynie Zeszyty Naukowe, Seria trezecia, 2 (2014): 85–98.

Fleming, Michael. *Auschwitz, the Allies and Censorship of the Holocaust* (New York: Cambridge University Press, 2014).

Fuchs, Abraham. *The Unheeded Cry: The Gripping Story of Rabbi Weissmandl, the Valiant Holocaust Leader, Who Battled Both Allied Indifference and Nazi Hatred* (Brooklyn, NY: Mesorah Publications, 1986, 2nd ed.).

Gerlach, Christian and Götz Aly. *Das letzte Kapitel: Realpolitik, Ideologie und der Mord an den ungarischen Juden 1944/1945* (Stuttgart: Deutsche Verlags-Anstalt, 2002).

Gilbert, Martin. *Auschwitz and the Allies* (New York: Henry Holt, 1981).

Gilbert, Martin. *The Holocaust: A History of the Jews of Europe during the Second World War* (New York: Henry Holt and Company, 1985).

Gilbert, Martin. „The Contemporary Case for the Feasibility of Bombing Auschwitz," in: Neufeld, Michael J. and Michael Berenbaum (eds.). *The Bombing of Auschwitz: Should the Allies Have Attempted It?* (Lawrence: University of Kansas Press, 2003), pp. 65–75.

Gilbert, Martin. "Should the Allies Have Bombed Auschwitz?" *The London Times*, January 27, 2005.

Gilbert, Martin. *Churchill and the Jews: A Lifelong Friendship* (New York: Henry Holt and Company, 2007).

Gonda, László. "The Service of Evangelism, the Evangelism of Service: The Influence of John R. Mott, Hendrik Kraemer, Willem A. Visser 't Hooft and Johannes C. Hoekendijk on the Development of the Understanding of Mission in the Reformed Church in Hungary (1910–1968)" Ph.D. diss. 2008.

Hantó, Zsuzsa and Nóra Szekér (eds.). *Páncélosokkal az életért. "Koszorús Ferenc, a holocaust hőse"* [Saving Lives with Tanks. "Ferenc Koszorús, "the Hero of the Holocaust."] (Budapest: Kiskapu, 2015).

Haraszti, György. *Auschwitzi jegyzőkönyv* [The Auschwitz Protocols] (Budapest: Múlt és Jövö Kiadó, 2016).

Herczl, Moshe Y. *Christianity and the Holocaust of Hungarian Jewry*. Translated by Joel Lerner (New York: New York University Press, 1993).

Horthy, Miklós. *Memoirs* (London: Hutchison, 1956).

[Horthy, Ilona] Cf. Edelsheim Gyulai, Gróf Ilona.

Jeszenszky, Géza (ed.). *July 1944: Deportation of the Jews of Budapest Foiled* (Reno, NE: Helena History Press, 2017).

Kanawada, Leo. *Holocaust Diaries, V*. (Bloomington, IN: Author House, 2010).

Karsai, Elek. *A Budai vártól a gyepűig. 1941–1945* (Budapest: Táncsics Könyvkiadó, 1965).

Karsai, Elek (ed.). *Szálasi naplója. A nyilasmozgalom a II. világháború idején* [The Diary of Szálasi]. The Arrow Cross movement during the Second World War] (Budapest: Kossuth Könyvkiadó, 1978).

Karsai, Elek. *Végjáték a Duna mentén* [The End Game on the Shores of the Danube] (Budapest, 1982).

Karsai, Elek. "Soos Géza és Hadnagy Domokos tájékoztatása a magyarországi helyzetről és a Magyar Függetlenségi Mozgalomról 1944 decemberében" [Report of Géza Soos and Domokos Hadnagy about the Hungarian Situation and the Hungarian Independence Movement in December 1944], in: *Raday Gyüjtemény Évkönyve*, IV-V (Budapest, 1986), pp. 238–287.

Karsai, Elek and Ilona Benoschofsky (eds.), *Vádirat a nácismus ellen. Dokumentumok a magyarországi zsidóüldözés történetéhez* [Indictment of Nacism in the context of the history of Jewish Persecution in Budapest] (Budapest: Balássi Kiadó, 2017, new edition), vols. III and IV.

Karsai, László and Judit Molnár (eds.). *Az Endre-Baky-Jaross Per* (Budapest 1994).

Karsai, László and Judit Molnár (eds.). *A magyar Quisling-kormány. Sztójay Döme és társai a népbíróság előtt*. (Budapest, 1956-os Kht., 2004).

Karsai, László. "Horthy Miklós (1868–1957). Legendák, mitoszok és valóság." In: *Beszélö* 12/3 (2007): 72–91. http://www.hdke.hu/files/csatolmanyok/Karsai_Horthy.pdf Accessed August 11, 2020.

Karsai, László. "Koszorús és a pesti zsidók," [Koszorús and the Jews of Budapest] *Népszabadság*, June 8, 2014.

Karsai, László. „Jeszenszky és a Holokauszt." In: *Publicisztika* 63 (2019).

Kastner, Rudolf. *Kastner-Bericht über Eichmanns Menschenhandel in Ungarn* (Munich: Kindler, 1961).

Klein, George. "Confronting the Holocaust: An Eyewitness Account," in: Randolph L. Braham and William vanden Heuevel (eds.), *The Auschwitz Reports and the Holocaust in Hungary*, pp. 255–284.

Klein, George. *Pietà* (Cambridge: MIT Press, 1989).

Koszorús Ferenc. Emlékiratai és tanulmányainak gyüjteménye [Collection of Memoirs and Essays] Istvánné Varsa (ed.). (New York: Universe Publishing Company, 1987).

Kovács, Gellért. *Alkonyat Budapest felett. Az embermentés és ellenállás története 1944–45-ben* [Dusk over Budapest: The History of Rescue and Resistance in 1944-45] (Budapest: Libri, 2013).

[Kovács], [Valéria] Istvánné Kováts. *Visszapilantó Tükö*r [The Mirror Looking Back in Time] (Budapest: GO-Press, 1983).

Kranzler, David. *The Man Who Stopped the Trains to Auschwsitz: George Mantello, El Salvador, and Switzerland's Finest Hour* (Syracuse: Syracuse University Press, 2000).

Külügyi közlöny (A m. kir. Külügyminisztérium ügybeosztása [The Royal Hungarian Foreign Ministry Organisation]), Budapest, 1943).

Laczó, Ferenc. "The Foundational Dilemmas of Jenő Lévai. Lévai: on the Birth of Hungarian Holocaust Historiography in the 1940s," in: *Holocaust Studies* 21 (2015): 93–119.

Laczó, Ferenc. *Hungarian Jews in the Age of Genocide: An Intellectual History, 1929–1948* (Leiden: Brill, 2016).

Lantos, Tom, "Ferenc Koszorús, a hero of the Hungarian Holocaust." In: *Congressional Record*, 103rd Congress (1993–1994).

Lanzmann, Claude. *Shoah: An Oral History of the Holocaust* (New York: Pantheon Books, 1985).

Laqueur, Walter and Richard Breitman. *Breaking the Silence* (New York: Simon and Schuster, 1986).

Lendvai, Paul. *The Hungarians: A Thousand Years of Victory in Defeat* (Princeton: University Press, 2003.

Lévai, Jenő. *Fekete Könyv a Magyar zsidóság szenvedéseiről* [Black Book about the Suffering of the Jewish People] (Budapest: Officina, 1946).

Lévai, Jenő. *Fehér Könyv* [White Book] (Budapest: Officina, 1946).
Lévai, Jenő. *Szürke Könyv* [Gray Book] (Budapest: Officina, 1946).
Lévai, Jenő. *Zsidósors Európában* [The Fate of Jews in Europe] (Budapest: Magyar Téka, 1948).
Lévai, Jenő. *Zsidósors Magyarországon* [The Fate of Jews in Hungary] (Budapest: Magyar Téka, 1948).
Lévai, Jenő. *Eichmann in Hungary: Documents* (Budapest: Pannonia Press, 1961).
Lévai, Jenő. *Abscheu und Grauen vor dem Genocid in aller Welt* (New York: Diplomatic Press, 1968).
Macartney, C. A. *October 15th: A History of Modern Hungary. 1929–1945* (Edinburgh: University Press, 1957), II.
Marrus, Michael R. (ed.), *The "Final Solution" Outside German*, II, in: *The Nazi Holocaust* (London: Meckler, 1989).
Matthaeidesz, Konrad. "Egy legenda valósága" [The Truth about a Legend]. In: *Historia* 2 (1982).
Matz, Johan. "Sweden, the United States, and Raoul Wallenberg's Mission to Hungary," *Journal of Cold War Studies* 14 (2012): 97–148.
Medoff, Rafael. *The Jews Should Keep Quiet: Franklin D. Roosevelt, Rabbi Stephen S. Wise, and the Holocaust* (Lincoln, NE: University of Nebraska Press, 2019).
Mester, Miklós. *Arcképek két tragikus kor árnyékában* [Portraits in the Shadows of Two Tragic Periods] (Budapest: Tarsoly Kiadó, 2012).
Miland, Gabriel. "The BBC Hungarian Service and the Final Solution in Hungary." In: *Historical Journal of Film, Radio and Television* 18 (1998): 353–373.
Miryam-Goldberg, Caryn. *Needle in the Bone: How a Holocaust Survivor and Polish Resistance Fighter Found Each Other* [Lou Frydman and Jarek Piekalkevich] (Lincon, NE: University of Nebraska Press, 2012).
Molnár, Judit. "Nazi Perpetrators: Behavior of Hungarian Authorities During the Holocaust." In: Jewish Virtual Library. https://www.jewishvirtuallibrary.org/behavior-of-hungarian-authorities-during-the-holocaust Accessed 9/13/2020.
Molnár, Judit. "Deportáljunk humánusan: A Horthy-rendszer és a Magyar holokauszt." Publicisztika 63/9 (2019). https://www.es.hu/cikk/2019-03-01/molnar-judit/deportaljunk-humanusan.html Accessed 9/13/2020. Accessed 9/13/2020.
Molnár, Judit. "Jeszenszky kontra Karsai," In: *Visszhang* 63/33 (2019). https://www.es.hu/cikk/2019-08-16/molnar-judit/jeszenszky-kontra-karsai.html Accessed 9/13/2020.
Munkácsi, Ernő. Ed. by Nina Munk, annotated by László Csösz and Ferenc Laczó. *How it Happened: Documenting the Tragedy of the Hungarian Jewry* (Montreal: McGill-Queen's University Press, 2018).

Nagy, Edit. *A Dunamelléki Református Egyházkerület Ráday Levéltárának repertóriuma* [The Records of the Calvinist Raday Archives] (Budapest: Nemzeti Kulturális Örökség Minisztériuma, 2002).

Neufeld, Michael J. and Michael Berenbaum. *The Bombing of Auschwitz: Should the Allies Have Attempted It?* (Lawrence: University of Kansas Press, 2003).

Nižňanský, Eduard. "The History of the Escape of Arnošt Rosin and Czeslaw Mordowicz from the Auschwitz-Birkenau Concentration Camp to Slovakia in 1944." In: *Resistance of Jews and Efforts to Inform the World on Genocide Conference Proceedings in Žilina, Slovakia, 25–26 August 2015 International Christian Embassy Jerusalem Historical Institute of Slovak Academy of Sciences.* http://vrbawetzler.eu/img/static/Prilohy/Proceedings_from_Conference_Zilina_2015.pdf Accessed on July 15, 2020.

Oláh, András Pál. "A magyarországi légiháború és a magyar zsidók deportálásának kapcsolatai a II. Világháború idején," [The connection between the deportation of Hungarian Jews and the air war over Hungary during World War II] In: *Belvedere Meridionale* 30 (2018): 69–87.

Pastor, Peter. "A New Historical Myth from Hungary: The Legend of Colonel Ferenc Koszorús as the Wartime Savior of the Jews of Budapest." In: *Hungarian Cultural Studies.* e-Journal of the American Hungarian Educators Association, Volume 12 (2019): 133–149.

Peteresen, Neal H. *From Hitler's Doorstep: The Wartime Intelligence Reports of Allen Dulles, 1942-1945* (University Park: Pennsylvania State Press, 1996).

Raday Gyüjtemény Évkönyve [The annual of the Raday Collection], IV–V (Budapest, 1986).

Ránki, György et al. (eds.) *Wilhelmstrasse és Magyarország. Német diplomáciai iratok Magyarországról* [Wilhelmstrasse and Hungary. German Diplomatic Papers about Hungary] (Budapest: Kossuth, 1968).

Rees, Lawrence. How *Mankind Committed the Ultimate Infamy at Auschwitz* (New York: Public Affairs, 2005).

Riegner, Gerhart M. Interview of April 1995 at the Jewish World Congress in Geneva.

Riegner, Gerhart M. *Never Despair: Sixteen Years in the Service of the Jewish People and the Cause of Human Rights* (Chicago: United States Holocaust Memorial Museum, 2006).

Sakmyster, Thomas. *Hungary's Admiral on Horseback: Miklós Horthy 1918–1944* (Budapest: Columbia University Press, 1994).

Schmidt, Mária. *Kollaboráció vagy kooperáció. A budapesti Zsidó Tanács* [Collaboration or Cooperation: The Jewish Council of Budapest] (Budapest: Minerva, 1990).

Schön, Dezső. *A jeruzsalemi per* [The Jerusalem Trial] (Tel Aviv, 1946).

Sebők, János. *A titkos alku. Zsidókat a függetlenségért. Horthy-mítosz és a holocaust* [The Secret Bargain: The Jews for Independence; Horthy-Myth and the Holocaust] (Budapest 2004).

Smith, Richard Harris. *The Secret History of America's First Central Intelligence Agency* (Guilford CT: The Lyons Press, 2005).

Suhl, Yuri. *They Fought Back: The Story of the Jewish Resistance in Nazi Europe* (New York: Crown Publishers, 1967).

Świebocki, Henryk. *London Has Been Informed . . . Reports by Auschwitz Escapees* (Auschwitz: The Auschwitz-Birkenau State Museum, 2008).

Szabó, Zoltán Tibori. "The Auschwitz Reports: Who Got Them, and When? The Auschwitz Reports and the Holocaust in Hungary," in: Randolph L. Braham and William J. vanden Heuvel (eds.), *The Auschwitz Reports and the Holocaust in Hungary* (New York: Columbia University Press, 2011), pp. 85–120.

Szekér, Nóra. "A Magyar Közösség Története" dissertation of the Péter Pázmány University in Budapest, 2009.

Szekér, Nóra. "A Magyar Függetlenségi Mozgalom tevékenysége," [The Activities of the Hungarian Independence Movement]. In: Zsuzsa Hantó and Nóra Szekér (eds.). *Páncélosokkal az életért,* (Budapest: Kiskapu, 2015), pp. 64–91.

Szekér, Nóra. "Vasdényey István, a Kistarcsai táborparancsnok embermentő tevékenysége, in: *Betekintő* 13/1 (2019): 58–79.

Szekér, Nóra (ed. with Gyula Kodolányi). Cf. Szent-Iványi, Domokos. *The Hungarian Independence Movement 1939–1946.*

Szenes, Sándor. " . . . akkor már minden egyházfő asztalán ott volt az Auschwitzi Jegyzőkönyv . . . " [At that time the Auschwitz Report was on the desk of every church leader] *Valóság* 10 (October 1983): 75–90.

Szenes, Sándor. *Befejezetlen múlt* [The Unfinished Past] (Budapest, 1994, 2nd ed.).

Szenes, Sándor and Frank Baron. *Die verschwiegene Warnung* (Münster: Westfälisches Dampfboot, 1994).

Szent-Iványi, Domokos. *The Hungarian Independence Movement 1939–1946* Edited by Gyula Kodolányi and Nóra Szekér (Budapest: Hungarian Review Books, 2013).

Szent-Iványi, Domokos. *Visszatekintés 1941–1972.* [Taking a Look Back] Edited by Nóra Szekér and Gyula Kodolányi (Budapest: Magyar Szemle Könyvek, 2016).

Szent-Iványi, Domokos. "A Bárczy elleni merénylet [The Assassination Attempt against Bárczy], 1944. június 28–29." In: *Magyar Szemle,* New series, 25, 3–4 (2014).

Szent-Miklosy, Istvan. *With the Hungarian Independence Movement (1943–1947): An Eyewitness Account* (New York: Praeger, Westport, 1988).

Török, Bálint. "Legenda vagy tény?" [Legend or Fact]. In: *Magyar Szemle* New Series 9, 5–6 (2000).

Török, Bálint. "Az Auschwitzi jegyzőkönyv 1," [The Auschwitz Protocol, part 1]. In: *Magyar Szemle,* New Series, 12 (2003).

Török, Bálint. "Az Auschwitzi Jegyzőkönyv 2. A Magyar Függetlenségi Mozgalom zsidómentő tevékenysége." [The Auschwitz Protocol, part 2. The Actions of the Hungarian Independence Movement to Save Lives of Jews] *Magyar Szemle*, New Series, 12 (2003).

Török, Bálint. *Farkas esz meg, medve esz meg . . . Szent-Iványi Domokos és a Magyar Függetlenségi Mozgalom* [The Germans and Then Russians Devour Us . . . Szent-Iványi Domokos and the Hungarian Independence Movement] (Basel and Budapest: Európai Protestáns Magyar Szabadegyetem, 2004).

Tüdős, Ilona [Mrs. Géza Soos] (ed.). *Evangéliumot Mayarországnak, Soos Géza Emlékkönyv* [The New Testament for Hungary: The Legacy of Géza Soos] (Budapest: Bulla, 1999).

Ullein-Reviczky, Antal. *German War; Russian Peace: The Hungarian Tragedy* (Paris: Éditions de la Baconnière, 1947).

Ullein-Reviczky, Antal. *German War; Russian Peace. The Hungarian* Tragedy (Reno, Nevada: Helena History Press, 2014).

Ungváry, Krisztián. *A Horthy-rendszer mérlege. Diszkrimináció sociálpolitika és antiszemitizmus Magyarországon.* [The Evaluation of Horthy's Legacy: Discrimination, Social Politics, and Anti-Semitism in Hungary] (Pécs: Jelenkor, 2012).

Ungváry, Krisztián. *Horthy Miklós—a kormányzó felelősége 1920–1944* [Miklós Horthy—the Regent's Responsibility] (Budapest: Jaffa Kiadó, 2020).

[United States], *Trial of the Major War Criminals before the International Military Tribunal. Nuremberg*, vol. 3 [Nov. 14 – Oct. 1, 1946] and (Nuremberg: US Printing Office, 1948),

[United States], *Trial of the Major War Criminals before the International Military Tribunals Under Control Council Law No. 10*, vol. 14 [in Oct. 1946–Apr. 1949] (Washington: US Printing Office, 1949–1953).

Vági, Zoltán et al. *The Holocaust in Hungary* (Lanham, MD: AltaMira Press, 2013).

Vago, Bela. "Budapest Jewry in the Summer of 1944: Ottó Komoly's Diaries," in: *Yad Vashem Studies* 8 (1970): 81–105.

Varsa Istvánné (ed.). *Koszorús Ferenc. Emlékiratai és tanulmányainak gyüjteménye* [Collection of Memoirs and Essays] (New York: Universe Publishing Company, 1987).

Visser 't Hooft, Willem A. *Memoirs* (Philadelphia: The Westminister Press, 1973).

Vrba, Rudolf. *I Cannot Forgive* (Vancouver: Regent College Publishing, 1964).

Vrba, Rudolf. "Preparations for the Holocaust in Hungary: An Eyewitness Account." In: Randolph L. Braham (ed.) with Scott Miller: *The Nazis' Last Victims: The Holocaust in Hungary* (Detroit: Wayne State University Press, 1998), pp. 55–101.

Waller, Douglas, *Disciples: The War II Missions of the CIA Directors Who Fought for Wild Bill Donovan* (New York: Simon and Schuster, 2015).
Wetzler, Alfred. *Escape from Hell: The True Story of the Auschwitz Protocol* (New York: Berghan, 2007).
Wyman, David S. *The Abandonment of the Jews* (New York: Pantheon Books, 1985).
Zakar, András. "Elhallgatott fejezetek a magyar történelemből" [Silenced Chapters from Hungarian History]. (Fahrwangen: Duna Könyvkiadó, 1976).
Zweig-Strauss, Hanna. *Saly Mayer (1882–1850). Ein Retter jüdischen Lebens während des Holocaust* (Köln: Böhlau, 2007).

Index of Names

Akrell (Acrel), Thorston 51

Agrell, Wilhelm, 48–51, 53, 56–57

Anger, Per, 31, 46–47, 51, 93, 108, 109, 111

Apor, Gábor, 54, 120

Apor, Gizella, 203–204, 206–207

Apor, Vilmos, 182, 202

Aradi, Zsolt 54, 119, 120

Arnóthy-Jungerth, Mihály, 40, 92, 94

Aronson, Schlomo, 50

Bajtay, Péter 29, 31, 93, 108, 112

Bakách-Bessenyey, György, 53, 69

Baky, László, 8, 27–29, 33, 40–41, 65, 76, 78–79, 88–89, 91, 95–104, 106, 108–111, 119

Bangha, Ernő, 33, 95

Bárczy, István, 28, 77–80, 88, 109

Bare, Duncan, x, 27, 47, 49, 53, 57–59, 119

Baron, Betty, x

Baron, Frank, x, 2, 177

Beleznay, László, 82, 83, 89, 91, 97, 100, 102, 105

Benoschofsky, Ilona, 29, 95

Ben-Tov, Arieh, 178

Bentinck, Johannes (John) Adolf, 57, 114, 117

Berecky, Albert, 185, 188

Berenbaum, Michael, 19, 30, 84

Ber[é]nyi, Tibor, 118

Bleakley, Fred, x

Boér, Elek, 53–54

Böhm, Vilmos, 47–48, 50

Bokor, Péter, 177

Bonhardt, Attila, 34–35, 98–100, 102, 105–106

Bothmer, Károly, 40

Braham, Randolph L., vii–viii, 4, 6, 22, 27, 31–32, 36, 38, 40–42, 71, 74, 76–77, 80, 88, 91, 96, 104, 108, 110, 111, 176, 177, 188, 189, 195–197, 200, 201

Breitman, Richard, 55

Burks, Richard, 58

Carlberg, Ingrid, 50

Cavallier, József, 26, 182–184, 198, 204, 208–210

Chemez, Károly, 82, 83, 91

Cole, R. Taylor, 50

Conway, John S., 19

Csicsery-Rónay, István, 81–82

Csikós [Colonel], 100

Curtis, Lori N., x

Davis, Richard, 30, 84

de Bavier, Jean, 178

de Jong, Alfred R. W., 10

Deák, István, 100

DeHuszar Allen, Marguerite x

Dulles, Allen W., 15–18, 21, 49, 54–55, 68–69, 118, 120

Eckhardt, Tibor, 118, 120

Ehrenreich, Robert M., viii

Eichmann, Adolf, 9, 13, 27, 37–38, 41–42, 62, 77, 85, 104, 110, 112, 177

Éliás, József, 4, 7, 25–26, 42, 46, 65, 68, 177–87, 193–194, 198, 206

Ember, Mária, 46–48, 52

Endre, László, 8, 29, 31, 69, 74, 76, 80, 86, 109

Erbelding, Rebecca, 46

Erez, Tsvi (Zwi), 22, 27, 31, 38,

Esty, Miklós, 198–199

Faragho (Faraghó), Gábor, 8, 27, 30–31, 40, 52, 74, 80, 93, 94

Fenyo, Mario D., 8–9, 41, 79, 92, 95

Ferenczy, László, 96

Fleischmann, Gisi, 9, 11

Fleming, Michael, x, 2, 5, 11, 13–14, 76, 79

Flues, Abraham G., 58

Foat, Andrew, x, 66

Fodor, Eugene, 58

Freudiger, Fülöp, 107

Friedman, Jonathan C., 107

Frojimovics, Kinga, 107

Frydman, Jane, x

Garrett, David, 18

Gellért, Andor, 40, 47–51, 53–54, 56, 58–59, 114

Verolino, Gennaro, 177

Gilbert, Esther, x

Gilbert, Martin, 12–15, 22–24, 26–27, 38, 75–76, 104

Goda, Norman J. W., 55

Goebbels, Joseph, 40

Gonda, László, 54

Gripp, Colonel, 38

Günther, Christian, 31, 93, 108

Gustaf V (king of Sweden) 29, 79

Gyulai, Ilona Edelsheim, 5, 7, 9, 26, 70, 71, 186, 202–203, 206

Hadnagy, Domokos, 53, 56–59, 111, 114, 117, 120–121

Hantó, Zsuzsa, 32, 34, 91, 98, 102, 104

Haraszti, György, 5–6

Harrison, Leland, 5, 19–21

Hellebronth, Vilmos, 56, 117

Himler, Márton, 58

Hitler, 7–9, 17–18, 41–43, 49–50, 55, 56, 62–64, 69, 109, 117, 196, 209

Hoekendijk, Johannes C., 54

Horthy, Jr. Miklós, 5, 7

Horthy, Miklós, vii–ix, 5, 7–9, 22–29, 30–35, 37, 39–43, 52, 56, 59–60, 62–64, 69, 70, 71, 74–75, 79–82, 84, 85, 87–89, 90, 92, 93, 95, 97, 98, 100, 101, 104, 105, 108–110, 116, 120, 177, 187, 194, 202, 206

Horv[á]th, L[á]szl[ó], 119

Huddle, J. Klahr, 11

Hutchins, Russ, x

Jaeger, Stephen, x

Jánosi, József 182, 204, 208–210

Jaross, Andor, 8, 29, 31, 41, 69, 74

Jeszenszky, Géza, 34–35, 83, 98, 104, 107

Johnson, Herschel, 46, 48

Kállai, Gyula, 185

K[á]llay Kristof, 120

Kállay, Miklós, 49, 54

Kaltenbrunner, Ernst, 38

Kanawada, Leo, 40

Kárpáty, Géza, 184

Karsai, Elek, 29, 53, 58–59, 94, 106, 111, 120–121, 176

Karsai, László, 8, 29, 31, 34, 69, 74

Karski, Jan, 2, 16

Kastner, Rudolf (Kasztner, Rezsö), 4, 13, 109, 110

Kem[é]ny, Gy[ö]rgy, 120

Kemény, Lajos, 182, 184, 186

Khuen-Héderváry, A. H., 78

Kirchner, Andrea, x

Kis, Görgy, 200

Klein, George, 6

Kodolányi, Gyula, 8, 28, 79, 81, 87, 96, 100

Koestler, Arthur 2, 16

Kohn, Zoltán, 6

Komoly, Ottó, 109, 185–187

Kopecky, Jaromir, 6, 12–13, 25, 42, 69

Kos[á]ry, Domokos, 120

Koszorús, Ferenc, 26, 29–32, 34–35, 41–43, 60, 81–83, 86–87, 89, 91–93, 96–103, 106–107, 121

Kovács, Gellért, 49–50

Kov[á]cs, P[é]ter, 120, 122

Kovács, Valéria (Kováts Istvánné) 26, 29, 85–86

Kraemer, Hendrik, 54

Kranzler, David, 10, 19

Krausz, Miklós (Moshe), 4, 16–17

Kudar, Lajos, 28–29, 81

Kulka, Erich, 14–15

Küllői, László, x

Küllői, Péter, x

Laczó, Ferenc, x, 73

Láday, István, 28–29, 34, 98, 105

Lázár, Károly, 28, 30, 32–33, 81, 87–91, 93, 95–97, 100, 107

LeRow, Pam, x

Lendvai, Paul, 100

Lévai, Jenő, 33, 36, 38, 40, 41, 75, 105, 108, 110, 176

Lichtheim, Richard, 5, 23–26, 37–39, 42, 76, 94, 101

Macartney, C. A., 7, 11, 27, 31, 49, 52, 63–64

Mantello, Georg(e) (György Mandel), 6, 10, 16, 18, 19, 25, 38–40, 42, 69

Martilotti, Mario, 5

Mátrai, Gyula, 200

Matz, Johan, 46, 50

McClelland, Roswell, 5, 10–11, 15–17, 19–21, 25, 69

McCloy, John, 20

Medoff, Rafael, 18

Miller, Scott, vii

Mohi, Zsolt, x

Molnár, Judit, 8, 29, 31, 69, 74, 96

Mordovicz, Czeslaw, 12–13, 16, 76

Mott, John R., 54

Munkácsi, Ernő, ii, 7, 29, 32–33, 65–67, 69–70, 72–73, 86, 96, 110

Muschner, Michael, 6

Naftali, Timothy, 55

Neufeld, Michael J., 19, 30, 84

Nicosia, Francis R., 38

Nižňanský, Eduard, 13

Norton, John Clifford, 38

Oderscalchi, Prince Paul, 118, 120

Oláh, András Pál, 22

Olsen, Iver, 48

Paksy-Kiss, Tibor, 32–33, 96, 100

Pastor, Peter, 34–35

Pehle, John W., 20

Perczel, Tamás, 54, 119–120

Perényi, Zsigmond, 187

Petersen, Neal H., 17, 55

Pető, Ernő, 5, 7

Pirhy, Janos, 118

Pius XII, 75, 196

Pontius (Pilate), 7, 64

Raffay, Sándor, 185, 187, 202

Rakolczay, László, 38–39

Rákovits, István, 57, 117, 119

Ravasz, László, 5, 9, 53–54, 64, 69–70, 121, 180, 185, 187–188, 202, 207, 211

Riegner, Gerhart, 2, 5, 12–15, 22, 24–25, 42

Franklin D., 10, 11, 17–18, 21–22, 30, 43, 46, 50, 75, 110

Rosin, Arnošt, 12–13, 16, 76

Rotta, Angelo, 70, 203, 209–210

Sakmyster, Thomas, 52

Saláta, Kálmán, 55, 80–81, 112

Schmidt, Mária, 108, 109

Schön, Dezső, 176

Schultz, Elizabeth, x

Schwalb, Nathan, 4, 10–11, 25, 173

Sebestyén, András, 26

Sebők, János, 8, 33, 40, 74, 84, 95

Serédi, Jusztinián, 4–5, 75, 177, 180, 184, 185, 187, 192, 195–197, 200, 208–210

Shapiro, Paul A., viii

Shaw, Michael and Anne, x

Smith, Richard Harris, 17

Soos (Soós), Géza, 4, 7–8, 25–26, 35, 42–43, 45–48, 50–60, 65–69, 80–84, 87, 91–93, 107, 111–121, 181–186, 193

Stark, Tamás, 107

Stern, Samu, 72, 109

Suhl, Yuri, 15

Świebocki, Henryk, 14, 16

Szab[ó] Istv[á]n, 118, 122

Szabó, Zoltán Tibori, 4, 6

Szakasits, Arpád, 185

Szálasi, Ferenc, 106

Székely, Mária, ix, 4, 67–68, 177–178, 182, 184, 189–194

Szekér, Nóra, x, 8, 28, 32, 34, 79, 81–82, 87, 91, 96, 98, 100, 104

Szenes, Sándor, ix–x, 4–5, 66, 68, 71, 175–211

Szent-Iványi, Domokos, 4, 8, 25, 28, 52, 56, 59, 71, 77–78, 81, 87, 91, 96, 100, 187

Szentiv[á]nyi, S[á]ndo[r], 120

Szladits, Károly, 191–193

Szőnyi, György, x

Sztójay, Döme, 23–24, 26, 32, 35–38, 103–104, 178, 183, 187

Tabeau, Jerzy, 15–16

Tahy, Imre, 39

Tarics, Sandor, 118

Taubert, Eberhard, 40

Teleki, Pál, 180

Tildy, Zoltán, 185

Tölgyessy, Győző, 32, 96, 100

Toperczer, Árpád, 57, 114, 117

Török, Bálint, 8, 26, 35, 69, 91

Török, Sándor, ii, 5, 7, 69–70, 75, 177–178, 186–188, 201–211

Toth, J[á]nos K. 120

Tüdős, Ilona, 47, 50, 52, 55, 58, 60, 80, 84, 121

Ullein-Reviczky, Antal, 49–50, 56. 118, 120

Ungváry, Kristián, 97, 105

Vági, Zoltán, 29, 79

Vago, Béla, 109

Vállay, Gyula, 202–204, 206–207

vanden Heuvel, William J., 4

Varga, Imre, 72–73

Veesenmayer, Edmund, 23–24, 27, 31, 35–38, 41, 63, 64, 71, 76, 101, 103–104, 108–109

Veress, László, 49

Visser 't Hooft, Willem A., 25, 54–55, 68–69, 117, 120

von Postnak, Erik, 109

Vörös, János, 32, 78–79, 92, 95

Vrba, Rudolf, 2–4, 6, 10–13, 15–16, 19, 20, 73, 76, 173–174

Wagner, Horst, 38

Wallenberg, Raoul, 45–60, 111–112

Waller, Douglass, 16

Weissmandl, Rabbi Michael Dov (Weissmandel), 9–11, 173–174

West, F. M., 38

Wetzler, Alfred, 2–4, 6, 10–13, 15, 16, 20, 73, 76, 173

Wiskeman, Elizabeth (also Elisabeth), 2, 5–6, 13, 15–17, 23–26, 37, 39, 42, 43, 55, 68–69, 76, 94 118, 120

Wolfe, Robert, 55

Wyman, David S., 10, 20

Zakar, András, 177–178, 195–200